HALFWAY *to* EACH OTHER

How a year in Italy brought our family home

SUSAN POHLMAN

Halfway to Each Other

ISBN-13: 978-1-7346132-0-9

Published by Riviera Communications Group

Acknowledgments

Lines from "Train in the Distance" by Paul Simon are copyright © 1981 Paul Simon. Used by permission of the publisher: Paul Simon Music.

Cover design by Katie Bussoletti
Cover photograph by Sanga Park
Interior design by Laura Klynstra
Typeset by Nancy Tardi

Printed and bound in the United States of America

For Tim, Katie and Matthew

Sometimes humans beg for battles to be taken away from them,

not realizing that only in struggling with shadows

is the Light made manifest.

W. MICHAEL GEAR

prologue

My husband Tim and I planned our wedding Mass together. He chose a couple of the readings and relatives to read them, and I did the same. Ordinary prewedding stuff, or so I thought. The only detail questioned by anyone was my choice of the Gospel. I was curiously drawn to Matthew 6:25–34, a passage about reliance upon God and how he would take care of us as well as he took care of the lilies of the field and the birds in the air if we placed our trust in him. I handed the verse, neatly typed in cursive font, to the priest who took one look at it and said, "This is a first. Are you sure you want this one?"

I nodded.

"There are a lot about love to choose from."

"I can't explain it," I said. "I had this overpowering feeling that this one had to be the one." He adjusted his glasses, reread the passage and then shrugged, exhaling loudly.

I am sure, now, that it was a message from God. For some reason, he wanted me to place that reading permanently in my spiritual back pocket. The second message came on the morning of the big day. I awoke on October 19, 1985, to an earthquake. New Jersey never has earthquakes. I took out my little Gospel verse, looked it over and felt better. I was very much in love with my husband-to-be and had no second thoughts about marriage, so it never entered my mind that we would struggle in the years to come, but God knew.

Eighteen years and two children later, I took that Gospel verse, tattered and worn, and threw it in the garbage. I was empty, disillusioned and heartbroken that we would not be among the few couples who made it all the way through life side by side. I was sick of the lilies of the field, and the birds could fly away for all I cared. Our marriage was over and, as far as I was concerned, God had not held up his side of the bargain. I was done.

But God was not. He slyly took my discarded verse and slid it back into its place, knowing that soon I would reach for it instinctively and finally read it with open eyes. And I did. On the eve of our divorce, my husband and I made a most unexpected decision fueled by faith, grace and hope. We moved our family to Italy.

Our marital therapist called it "an elaborate scheme of avoidance at best." And when she pressed for a reason, we said, "We can't explain it. We had this overpowering feeling that we had to do this."

"I see." Her blue eyes darted back and forth between us as the clock ticked away our final appointment. "Well, you know where to find me when you get back."

People who have lived through a personal crisis often say that faith is what got them through it. I know now that God sends us messages and overpowering feelings every day but we only hear him in fits and starts, and we listen even less. I did not take Matthew 6:25–34 to heart until I was an emotional train wreck and then I was all ears, listening like a child with a cup to the wall.

1   the background

It was the last week in May 2003. My husband, Tim—a highly successful radio executive—and I were hosting a six-day business trip for the clients of a local radio station in Los Angeles. Playing the role of the dutiful wife, I helped Tim ensure that approximately forty clients had the time of their lives in Florence and Portofino. Tim was a larger-than-life kind of guy whose great claim to fame, other than running radio stations, was knowing his way around a party. And I, after having been married to him for so long, was well versed in the art of schmoozing as well. We'd done quite a few of these incentive trips over the years, so other than meeting some new people, we expected business as usual: fancy hotels, fine meals and pleasant excursions—all on the company tab.

We were here to do a job, not to search for romance under the Tuscan sun. Those days were long over for us. As we explored Italy, my lawyer back home explored my strategies to exit a marriage that had ended years earlier.

We had landed at our emotional ground zero after a series of spectacular fights and discussions about who was working harder, who was ignoring the other person, who was the more invested parent, who was spending what and who just didn't care about being married anymore. We had finally looked at each other across the highly polished dining room table and admitted it. We were tired of each other. Tired of wondering what was missing. Tired of pretending that we were happy. Tired of the

1

stresses of life together. Tired of trying to work through our differences in therapy. After more than twenty years as a couple, we had become character actors in our own lives, starring in the roles of Husband and Wife. And our two children, fourteen-year-old Katie and eleven-year-old Matt were suffering the consequences of living in an environment of silent rage. When we asked each other what we wanted to do about our marriage, we both agreed to keep going. I was lying.

In Florence, though, for the sake of developing relationships with people who could positively affect future radio budgets, and therefore my alimony checks, I pretended that none of this was happening. We worked as a team on the surface only. My heart was off limits.

So I helped Tim arrange the perfect tour of the duomo for our group of car dealership owners and agency representatives, but I was not prepared for the unexpected tears that sprang to my eyes as I walked through it, overwhelmed by its huge scale and the beauty of its frescoes and paintings and sculpture. I printed up perfect little maps so that our charges could easily navigate the cobblestoned streets, but as I ventured out behind them, I didn't expect to be charmed by the medieval alleyways, palaces and churches that held the footprints of Michelangelo and da Vinci and that had listened once to their whispers.

I dutifully included the many basic landmarks, like the Basilica di Santa Croce, as recommendations on the little typed itineraries that I slid under the clients' doors each morning. But I was struck dumb when we entered the basilica, a fourteenth-century Gothic church, and stood at the feet of Galileo, Michelangelo, Rossini, Machiavelli and other famous Florentines buried there. What was it about these men who didn't give up when the odds were stacked against them, or shrink back in fear as they teased open the doors of groundbreaking philosophy and invention? All of a sudden, Florence was not just about artwork. Unbeknownst to me, Tim's inner orientation was changing too. Neither of us had the words for it yet, just the feeling that something was different.

I awoke on day four of the trip in an aristocratic hotel called The Miramare in Santa Margherita Ligure on the Italian Riviera. While Tim slept, I sat up in bed and gazed out the narrow window, its hard edges softened by sheer white curtains softly billowing in the sea breeze. From our third-story vantage point, I watched a lone sailboat turn from gray to orange to white as it cut its way across the expansive harbor, bathed by the changing light of the rising sun on the Ligurian Sea. I felt strangely calm. Peaceful, even. This was not normal. I found myself snuggling back under the covers next to Tim.

"Hey, you." I whispered.

Grunt. Snore.

"Wake up."

Tim slowly opened one eye and peered at his nifty travel clock perched on the bedside table.

"We just went to bed."

"The mountains and the sea look like a painting."

"This is not on the itinerary."

"Trust me."

We had coffee delivered to our room as we put on our matching white robes from the tiny closet. We carried the tray outside and sat on our balcony in the crisp spring air like we were movie stars.

"This view is killer."

"Told you," I said as I poured real cream into my coffee. "Close your eyes for a minute. Just listen." Silence, birds, wind through the trees. The musical quality of the Italian language between two friends far below us. He opened his eyes and we laughed.

"Florence was…"

"I know."

"You don't even know what I was going to say."

"Yes, I do."

"Okay, then what?"

"Overwhelming, unsettling, amazing, life-changing?"

"Fine. All of the above."

Whoa, whoa … now wait a minute here. Were we actually enjoying this moment together? Easy, sister. Get back on track.

"So what's on the agenda for today?" I asked.

"Nothing planned until evening. Wanna do something?"

"Together?" *That's a long time.*

"What is that supposed to mean?

"I didn't mean it that way."

"Like there's another way to mean it?"

"So what do you have in mind?"

"Why don't we rent some Vespas?"

Hmm. That would be just the right amount of motion and separateness to ensure a successful and emotionally insulated afternoon.

"Okay."

"We can ride through the mountains and find a tiny restaurant off the beaten track somewhere." This sounded romantic. It made me nervous.

After a leisurely breakfast, we got directions from the concierge and walked down the palm-lined beach promenade through town in search of the Vespa shop. This once small fishing community had blossomed over the years into a charming tourist town; its narrow streets boasted elegant boutiques and galleries tucked amid local markets and bakeries. We found the rental place up a dark, tiny side street, but it was closed, the scooters chained outside together like a string of paper dolls. We waited awhile, but it soon became apparent that the "hours of business" sign in the window was merely a suggestion.

We headed back to the hotel. The sun was climbing high in the sky, so we agreed that a few hours by a pool overlooking the sea would be a fitting substitute. We ambled slowly along the coast road and drank in the details that make this region of Italy unique. The brightly colored buildings with their trompe l'oeil facades and painted details tricked the eye into seeing cornices, carvings and shutters that didn't really exist. Flowers cascaded from windows, walkways and archways. The sun glinted off the sea in sprays of glitter. This was where Christopher Columbus had learned to sail as a boy. Tim reached for my hand, and it felt right to hold his. This was not the type of scenery that a soul could handle alone. Even souls who were trying to ignore each other.

And then the conversation. The one we have had on each and every vacation we have ever taken.

"I could live here," said Tim.

"Me too."

And then the fateful change of inflection.

"No, I really *could* live here."

"Yeah, right."

We walked the rest of the way back to the hotel in silence. He was suggesting something unfathomable. Why couldn't we make this charmed life here ours?

No, no, no. I'm leaving you, remember? I've invested too much time and pain in that decision. I was not going to be derailed by some romantic stroll along the sea. I told myself to get a grip. But soon there were three of us walking along. On the left I was holding Tim's hand, but on the right I was holding the hand of the memory of my recent experiences in the lawyer's office. My left hand was starting to feel more comfortable.

I remembered sitting in the waiting room while other clients commiserated in whiny voices about exes and child support. My mind drifted to the guy with gray chest hair caught in his big gold chain who had winked at me. I remembered the people's eyes and how they didn't smile along with the rest of their faces. Eyes that held the grief that comes from realizing that "happily ever after" is just three fragile words after all. I had recognized the pain hidden behind the bravado and the jokes of those who tried to hold the two halves of their children's hearts together with unsteady hands. I didn't really want to join this club, but I didn't know what else to do with my emptiness.

Twenty minutes later, Tim and I were side by side on two blue-striped lounge chairs facing the sea at the hotel pool. We were the only ones there except for a young pool cleaner who I couldn't help but notice since he wasn't exactly ugly.

"I really meant what I said before," Tim said in all seriousness.

"Me too." Even as I said it, I thought, *Stop all of this nonsense.* I would have left months ago, if it hadn't been for Katie and Matt. I had no problem visualizing myself in a new marriage, but I was having profound difficulty visualizing myself in a new family. No matter how many articles I read that reassured me that children of divorce ended up just fine, I didn't believe one of them. As a teacher, I had encountered many children of divorce. I wondered how many of those writers had ever sat in a classroom with a student like Kyle, whose vacant green eyes stared me down when I asked him why he continued to hit other children and say mean things for no apparent reason, or had hugged a tearful Cynthia when she confessed that the reason she kept falling asleep during Language Arts was because she had been up all night waiting for her dad to come home even though the divorce had been final for over a year.

"I could quit my job. We could live off the profit from the sale of our house," said Tim.

"Are you crazy?"

"I don't know. These past few days, I'm just ... I am miserable at that job. It just hit me like a ton of bricks yesterday while we were crossing the Ponte Vecchio. I have not been happy there for a long time. It's like someone slapped me across the face and told me to wake up."

"I've been doing that for years."

"I'm trying to be serious. Other people do crazy things. Why can't we?"

"Because we don't know how to work as a team. We're terrible at compromise. Our communication skills are prehistoric. We don't even like each other that much anymore, remember?"

"Just think about it. That's all I'm asking."

I sat back and closed my eyes. I felt the hot sun wash over me. A heartbeat later, an internal voice boomed, *Do this.* It was so unexpected that I sat up, opened my eyes and peered around. Tim's eyes were still closed. The pool guy was still cute. I lay back down and told my conscience or whatever it was to shut up.

But it didn't shut up. This commanding voice inside my head started to badger me incessantly with one simple question: *Why do you want to stay anchored to a lovely lifestyle in Los Angeles that's brought you nothing but distance from the man you used to love and is teaching your children a world of skewed values?*

"Tim," I whispered. "Did you ever think that maybe, the life we built together, the American Dream so to speak, is the reason why we're so miserable?" Tim propped himself up on his elbow to listen, his steel blue eyes intent. "You just kind of get lost in the repetition of it all. But you don't really know you're lost until you're so lonely that you can't take it anymore. The layers of your life slowly suffocate you. And then it all falls apart. The marriage, the family, the house..."

Silence. Then Tim's eyes started to tear, which of course made mine water up as well. "I think it's safe to say that we're in the 'lost' part. Really, really close to the falling apart part," he said. I nodded and tried to blink back my tears. "So let's try something different."

"You're asking me to give up everything. Leave all of our friends and family. I don't know, Tim. Katie's in high school. Besides, if we can barely be civil to each other in our own home, how would this kind of stress be any easier?"

"We'd be doing something that counted, and we'd be doing it together. The kids could see some of the world beyond Ventura Boulevard. Think about it."

I lay back down, turned my head to the side away from Tim and quietly proceeded to have a nervous breakdown. I could continue the secret divorce proceedings and take half of everything we owned and probably be financially set. I could make a new life for myself and in thus doing, ask Katie and Matt to live with hearts forever broken. Or I could look at this person as the man I used to love and know that deep down we were both lost and scared.

I realized then, on those blue-striped lounge chairs at the edge of the sea that had cradled Christopher Columbus, if we had even an ounce of his courage, we, too, could set sail for the unknown. Maybe we were drowning in the very life we had built for ourselves. Something had to give. Either our lifestyle or our family. Our marriage, all of those years, might be worth at least this … giving it all up for each other to see if our life was in the way of our love.

Then, in a voice I barely recognized as my own, I said, "If there's an American International School in the area, I'll consider it." We looked at each other, and I felt our souls connect at the thought of the impossible. It was like a greeting between old friends, tired soldiers finally back from the war.

We sat up in our chairs and giggled with nervous laughter. I called to the pool guy, "Is there an American International School nearby?" He thought awhile and then slowly nodded "Genoa."

2 ✽ the decision

I awoke before dawn the next morning and lay still in the bed listening to Tim snore softly as I waited for the sun to rise and shine rays of common sense upon us. My lightness of being from the day before had dissipated like a vapor in the Sahara. The glossy white and blue folder that held Katie and Matthew's enrollment paperwork for the American International School of Genoa lay atop crumpled clothes in my open suitcase on the floor. I tried to imagine the various facial expressions of our children as we told them they would be going to school in an old villa on the other side of the world next year. None of their imaginary expressions exuded happiness. Everything inside of me was screaming with strict instructions to run as far as I could in the opposite direction. As soon as Tim woke up, I would put my foot down and stop this craziness.

Restless, I got out of bed and sat alone on the balcony, my sheet wrapped around me against the cool air. Ordinarily I would have sent an immediate SOS to heaven to beg for strength and help with choosing the right words to use in this upcoming conversation with Tim, but I was angry at God for letting me down all of the time and leading me astray from the very beginning with that Gospel reading from our wedding. I should have listened to the priest when he suggested that I choose something else. Matthew 6:25–34 had turned out to be a complete bust. All the faith in the world had not helped us forge a meaningful and lasting relationship.

I rested my head on the back of the chair and drank in the starry sky twinkling above the water, the beauty of which filled me with a sense of peace that erased all worry. And I sat this way, marveling at the power of nature to calm the mind and fill the heart with its divine presence until the sun rose and Tim appeared in the doorway with the school folder in his hand.

"Hi," he said.

"Hi."

"Trouble sleeping?"

"Kind of."

"I know. This is so exciting." He plopped into the chair next to me and started to rifle through the paperwork. "What are the chances that the only two classes that had openings for next year were Katie's and Matt's grade levels? Definitely a sign from God."

"Tim."

"Right after breakfast, we'll find that Realtor the school secretary mentioned."

"Tim."

He fished a business card out of the folder and held it up. "They help find housing for many of their teachers every year. We'll see what rental listings they have available."

"Tim, stop." He looked at me. "We need to talk."

"You're backpedaling now, aren't you? You sat up all night and thought of all the reasons why this won't work. This is a perfect example of why our marriage is crumbling. Your constant overanalyzing and negativity."

"Excuse me?" I hated these surprise attacks. They made me completely forget all of the things I planned to say. "Overanalyzing? Well, someone has to keep you from your stupid impulsivity. Shall we rehash some of *those* decisions, like the three-thousand-dollar telescope you had to have that would miraculously bring you happiness and give you a hobby that you could share with the kids? You set it up in the backyard once." *Where did that come from? I haven't thought about that telescope in three years.*

"If I remember correctly, you bought that for me for Christmas."

"Yeah, but you pestered me for it like a five-year-old."

"Pestering—which takes time—would imply the opposite of impulsivity." He stood up and pointed the folder at my nose like a huge glossy finger. "And by the way, impulsive people are fun. You do not have one fun bone in your body."

"I do too," I shouted after him as he stomped away. *I'm fun. I like jokes. I'll show him.* I followed him back into the room where he was angrily pulling on his tan cargo shorts. "And for your information, I was sitting out there imagining the looks on Katie's and Matt's faces when we tell them the news. That's what I was thinking about."

"Right."

"And you're picking this fight because you're getting cold feet and want to blame me for backing out so you can go home and be Mr. 'I would have done it if it weren't for you.'" *Okay, Susan. Stop while you're ahead. This is going nowhere.*

"You know that's not true."

We stood and glared at each other for a long moment. Then Tim pulled on his shirt and said, "Last night we promised each other that we'd at least see it through today before we made our decision. Can we at least do that?"

"Fine." That was not at all the conversation I had pictured. But what would one more day hurt?

It took all morning to locate the *immobiliare* (Realtor). When we found Studio Massa hidden down a little cobblestoned street by the port of Nervi, we had a hard time communicating with Umberto, a soft version of Gene Wilder, who spoke very little English. Eventually he figured out that we were interested in a fully furnished apartment for four people, near the school for one year. He said that they had only one listing that would come available in July, but we could not go look at it until 6:00 PM.

We decided to spend the afternoon walking around Nervi and the neighboring town of Quinto to get a feel for what life would be like here. Unlike Santa Margherita, which was a quiet haven for tourists, this locale, just a few minutes up the coast toward Genoa, was more urban, though still color-washed and charmed by the beauty of the sea. And in addition to the cascading flowers and trompe l'oeil cornice work, it was filled with one other thing: sound. We strolled down the uneven sidewalks of the busy thoroughfare to the roar of buses, cars and Vespas, climbed up hillsides through neighborhoods of high-rise apartment buildings to the sounds of neighbors squawking at each other, children laughing and babies crying and wandered by a few parks with elderly people lined up on benches whispering and cajoling each other. We drew our share of stares and finger pointing. I was sure that it was not every day that these people saw a six-foot-eight bald guy and a five-foot-eight blonde crisscrossing their environs from all angles.

Throughout our grand tour Tim droned on, persistent and passionate about our starting over and thinking outside the box while I remained petty and small-minded as I walked along beside him making mental lists of all the things about him that bugged me, like the way he scraped his teeth against the fork every time he took a bite of food at the dinner table. Despite myself, however, little thoughts of intrigue and possibility started to push their way through my psyche like blades of grass through tiny cracks in the pavement. Something was pressing me beyond logic. The presence was palpable and it was like nothing I had ever felt before. No matter what words raced through my mind to argue against this preposterous idea, the momentum toward it increased. It was as if my limbs and mouth were not connected to my brain anymore. I even heard myself throw in a few inanities like how much money we could get for our car and how far that would go in helping us afford to travel on weekends to places like Germany and Switzerland. I felt like a marionette with a painted face unsure of who was in control of my strings.

Then I wondered if I was really just having a nervous breakdown, and fantasy and reality were now blurring their borders. *Is this how it feels to go insane? How could I be signing documents in a lawyer's office one week and then consider moving across the ocean with the very person I'm trying to divorce the next week? What on earth is going on here?*

Physically and emotionally drained by midafternoon, we took a break to get a bite to eat. Tim and I sat across from each other at a small square table in a little restaurant with crisp white tablecloths and windows like oversized portholes that looked out at the choppy blue water. Ordinarily I would have found it delightful, but right now, with my entire future hanging in the balance, I was not in the mood. I put my fingers to my temples and tried to knead away an encroaching headache. Tim got busy crunching numbers, his jaw clenched and brow furrowed. The yellow number two pencil whipped up and down the paper place mat, creating columns and lists. He loved to do this, proving or disproving on paper why we should or should not do something. Even the sound of the graphite scratching against the paper made my skin crawl.

"The rent's half of our house payment, and if you count up all of the utilities, transportation, insurance … Are you listening?" Tim waved the pencil in my direction.

"I'm sitting three feet from you. Obviously I'm listening."

"It would be nice if you would look at me."

I stopped kneading my temples and looked at the place mat. The columns were so straight and neat that I suddenly had this vision of myself grabbing the pencil and scribbling all over it just to see what he would do.

"As I was saying, we could probably afford to live here for two years if we really scrimped."

"Are we really doing this?"

"I just want us to have all of our information gathered so we can make an informed and intelligent decision."

"Let's take intelligence out of it."

At 5:45 we went back to Studio Massa and jumped into Umberto's tiny silver car. He drove on winding roads up a hillside until we parked next to a seven-story building on Via Fratelli Coda. It had a 1970s kind of feel to it, a mixture of slate, stone and brick with gray steel balconies flat across the front.

I took a deep breath, wiped my sweaty palms on my jeans and tapped

Tim on the shoulder. "If the place is a dump, then it wasn't meant to be. We leave tomorrow and drop the idea permanently. Okay?"

"If it isn't a dump?"

"Then that's a sign that we should do it."

"Deal."

I was confident that it would be a dump. The three of us walked into the cavernous lobby, past a mirrored wall and stood before a narrow elevator door, smiling nervously at each other. The doors opened and we squeezed inside. It felt claustrophobic, like a coffin for four, a phone booth that traveled between floors. Umberto pushed the button, and as the elevator climbed unsteadily toward the seventh floor, I was reminded of the story of the hanging elevator. It is a common metaphor used in movie writing where you have the unsuspecting people riding in the elevator, all happy and isolated in their own lives, sure that they are in complete control of their destiny, but the viewer sees that the elevator cable is starting to unthread and soon the elevator will plunge to its demise. The people inside begin to argue over something petty and the audience sits on the edge of their seats aghast that the passengers are wasting the last moments of their lives on something useless and without virtue.

I knew in that instant that Tim and I were those people missing the point of life entirely. And it became undeniably clear that I was not in complete control of this decision, that there was a greater force at work. All of a sudden everything that was wrong between us seemed trivial in contrast to the importance of preserving the sanctity of our family. I was overcome with such desperation that I forgot about being mad at God and cried to him for help. Then out of nowhere floated snippets of words from Matthew 6:25–34, *Can any of you by worrying add a single moment to your life…why are you anxious…seek first the kingdom…and all these things will be given you…*

Then it was me and God, face-to-face in the elevator and I knew that this was going to be my defining fork in the road. After forty-four years of Christian living, how much did I really believe in love? How much faith did I really have? Did I have the courage to surrender and put my life in God's hands?

And he said to me "You and Tim are emotionally and spiritually lost, your family is falling apart, your children are hurting, and you want to run away from that pain."

"Yes, I do. I'm worn out. I can't pretend for even one more day. Look at me. I don't even know who I am anymore. I can't remember what it feels like to be truly, deeply happy."

"What about Katie and Matthew? Will it make you truly, deeply happy to see them broken and shuttling back and forth between two homes?"

"How can you ask me such a painful thing? How does a parent balance her needs against her children's?"

"Answer the question."

"I was just going to handle it the way the world handles such matters. We'll adjust."

"You can do that if you'd like, but I am laying before you a chance of a lifetime."

"I'm afraid."

"Of what? As it stands, you've got nothing more than a lot of brokenness and a few bucks in the bank, which, by the way, is not the currency we use up here."

"What if I do this and nothing changes?"

"And what if it does?"

"What if I rely on faith like I did for the past eighteen years and end up here again. I've turned to Matthew 6:25–34 over and over, and nothing ever changed."

"You relied on faith?"

"I prayed to you for answers, for help with decisions."

"You prayed to me after you had already made your own decisions and they weren't working out. Your prayers were always after the fact."

"They were?"

"How come you never prayed at the beginning of a situation, before you made your choices? Why didn't you feel me guide you?"

"I thought I knew the right path. I went to church. I heard the sermons."

"But did you listen?"

"Is this a trick? Is this elevator hanging from a thread? Are we getting ready to plunge to our deaths?"

"Why won't you trust me?"

"I will trust you if the place is not a dump."

The longest elevator ride of my life halted, and the doors opened to an open-air staircase. We ascended three steps to the front door and took one last breath together. The Realtor jiggled the key left and right, and the door opened to an expansive view of sea and sky and sun-washed coastline visible through floor-to-ceiling glass doors that ran the length of the entire apartment. Tim and I gasped in awe and looked at each other, petrified.

"Oh no," I said. "Now we have to do this."

With shaky hands, we signed a preliminary lease (in Italian no less) and then headed back to our hotel to host our final client dinner. It was outrageous and unthinkable. It was gutsy and stupid. It was the best I had felt about anything in years.

We went home and broke the news to our stunned children: We were moving to Italy. Tim resigned from his job the next day. We sold our house and some of our belongings, threw the rest in storage and left our sweet dog, Carmel Corn, with the generous family that had bought our home and offered to take care of her for the year. We were back on a flight to Italy two months later. The whole thing was downright shocking. People wondered if we had lost our minds. We were hoping that we had finally found them.

3   the first day

After flying all night from Los Angeles, we arrived in Paris at 5:00 AM. We tracked down all of our fourteen huge, cherry red suitcases at the baggage belt and headed for the front door. Ronit, a beautiful Israeli who had lived in France for the past ten years and was married to Tim's best friend, Jack, met us with a large van to drive us to our train connection at one of Paris' many stations. The train station, Gare de Lyon, was quite a distance from the airport, so we were grateful for her help.

On the way, she took us on a mini tour of Paris at dawn. We tried to muster enthusiasm, but we were all battle weary from the long flight and eight hectic weeks of packing up our lives. Matt could barely focus or form a word. We kept saying things like: "Look over there, the Arc de Triomphe!" and "We're on the Champs-Elysées!" to which Matt would grunt his pat answer for everything those days, "Who gives? It's just a street."

Katie, coming to life between tracks on her newly burned CD, showed hints of interest about the ornate buildings and quaint cafés. Her best friend had made the CD for her the day before we left, and I suspected it was filled with songs that no mother wanted her children to hear. I made a mental note to check it later and decided to pretend that she was listening to Vivaldi.

We eventually made it to the train station and, with some doing, onto our train. Ronit, with her serious brown eyes and wide smile, stood on the platform and waved as the doors closed. The train lurched and started to glide out of the station. She blew us a kiss and walked alongside awhile with her palm pressed to the glass. We watched as she faded to a pinprick in the distance. We were now officially alone on a strange continent.

We settled into the plush red seats on the sleek, modern train, Tim and Katie on one side of the aisle and Matt and I on the other.

"My seat doesn't recline," complained Matt as he looked toward Katie. "How come you always get the better seat?"

"I don't always get the better seat, yours is just broken," Katie responded as she wrapped her long blonde hair into a knot on the top of her head.

"There's a whole train full of seats. Just find another one," Tim said. "And stop whining all of the time." Matt got up and repositioned himself on the other side of the aisle with Tim and Katie.

"How long is this going to take?" Matt asked. "That wasn't a whine, it's just a question."

"It'll be a nine-hour ride to Genoa," I explained. "Why don't we all relax and try to get some sleep. I think we're beyond exhausted." Soon we were settled and lost in our own thoughts. Pushing back the beige curtains on the windows, I gazed at the passing countryside. Ivory cows grazed on golden hay fields. They looked ghostly against dark green trees and a stormy sky.

"Matt," I whispered across the aisle so as not to disturb the other passengers, "look at the color of the cows. Their black splotches are missing."

Silence.

"Matt?" He looked at me across the aisle through big, dark pupils. Something was wrong.

"I don't feel so good." His little eleven-year-old face started to crumble.

"Come on over and sit on my lap," I said, though he was nearly as tall as I was. As he crawled into my arms, he began to shake all over.

"I can't stop shaking," Matt whispered.

"Honey, I think you're having a panic attack." This had never happened to him before. I struggled to appear calm. "Don't worry. It's just nerves. You're going to be okay."

"I'm afraid," Matt admitted, his voice cracked with emotion. "What does Italy even look like?"

"The part we're going to looks a lot like California. Only the buildings are older." I stroked his light brown crew cut and rubbed his neck as I did my best to describe some of the streets of his new home. He slowly drifted off to sleep. Though he was cutting off the circulation in my body, I didn't dare move him. I was overcome by his vulnerability and knew there would be few times left in his life when he would be able to seek solace in my arms so innocently. I glanced across the aisle and saw Katie watching us through flowing tears. She, too, was quietly trembling away.

"Mom?"

"You okay?" I whispered, so as not to wake Matt. Katie nodded at first and then shook her head.

"I don't want to talk about it," she choked out through her tears.

"Good. Me neither," I tried to joke.

I reached toward her and we held hands across the aisle. I kept glancing over at Tim in hopes of catching his eye, but he was snoring into his pillow. *Thanks for all of your help there, big guy.*

Unable to doze, I laid my head back and watched the scenery pass in a blur. Though the train car was crowded, the four of us seemed strangely alone. A family on an island. I gently placed Katie's arm on her armrest when she began to doze and shifted under Matthew's weight to improve blood flow to my lower extremities. Unfamiliar languages drifted around me as other passengers conversed. Tears started to drip down my cheeks, but I was not sure whether I was laughing or crying. The rhythm of the wheels on the track became a chant in my head. *Oh, God, what have we done? Oh, God, what have we done?...*

Fear and doubt filled the train compartment like poison gas. My hands shook and my heart thumped wildly in my chest. My turn for a panic attack. I made a conscious effort to breathe deeply and control my tears, vaguely aware that the conductor was eyeing me curiously. With my eyes closed, I tried to calm my panic by visualizing numbers as I slowly counted to ten. But instead of seeing numbers, I saw a paragraph from an article by Dr. Norman Vincent Peale that I used to use in the classroom years earlier when I taught Religion. During times of despair he said that we should frequently remind ourselves that God is with us, that he will never fail us and that we can count upon him. That we should actually say the words "God is with me, helping me" over and over to remind us of his power and great love.

So, with much effort, under the ever-probing eye of the conductor, I began to whisper those words under my breath. And the rhythm of the wheels on the track changed from "Oh, God, what have we done? Oh, God, what have we done?" to "God is with me, helping me. God is with me, helping me..." Within minutes, my heart stopped pounding and my tears slowed to a trickle, but I still felt achingly alone.

We arrived in Genoa around 9:00 PM. We and all of our fourteen giant red bags, of course, got off at the wrong station when we heard the conductor say the word *Genoa*. It didn't occur to us that there might be more than one station in this large city. We were at Genoa Principe. We should have been at Genoa Brignole.

"What the *heck* do you mean we're at the wrong station?" said Tim through clenched teeth as we double-checked our tickets. All of a sudden the word *heck* was popping up all over the place. "What the *heck* are we going to do now? We have no idea where the *heck* we are in relation to where we're staying for the night."

"Let's find a map." I tried to act calm. I looked around the station but saw only foreign words looming at us from every direction. There was a train schedule hanging on the wall, but no map. *Heck*, we could be anywhere.

"Look." Matt pointed to the corner where a neon sign advertised the one word that we could handle: *pizza*. Tim had been luring the kids to Italy with the promise of pizza from the gods.

"Great. Let's go get some while we figure out our next move." Tim said.

"I'm starving. This is going to be awesome." Katie smiled for the first time in hours. It took the four of us two trips each to drag our luggage down the long hallway that connected the train platform to the main hall and then around the corner to the pizzeria. This included an elaborate system of taking turns standing in strategic spots to make sure that some random thief didn't zoom over and steal anything in the process.

Standing at the counter before our first official Italian person—clearly annoyed that our luggage was taking up all of his floor space—we ordered the pizza with the verbal aplomb of cavemen.

"Pizza."

"One."

"Cheese."

"*Umm. Grande.*"

When it was delivered, it turned out to be a big piece of glop with a cup of olive oil poured on top.

"I thought you said the pizza was great here," Matt complained.

19

"This is disgusting," said Katie.

"It's not so bad," grumbled Tim. I could feel tempers rising as we chewed very slowly and peered at each other over our crusts.

"Let's just take a cab to Nervi. I don't care what it costs at this point," said Tim. "We have to get the kids to a bed."

"Great idea," I replied, visualizing us getting this luggage back on the train and off again at the next station.

"I'll go up and figure out the taxi situation. Can you guys handle getting the bags upstairs?"

Matt, Katie and I looked at each other and nodded. Tim headed out the door as Katie got up and emptied the rest of the pizza into the garbage can.

"Whew. Perfect timing. I thought we'd have to eat all of that," Matt said.

"Okay, guys, let's go," I said as I started piling some of the smaller bags on top of the larger ones with wheels. Somehow we managed to get it all over to the bottom of the escalator, which was at least two stories high.

"It feels like we're standing at the bottom of a roller coaster," Katie said.

"Here, Matt, we'll put half the bags on and then you get on. When you get to the top, just push them out onto the floor. The escalator will do all of the work, you just guide it," I instructed like I had done this before.

"Okay," said Matt. We all started to put bags on in succession. After about five bags, Matt got on and he and the bags started to rise. Katie and I went to work throwing a few more bags on the moving stairs when we heard a scream.

"Mom!"

Looking up, we could see that the first suitcase had fallen backward and pushed the rest, like dominoes, toward Matthew, who was now lying backward on the moving escalator, struggling to keep the bags off of his face.

"Help me!" Matt was now crying.

"Hold on!" I yelled, knowing this made no sense. With all of the bags in the way, I couldn't even run up to help. Matt and all of the bags were delivered, in a heap at the top. Katie and I were just seconds behind, but close enough to see that at least a dozen people had passed by him without offering to help. Matt stood and brushed himself off as Katie started to laugh.

"It wasn't funny." He grabbed the handles and wheeled two bags out the front door.

By the time we made it outside, Tim was in animated negotiations with a driver of a taxi that looked like it had been stolen from Fred Flintstone. The driver kept putting his hand high over Tim's bald head, trying to measure his height.

"Six feet eight inches," Tim kept repeating.

"Basket?" asked the driver with glee.

"Yes, basketball," Tim answered.

"Sì, sì, basketball, basketball. NBA," the driver kept repeating, his smile getting wider.

"He thinks dad's in the NBA," Matt whispered.

"We must look a lot younger in the dark," I said.

"Whatever," said Tim as he pointed to all of the bags on the sidewalk. The driver nodded as he went to the trunk of his cab and pulled out a long rope.

"Tim, don't you think we might need two taxis?"

"He said he could do it."

"You can't be serious."

"I'm not going to insult the guy. None of the other cabbies wanted to drive as far as Nervi." Tim motioned toward a line of cabs whose drivers were leaning against their cars pointing and laughing at our driver as he began to tie all of the bags to the top of the car. Obviously, people weren't too keen on helping each other around here.

"Fine. At this point, I don't even care if these bags fall off on the highway."

Moments later, we were zipping along the *autostrada* like a can of sardines on vacation, chatting up a storm with a cabbie who was clearly excited to have a famous NBA player in his presence.

"What teams are best? Can you believe those salaries? What position do you play?" The questions went on and on. Tim did his best with vague answers while we all jabbed each other in the backseat. Why burst this guy's bubble and ruin his night? Finally we saw the exit for Nervi and a hush fell over the car. This was it.

"Hotel?" he asked.

"We don't exactly have a reservation anywhere."

"You are crazy Americans. This is holiday time. The coast is already full of visitors."

"Oh." I vaguely remembered that someone had told me that Europe took the month of August for vacation. "Any ideas?"

"Yes, I will help you."

Thank goodness for the NBA. Like an angel sent from heaven, the driver took us from hotel to hotel to check for vacancies. Finally, we hit the jackpot at the Hotel Astor, a lovely place on a palm tree-lined street close to the sea. He untied the bags from the roof of his car, piled them before a horrified clerk who now had to figure out where to put them, and bid us a fond farewell.

The clerk crisply informed us that the rooms were small, with twin beds, so we had to take two. As the kids were too afraid to be alone, Katie and I would share one, and Tim and Matt would take another. He pointed us to a narrow stairwell and we started up.

"Oh no!" exclaimed Katie. We all stopped midstep.

"What?"

"My purse. Where is my purse?" Katie was frantic. We all scurried about searching for the purse. Nothing.

"Did you leave it in the cab?" asked Tim

"The train station. I hung it on the back of my chair when we got pizza." Huge tears started to roll down her face. "You're going to kill me."

"Why? What was in there?" I asked.

"All of my money."

"Oh, Katie."

"My friends. All of their pictures."

"Well, they can send more."

"And my brand new retainers."

I looked at Tim. Tim looked at me. A vision of the four-hundred-dollar check I had written just three days earlier when I picked them up flashed before my eyes.

"That's it. No one is allowed to talk to me for the rest of the night." I started to stomp childishly up the steps and headed toward my room with my best "don't even think about trying to explain how it happened" face on. I knew I was losing it, but I could not, try as I might, control myself.

I unlocked the door and Katie stomped in behind me. Before the door closed, we could hear Tim and Matt's door slam forcefully down the hall. Katie and I turned and looked at each other with bemused expressions.

"Please tell me that we're dreaming," Katie pleaded as we collapsed onto the beds and laughed until our stomachs ached. Twenty minutes later, just as we were finished showering and climbing under the covers, Tim knocked at the door. Matt was shaking again.

4 ✳ the apartment

We awakened to sunshine and had our first Italian cappuccino. Leaving all of our bags at the hotel, we set out on foot to find the Realtor. We wound through the maze of narrow paved streets that were lined on both sides with ancient two-story buildings painted in a palette of smeared pinks, oranges and yellows, with a little bit of dirt and grime thrown in for good measure. I doubted if a right angle existed anywhere in the town. The throngs of people were not glamorous vacationers dressed in designer clothes and the latest sunglasses. They were ordinary townspeople going about their ordinary errands, speaking a language that we didn't understand. In the midsummer heat and humidity, they carried sacks of groceries, pushed baby carriages and occasionally just stood in doorways or leaned out second-story windows watching us—and the morning—pass by. Things, in general, looked a little less adorable now than they had in May. I chalked this up to raw fear and kept it to myself.

With much effort, we found our way back to the alley near the old port of Nervi, entered Studio Massa and greeted Umberto with hugs and sign language. He grabbed our contract off his desk and ushered us into a contemporary conference room with sleek lines, lots of chrome and stale air thick with cigarette smoke. Unable to find the words in English, he held up an index finger, indicating that we should wait there while he called the owner of the apartment we had rented. Ten long, oxygen-deprived minutes later, Umberto returned with another man by his side. All I could see were muscles, brown eyes and soccer-player-tousled hair the color of chocolate. I couldn't stare at him hard enough. Suddenly the town was looking adorable again.

"Oh, you are all very tall!" He laughed, holding his hand up to mea-sure our heights compared to his. He stopped at Katie. "Even this girl she is taller than me. My name is Stefano," he said, looking at Tim.

"I'm Tim. This is Susan, Katie and Matthew." Stefano put his hand out and we all took turns shaking hands and doing the European "double kiss" greeting with a fair share of nose banging since we couldn't figure out which side of the face to kiss first.

"So you are from America," Stefano said, his manner warm and friendly. "Why are you here?" The four of us looked at each other and shrugged. How were we supposed to answer that?

"To see what Italy is like." I blurted out, knowing how stupid I sounded.

"*Vacanza?*" Stefano asked.

"No, we are here for a year or so." Tim responded.

"You play basketball?"

"College," answered Tim.

"University?"

"Yes, university," Tim said with a laugh.

"Your hair. Is gone like Michael Jordan."

"Yeah, he copied me," Tim joked.

"Stefano is famous footballer," Umberto said. "Genova, England, Milano."

Umberto held up the contract and instructed us all to sit around the conference table. He and Stefano went through each page with us. Luckily, Stefano knew quite a bit of English, so he could interpret the various sections. It was all standard, so we signed our names, wrote our first rent check and handed it to him.

"Do you have a way to get there?" Stefano asked as he stood and pulled his car keys from his pocket. Our blank looks said it all, and soon we were crammed into his BMW SUV and winding our way up a hill to the apartment where his wife, Sabrina, and two daughters were waiting.

Tim and Stefano talked sports while Matthew, Katie and I examined every detail of our new neighborhood out the car windows. We came to a sudden halt outside of our building.

"Don't tell me this is it," said Matt.

"I wouldn't exactly call this homey," added Katie.

"There's no basketball hoop. There's not even a yard," complained Matt.

"It's better inside, I promise," I said.

"I hope so," Katie mumbled.

We followed Stefano through the front door of the foyer, past the rows of brass mailboxes and into the infamous elevator. It was so narrow that when the five of us stood inside, our bodies almost touched, which was fine since I was standing next to Stefano.

"Matthew, hit button number seven," Tim said. The elevator started up with a jerk and a loud shudder. We looked at each other in alarm, but I consciously pushed all thoughts of the "hanging elevator" out of my head. *We're here, God, stop fooling around.*

Sabrina opened the apartment door with a grin and a warm greeting. Her brown hair fell loosely around her shoulders framing her wide blue eyes and round face. Tim and I could see Katie's and Matt's faces brighten as they entered and took in the expansive view of the sea through the wall of windows.

"Wow," said Matt.

"Not bad, huh?" Stefano said, laughing.

"This is awesome," said Katie. I sighed with relief as Katie and Matt went to explore.

"You must be tired. All of this travel," Sabrina said as she led us into the living room.

"It's a pleasure to meet you. I'm so glad you can speak English," I confided.

"A little bit. Not so good. When we lived in England, we had to learn. It was so difficult. We carried our little dictionary everywhere. This will be hard for you. We understand."

Katie and Matt returned with the two girls, whom they had found hanging out in the back bedroom. Quite stylish with their long brown hair and brightly colored outfits, they stood shyly by their dad as Katie introduced them.

"This is Stephanie, she's my age. And this is Nikki, she's the same age as Matt. They're showing us around the apartment and teaching us a few words."

"Thank you for making them feel at home," I said. Stephanie then led them out the door and onto the terrace to see the view.

Sabrina and Stefano walked us through each room, explaining as much as they could in their limited vocabulary. We couldn't believe our good fortune in finding such a fully furnished home with three bedrooms and three bathrooms on the top floor of a newer building perched high up on a mountainside. Sliding glass doors graced the front and sides, providing a view of the rocky coastline from Genoa to Portofino. The apartment had three terraces including the rooftop, where I envisioned throwing parties with foreign dignitaries that we would happen to meet along the way. It could not have been more unlike our one-story ranch home in Los Angeles. And less than half the price.

Stefano and his family took us to lunch at their favorite seaside restaurant, Mirabella, where they introduced us to both the family that ran the place and to one of the region's most famous dishes—focaccia di formaggio—a bread and cheese concoction that melted in our mouths. Suddenly, grilled cheese on Wonder bread embarrassed me.

At the end of the meal, I asked where I could buy things like sheets and towels.

"There is no place here." Sabrina sighed.

"You can't buy sheets?"

"Not in Nervi. You must travel about thirty minutes by car to Eekaya."

"Eekaya?" Sabrina took in my stricken look as I told her that we didn't have a car and didn't plan to get one. "Can we get there on the train?"

"It's too late. It would be too complicated for you." Sabrina checked her watch. "We are leaving now for our vacation home in Chamonix, but ... uh ... Stefano, we can drive them there first, no?"

First, they bought us lunch, now they were going to drive us to some far-off town to buy sheets? I simply couldn't believe how nice they were being. And it was not because they thought that Tim was in the NBA.

They dropped Tim, Matt and their two girls off at the apartment, and then drove Katie and me with our long shopping list to Eekaya—which to my amusement turned out to be Ikea pronounced Italian style—the only superstore in Genoa. We all grabbed carts and headed in different directions. Katie and Sabrina went to find kitchenware; Stefano and I headed over to the bedding department where an array of comforters and duvet covers hung from racks on display. Decorating decisions that usually took me days to mull over happened in minutes.

"What do you think about this one for the master?" I asked Stefano.

"Too many flowers for the husband." He laughed. "Something without"—he motioned his arms in front of all of the floral and geometric duvet covers—"all of this."

I pointed to a traditional white with simple red piping and matching shams. "Like this?"

"Perfetto."

I grabbed it and threw it into the cart. Farther down the aisle we quickly settled on two others for Katie's and Matt's rooms, one in blues and greens, the other in reds and oranges. As we pushed our carts toward the bathroom section, I laughed to myself and wondered how it was that I came to be picking out bedding and comparing color schemes with a handsome soccer star.

"Stefano, Stefano!" Someone recognized Stefano and waved to him as we went by. Stefano graciously waved back as others joined in on the greetings. I stuck right by his side and acted like we were old friends. This whole Italy thing was really coming together.

An hour and a half later, they dropped us off with our purchases and bid us farewell. They headed off to their vacation home in the French Alps while we started to unpack and settle in. The previous tenants had just moved out, and the apartment was less than spotless. The refrigerator needed to be cleaned, the drawers wiped out, the shelves and other surfaces dusted and the bathrooms disinfected. A quick tour before we began cleaning revealed no fewer than three to six air fresheners in every room! I'm not sure who the last tenants were, but deodorant had to be cheaper than that. Besides, how about opening a window or door?

We peeled the fresheners off the walls, pulled them from the electric sockets and out of drawers. We chucked them in the trash can and opened all of the doors and windows to let the stale air hitch a ride on the evening breeze. Tim and Matt had already organized the various suitcases and put them into the appropriate rooms. We had a lot of unpacking to do and not much energy left to get too excited about it.

"Why don't we just make up the beds. I'm beat," said Tim.

"Me too," said Matt.

"I don't really want to sleep in my room yet," Katie stated as she plopped down on one of the two low peach-colored couches that lined half the perimeter of the living room.

"Me neither," Matt concurred, plopping down next to her. Tim and I looked at each other as we started to get the picture.

"What if I move the kids' mattresses into the living room and we sleep on the couches? Like a campout," said Tim.

Twenty minutes later, we were all bedded down in our new Ikea sheets with the sliding glass doors opened wide and the fresh salt air blowing in from the sea.

5 ⚮ sunrise

A mosquito buzzing around my ear woke me up about four AM, the heat and humidity heavy and thick around me. The sheets were bunched in clumps and I could not, for the life of me, find my pillow. The sections of the couch had separated while I was sleeping and my body was holding them all together like sausage links. *Could I please be a little more uncomfortable?*

"You awake?" Tim whispered from the other side of the room.

"Yeah, you?"

"It's too hot to sleep. Want to watch the sun rise?"

"Let's make some coffee." We tiptoed into the kitchen and started to search the cupboards.

"Sabrina said they had a coffeepot. Has to be here somewhere." I opened a cabinet and saw a tiny silver one about the size of a large mug. I held it up like a prize.

"What is that?" Tim asked.

"That's the coffeepot."

"What does that make … like four sips?"

"How does this even work?" I opened the lid and stared inside.

"It kind of looks like a percolator."

"A percolator? Is this 1962?"

We attacked the problem in awkward silence like newly assigned lab partners on the first day of biology class. About five pots later, we had enough for two cups of coffee. We tiptoed, with our liquid gold, gingerly stepping around our sleeping children and out to the terrace. We sat down under the stars on two rickety looking Adirondack chairs, gazed at the orange line on the horizon that signaled the start of a new day and high-fived each other like we were ten. Like we were on the same team rather than the opposing ones we had become so used to.

With the sun came our first opportunity to survey the details of our surroundings. We gazed up and down the coast. The steep slope of the Apennine Mountains ran to the water. To the left, we saw the far reaches of a natural harbor that ended at the Monte di Portofino, a promontory that reached out into the sea. To the right we saw two tankers and a cruise ship steaming toward the port of Genoa and its densely populated suburbs that jockeyed for space along the narrow coast.

Liguria is shaped like an arc that sits at the northwestern top of the "Boot" of Italy, which is about the size and shape of New Jersey, on a diet. Genoa anchors the region and serves as the dividing line between its two sections: Riviera di Ponente (to the west) goes from Ventimiglia to Genoa, while Riviera di Levante (to the east) starts at Genoa and reaches to La Spezia. Most people come to Liguria for its seashore with its string of gorgeous towns like Portofino, Santa Margherita, Sori, Bogliasco and Chiavari strung along its coast.

"Check out those old homes," Tim pointed to the handful of boxy looking villas hidden among the numerous apartment buildings. "And the ancient stone walls." Like any urban area, there were clues here and there of a quieter life long ago. We counted the steeples of three churches within walking distance and tried to mathematically deduce how many times these hills have heard the echoes of their bells over the years.

"I love all of the thick foliage," I said already missing my garden in Los Angeles. I was surprised that the vegetation here included palm trees, pink bougainvillea and flowers of all sorts.

"It looks a lot like LA," Tim said matter-of-factly as the sound of an approaching train cut through the silence. It was haunting and comforting at the same time. We sat for a long moment and listened.

Tim began to softly sing an old tune I couldn't place.

"Two disappointed believers, two people playing the game.

Negotiations and love songs are often mistaken for one and the same." He looked at me like I should be singing along.

"What are you singing?" The whistle of the train was getting closer.

"From time to time he makes her laugh," he continues. "She cooks a meal for two..." Then, as the train came to a squealing halt at the station at the bottom of our hill, I remembered. It was a Paul Simon song we used to sing years ago when we were dating. We loved it for its soulful melody. Back then, all that mattered was that we both knew enough of the words to sing with abandon in an old, brown Buick LeSabre on a moonlit Ohio night. I did not understand or care about its lyrics lamenting a failed marriage. I understood them now.

"Everybody loves the sound of a train in the distance," I chimed in, as we finished the stanza together. "Everybody thinks it's true."

6 annalisa

Later that morning, about eight o'clock, while we were busy unpacking, there was a knock on our door.

"Who could that be?" I said as Tim went to open it. A second later a dark haired, middle-aged woman and her four children stood in our tiny foyer.

"I am Annalisa," she announced as her dark chocolate eyes examined us from head to toe. "We live ... under ... down." She pointed downward. She handed me a brown bag full of tomatoes and hugged Tim like she had known him for years. Everyone laughed as she introduced her children. There was elegant Elisabetta, fourteen, proud Carlo, twelve, shy Ester, eleven, and gentle Andrei, thirteen, a boy they had adopted from Russia.

"I'm Katie and this is Matthew, Tim and Susan. We're from Los Angeles." Clearly thrilled to have a girl her own age nearby, Katie beamed. Matt and Carlo sized each other up. I quickly thanked God for this little development, as a few friends in the neighborhood would be crucial to their happiness.

Though her children knew only a few English words from school, Annalisa knew enough to get by with the help of elaborate sign language.

"You speak Italian? Yes?"

We all shook our heads.

"No? You speak a *little* Italian, yes?"

"A couple of words," said Tim. "*Ciao, sì, arrivederci, grazie…*"

"Only *ciao, arrivederci!* You are crazy Americans."

We know.

"Why you come here? This little village. LA has everything, this village … nothing."

"The excess is what we are trying to escape."

All five of them stared at us blankly.

"Okay. We leave now. You,"—she motions to all of our bags and belongings strewn around the apartment—"do that."

I held up the bag of tomatoes. "Thank you, Annalisa."

"Is nothing."

As they started to leave, she startled us by pulling us close like we were all involved in some big secret and warned us in a fierce whisper, "You must not sleep with the doors open and the shades up. Beware of the Gypsies!"

After the door shut, Tim and I exchanged puzzled looks.

"Gypsies?" asked Katie.

"They don't have Gypsies anymore," Matt added with a disgusted tone in his voice as if he were the sudden expert on the state of Gypsies in the world. "They're only in the movies."

"I don't know, you guys," I said, "She didn't look like she was joking."

"Kind of a weird thing to say to someone you just met," added Tim. "It's so hot, there's no way we can sleep with all of the windows and doors closed."

"Hey, everyone, look," said Katie pointing out the window at all of the apartment buildings within sight. Most of the windows were sealed with shutters and shades as far as the eye could see. Okay, so maybe there were a few Gypsies.

"I have a feeling that what they call Gypsies are your basic burglars. I doubt they wear big gold hoop earrings and scarves on their heads," Tim said, intruding on my sudden fantasy about Johnny Depp sneaking into our place in the middle of the night.

"Let's not worry about it right now," I replied.

As I unpacked and cleaned, we were visited by a variety of people who already had copies of the keys to our place. No one seemed to feel that this was a safety problem. I found out that we had a suspender-wearing gardener, Roberto, whom we immediately held suspect as we had only about twenty containers with plants on the terraces, more than half of which were dead.

"So, Roberto, what is it exactly that you do?" I asked.

"You have problem with plants. I fix," he said proudly with a sweeping motion of his arms that pointed to our terrace planters filled with a straw-colored substance that was once lavender.

"Are you going to fix that?" Tim pointed to the lavender.

"No, that is fine. It will grow back. Sun is very hot now."

"Thank you, Roberto. We'll give you a call if something comes up."

"Ciao, ciao, arrivederci, ciao," he said as he left, carrying a tin bucket filled with digging tools of his trade.

Then there was a handyman, Andre, who spoke no English at all but knew how to smoke unfiltered cigarettes faster than any human being I'd ever seen. He showed up to check the electricity and show us how to work the state-of-the-art security system that didn't seem to be working. It still wasn't working when he left, but he acted like it was. I didn't really care since Tim had demonstrated to the rest of us that the "open the window and stick your head out" method of seeing who was at the door was just as effective. Both Andre and Roberto left us with a list of phone numbers of people to help us if we had an emergency. They even gave us numbers of "friends of friends" whom they *thought* spoke English, in case we needed something.

The previous tenants, Lucca and Maria, a young couple, stopped by to grab a few articles of clothing and some baby toys they had left behind and then promised to give up their copies of the keys in a few weeks after they were settled into their new place. I didn't really follow the logic, but they seemed harmless enough, though I couldn't seem to get the air freshener thing out of my head.

I decided not to care about the key situation. We had nothing to steal anyway. It was my first "letting go." We had come here to let go of life as we knew it, and this was as good a place as any to start. We would not change the locks, and I would not complain about it.

Midmorning, we embarked on our first foray into town. We needed to do a big grocery shopping and fill those empty cabinets. Matt and Katie wrote up a lengthy list of things they "absolutely had to have."

We put on our walking shoes and headed out the door. The streets were old, narrow and winding. There were no sidewalks on the way down the hill. You would think that drivers would practice caution and drive slowly so as not to endanger pedestrians, but instead, they drove with tires screeching as if they were spurred on by the sheer challenge of it.

We naturally fell into single file with Tim leading the way, shouting to us over his shoulder. "Always walk on the right-hand side in single file around the first two bends in the road. Then here,"—he pointed with his long arm—"cross the road and walk down the left side."

"I think we know how to walk," Matt grumbled.

"Seriously," agreed Katie.

"This isn't a joke. You have to walk where the drivers can see you around these bends. This isn't like Thousand Oaks Boulevard back home."

"We're not little kids, you know." Katie rolled her eyes. *Oh no, not the eye roll. Good, he didn't see it.*

"I'm just trying to keep you safe."

"Whatever." Katie glanced back at me with another eye roll.

"Don't you roll your eyes at me." Tim stopped and turned to face us, hands on hips. He glared at Katie and then at me.

"What did *I* do?" I asked.

"It's what you didn't do."

"Come on, we're all a little on edge, Tim. Just drop it."

"How about a little support here? I'm trying to start some new safety routines, and you just stand there and let them be disrespectful. It would be nice if you'd back me up."

"Back you up? You're making this bigger than it needs to be."

"I can't even imagine treating my father like that when I was fourteen."

"Fine. Dad's right. These bends are dangerous. Do what he says. There. Did that make you feel 'backed up'?"

More glaring.

"Sorry, Dad," Katie said.

"Me too." said Matt. Then Tim turned on his heel and we continued on, our tennis shoes squeaking on the far left side of the hot pavement.

We happened upon an ancient stairway lined with purple bougainvillea and vines sprayed with orange trumpet flowers. Much safer than the road, it looked like a secret passageway to somewhere good. A couple hundred single-file steps downward plopped us near the center of town.

Our first stop was at the *farmacia* to get some aspirin and toothpaste. Everyone else decided to wait outside since the place was tiny and filled with people over seventy-five. I got in line and marveled at the abundance of anti-cellulite products that filled the shelves while customer after customer cut in front of me. Apparently they didn't know about the "no cuts" rule. Finally it was my turn. I looked at the girl behind the counter. She looked at me. I had no idea how to say *aspirin* and *toothpaste*. I started to flip frantically through my trusty little dictionary.

"One moment," I said to the girl as she folded her arms and waited. All of a sudden, I became aware that the old man behind me was breathing conspicuously close to the back of my neck. I turned around and glared at him.

"Excuse me," I said, but he did not respond. I stared at him and gave a little shoving motion with my hands, but he continued to look right through me like a zombie. I turned my attention back to the dictionary, found the word for *aspirin* and pointed to it so the girl could read it. For *toothpaste* I gave a quick brushing pantomime.

"*Sì, sì,*" she said and went to get them. I kept turning again and again to glare at the man behind me, but he wouldn't move back. He had bad breath and terrible BO. I wondered if his wife had sent him to get air fresheners.

The pharmacist wrapped both items in paper like a Christmas gift and then put them in a bag. As I handed her a few euros, I could see Matthew knocking on the store window and pointing to his watch. I just shrugged in reply.

We continued on down the street. The sidewalks were crowded and narrow, so we again fell into single-file and made our way like a train of giant bobble-head dolls, attracting attention that we did not seek.

As we walked through the neighborhood, we stopped and peered into the butcher shop, the fruit store, the fresh pasta place, the bakery, the fresh fish store, the wine shop, the pizzeria, the coffee bar and the tobacco shop. Many of the doors were open, and their mouth-watering aromas made us take frequent stops to stand, close our eyes and breathe deeply though our noses, as if we were centering ourselves for an impromptu yoga experience.

"Does anyone see an actual grocery store?" asked Katie.

"I think we just have to go to each of these little shops instead," said Tim.

We all stood and looked at each other with trepidation. We were charmed. We were delighted. We were petrified. How were we going to do this when the only words we knew were *ciao* and *arrivederci*?

"Look over there," Matt pointed to a storefront down the street in the basement of an apartment building. "Doesn't that look like one?"

We headed toward the door, over which a large sign read *dì per dì* in bright red letters. "It is!" Katie exclaimed as we watched an elderly couple exit with white bags in their hands.

We walked down a long ramp into the store. Our collective height attracted attention from all of the people in line waiting to check out. We were the tall, thin, celery people invading the city of eggplants. We ignored their stares and acted like we knew what we were doing.

I grabbed a small cart whose wheels rolled kind of forward and sideways at the same time.

"These aisles are narrow."

"How come milk only comes in quart bottles?"

"The eggs aren't refrigerated. Can we eat them like that?"

"All of the packages are so small."

"Where's the list?" Katie pulled out the list, tore it into four equal pieces and handed one to each of us. Everyone set out to find their items. I rolled the cart over to the produce section and started to pick out a few fruits and vegetables. As I pinched and poked, I noticed a lot of huffing and staring going on. People were clearly annoyed at me. Was I taking too much? It's a store, for goodness' sake. I pretended not to notice and continued to fill my little plastic bags with all sorts of salad makings. Before I knew it, I was surrounded by a bevy of irate silver-haired shoppers, arms folded and toes tapping.

"What?" I asked, holding up my arms in surrender. One of them pointed an arthritic finger toward a box near the bananas. She reached into it and whipped out a large clear plastic glove. The rest of them then held up their plastic-clad right hands.

"Oh," I said as she handed it to me and they all waited until I put it on. Apparently, I wasn't supposed to touch the produce with my bare hands.

"Sorry," I mumbled as they shuffled back to their own purchases, shaking their heads and rolling their eyes.

I met up with Tim in the next aisle as he stood with a blank look on his face.

"I hate to tell you this," he said, "but you know what this store is full of?"

"What?"

"Ingredients."

As I looked around, I could see he was right. This place was not about prepackaging, preserving, home at five thirty, dinner on the table by six. There would be no buying frozen gourmet food and putting it in our own fancy dishware to pretend we made it. No siree.

"Mom!" Katie and Matt cried in unison as they came around the corner with a lone box of crackers. "Nothing on our list is even here!"

There were no Oreos, no spicy Cheetos and few recognizable candy bars. No Campbell's soup, no corn on the cob, no Chef Boyardee, no peanut butter. No baggies of any sort. No garlic salt, no Fruit Roll-Ups. No salad dressing or maple syrup. No pancakes or waffles. No Kraft Mac and Cheese. No cake mixes or frosting for Katie's upcoming birthday cake. It was going to be healthy eating all the way. We wondered if our bodies would recognize food without preservatives.

Variety, here, was not the spice of life. The exotic food shelf held only a few cans of kidney beans, corn chips and salsa. But what was offered was fresh and delicious. The cheeses, fresh meats, olives, marinated vegetables and pesto sauce were pictures from a gourmet magazine.

Soon enough our cart was full, and we headed to the little checkout counter. Embarrassingly, we had five times as much as every other customer in line. Finally it was our turn. The conveyor belt at the checkout was—no surprise—small. It immediately clogged with all of our stuff, but the checker kept going.

"Where's the bagger?"

Things started to tumble to the floor. We looked at each other in panic.

"Where's the bagger?" People were staring (again).

"Where's the bagger?!" The checker kept on checking away. Things kept falling.

Finally it dawned on us. We had to buy plastic bags (paper is not an option here) from the grocer and do it ourselves. Giggling, the four of us scurried to bag our items, piling the bags on the floor in the corner as we went. A mountain of white. As Tim paid the bill, I suddenly realized why everyone else had just a few things in their carts.

Up the hillside we trudged, laden like donkeys with our white bags, in the soaring temperatures of the afternoon. The tall, thin, celery people began to wilt. The eggplants were amused.

7 ✦ opera

Still not fully adjusted to the time change after five days in our new home, I awoke just after dawn and decided to finish the final phase of cleaning while the rest of the family slept. Everything had been unpacked and put away; all that was left to do was to clean and polish the dark wood floors and abundant shelving. When the residue from past inhabitants was wiped away, the place would feel like it was ours. I looked through cabinets and under the sinks for supplies. All I found was one Swiffer without accompanying wipes, an old broom with bristles that resembled Alfalfa's hair, and a vacuum cleaner with a hose attached to the body with white tape, Windex and water. No Murphy Oil Soap, no orange oil, no Pledge.

If I had been in LA, I would have driven over to the twenty-four-hour Rite Aid and bought the largest box of premoistened Swiffer sheets I could find. But that option was now in storage with the rest of our belongings. Feeling very ingenious and thrifty, I cut one of Tim's old T-shirts into small rectangles to use in the Swiffer. Since I figured I had just saved about seven euro, I made a mental note to reward my cleverness by hiding that amount away to spend on a trinket at the open air market that comes each Tuesday. Hopefully, Tim would not miss his T-shirt.

I decided to put on some music. A little rhythm always helped me clean faster. I turned on the small Bose radio that we had brought with us from home and found a station that was playing American songs. I adjusted the volume so as not to disturb the rest of the family and went to work. Deciding it safest to use only water, I wiped and mopped away to the beat of "Jeremiah Was a Bullfrog."

A knock at the door surprised me. Who now? I opened it to find Annalisa with her infectious smile and her arms filled with more house-warming gifts. She handed me another big bag of ripe tomatoes and a bottle of limoncello, a traditional lemon liqueur, homemade from the lemon trees planted on the terraced gardens she had carved from the mountainside behind our building. I felt embarrassed because this was the second time she had brought us gifts, and I had yet to reciprocate. I quickly scanned the area for something I could give in return. I spied our last PowerBar on the counter but decided against it.

"Thank you!"

"Everything. Is ripe all at once."

"I love garden tomatoes."

"Tim, Katie and Matthew. They are still sleeping?"

I nodded and shrugged my shoulders pretending to be miffed that they would all still be sleeping at seven in the morning. I wracked my brain for something else to say. The language barrier had made me tentative. We stood for a moment just smiling at each other.

"Your family. I want you come to dinner at my house. I teach you make pizza. Italian pizza, not American."

"We'd love to come! Thank you! That sounds like great fun."

"*Umm.* Next Thursday."

A week away, obviously she liked to plan ahead. I paused a moment to pretend that I had to mentally check my calendar. I didn't want to let on that we were drifters with no immediate or long-term plans on the docket.

"I think Thursday would work great!"

"Okay, *ciao.*"

"*Ciao.*"

"*Ciao, ciao, arrivederci, ciao!*"

"Okay, *ciao, arrivederci.*"

"*Ciao.*" She turned and walked off. I was having trouble understanding how many times we needed to say *ciao* and *arrivederci* before leaving someone. I made another mental note to research this, as the single American good-bye was obviously not enough to truly disconnect from social encounters over here.

I closed the door and went back to my mop and the view of the sparkling Mediterranean from the living room. Suddenly the radio changed format. The American music gave way to the Opera Hour, so I rushed to change the station. As I stood, pressing the scan button over and over, the red tile roofs, the churches in the distance and the multicolored buildings down below caught my eye. For some strange reason a twinge of guilt compelled me to turn back to the opera station.

A woman began an aria, soulful and haunting. The notes dripped down the walls. I had no idea what she was saying, but the music stirred me somewhere deep in the core of my being. I recalled the scene in *Shawshank Redemption* when Andy played Mozart's *The Marriage of Figaro* over the loudspeaker and treated the inmates to a few moments of humanity and dignity.

Propped up by my Swiffer handle, I rested a moment and said a prayer thanking God for our many blessings. For leading us to this threshold of opportunity and then giving us the courage to walk through Door Number 2. I had made peace with the fact that Tim and I felt unfulfilled and inept in our marriage. I had wrapped up that bitter disappointment and handed it to God with a note card that said "No backsies." I did not want to live in the mire of negativity and blame anymore. I had, instead, chosen to embrace hope with the knowledge that we were trying to do something about it. I felt we were poised on the edge of a year filled with finer moments. M. Scott Peck said that our finest moments are most likely to occur when we are feeling deeply uncomfortable, unhappy or unfulfilled. For it was only in such moments, propelled by our discomfort, that we are likely to step out of our ruts and start searching for different ways or truer answers.

So far so good. I felt strangely peaceful, as if this deep cleaning was reaching all the way down to my soul and wiping away some of my accumulated unrest and disillusionment.

"What the heck are you listening to?" Tim broke my reverie as he stood, sleepy-eyed in the hallway at the edge of the room. I had no idea how long he had been standing there.

"Opera." Avoiding his perplexed stare, I put the Swiffer back to work scrubbing at imaginary stains.

"Opera? I hate opera." He shuffled over and changed the station.

"I was listening to that."

My strangely peaceful moment vanished with the push of that button. "I said I was listening to that."

He plopped down on the couch, toppling my carefully arranged stack of rectangular pieces of cloth. We both reached for them at once. "You cut up my T-shirt?"

8 ✦ the heat wave

The windows of the houses and apartments were covered with electronically controlled shades of horizontal, slatted wood that you raised and lowered with the push of a button. When they were shut, it was so dark that you couldn't see your hand in front of your face. At night and upon leaving during the day, you had to lower them. That, I deduced, was the rule.

The only problem with that was the soaring heat. Europe was having its worst heat wave ever. With August temperatures close to a hundred and humidity at ninety percent, people in Italy and surrounding countries were dying in large numbers. Umberto had told us that our apartment came with air conditioning, but he forgot to mention that it hadn't worked since 1977. So we were faced with the ultimate dilemma: Should we sleep with the doors open in order to breathe and thus risk the unlawful entry of the Gypsies? Or should we protect ourselves from intruders and suffocate?

Tim and I researched this Gypsy situation by asking the few people we had met about it. In my heart, I couldn't imagine that it was a real threat. Come on. Surely Annalisa must have been exaggerating.

But the answers were unnerving. The girl at the coffee shop said, "They scale the buildings on fire escapes. Then they take their shoes off so they won't make noise as they slink thorough your home while you sleep."

The man at the fruit stand informed us of a secret spray. "They will come into your house while you're sleeping and spray your faces with a mist so fine that you will not feel it. You will not wake up for hours, and they will steal everything."

Annalisa, in our second conversation on the subject, assured us that they had "come into the man's apartment on the fourth floor of our very building dressed like Dracula." So, after this very unscientific study, Tim and I could only conclude one thing. There *were* Gypsies, tramps and thieves. Yes, we heard that from the people of the town. They told us, beware of Gypsies, tramps and thieves. So every night we had to lock our windows up and put our shades down.

Tim set out on a mission to find some fans. Every single store in Nervi had sold out. The various shop owners told him that this area had never had to deal with such temperatures, and it was just not equipped to handle them. The part that made Tim crazy was that none of the shop owners seemed to feel the urge to restock or capitalize on the situation. The minor fact that people were dying all over Europe didn't seem to faze anyone. They sold their fans. End of story.

The heat and humidity made everyone cranky. Katie and Matthew were at each other constantly.

"Matt, move over. You're breathing too loud."

"Yeah? Well your breath smells."

"I'm serious. Move over to that couch over there."

"No. If it bothers you that much, you move."

"Fine."

"Fine."

We spent the next few nights camping together in the living room, our heads close to a tiny crack we had left open in one door, booby-trapped to make noise if someone came in. I slept fitfully, woke up drenched in sweat and took cold showers at all hours of the night. It was a relief to get up in the morning, though I was anything but rested.

On the fourth morning Tim got up and disappeared in a huff. He returned two hours later with a standing air conditioner the size of a

43

small Volkswagen. He wheeled it into the foyer and stood beside it like a proud car dealer showing off his latest model.

"What the heck is that?" asked Matt.

"It's an air conditioner." Tim said. We all cheered as he took a bow.

"Why is it so big?" asked Katie. It occurred to me that our children had never even seen a window air conditioner before.

"What are we going to do, cool down the whole building?" teased Matt.

"Where are we going to put it?" I asked.

"I just spent two hours combing the entire area. This was the only air conditioner left, and it wasn't even for sale. I convinced them to sell it to me." Tim could sell stripes to a zebra.

"You are awesome," I said.

"Was that a compliment?" Tim said as we both looked at each other with raised eyebrows.

"Oh my gosh, I think it was." I said with a giggle. It had been a while. "Thank you."

"You're welcome."

"It was the floor model from a store down near the train station in Nervi. The sales guy even drove me back here with it in his own car and helped me get it into the elevator. Talk about service."

"Let's figure out how it works," said Katie. We all gathered around and examined its every detail like it was a spaceship that had landed unexpectedly. I opened the instruction manual and found that it would cool a room about seven by seven.

"We'll put it in our bedroom," Tim said as he pushed it down the hallway. "We can all sleep in there." Tim and Matt dragged the kids' mattresses from the living room into our bedroom and laid them on the floor at the side and foot of our bed. Tonight we would cool this one room down and sleep soundly in comfort without fear of Gypsy invasion.

Late in the evening, Tim decided to get the room ready. Matt and I lowered all of the shades and locked all of the doors. Then Katie made a great ceremony of plugging in the air conditioner and turning it on. BOOM! All of the lights in the entire apartment went out! I screamed and ran through the pitch black darkness in search of the front door. I was suddenly ten years old playing Murderer in the Dark with my three older brothers in my New Jersey basement. I jerked open the front door, and within moments we were all standing together in the moonlight.

"What happened?" asked Matt.

"What do you think happened?" Katie answered sarcastically.

"You're the one who plugged it in," Matt chided. "It's probably your fault."

"It's not my fault. Dad told me to."

"It's nobody's fault," I cut in. "It's the air conditioner. It blew all of the fuses."

"Let's find some matches, light a few candles," said Tim.

"Did we buy a flashlight at Ikea?"

I found a few tea lights in the kitchen and lit them. I held them up high like I was asking for an encore at a concert. "Where's the fuse box?"

"I can't find it," said Tim, rummaging through the closets in the dark.

"Crap." said Matt. "How are we going to fix it?"

"We'll have to ask for help." I said.

I grabbed our Italian dictionary, and all four of us tromped downstairs where the lights were still on. Tim knocked at Annalisa's door. A thin, unassuming man with short brown hair and wire glasses opened it. In his rumpled dress pants and white collared shirt, it looked like he had had a long rough day. He looked at us with a blank stare.

"Hi...uh *buona sera, um* we are from upstairs," Tim stammered as the man narrowed his eyes and started to nod his head. Annalisa came up behind him.

"Tim! Susan! This is my husband, no?" she said. Her husband took control and spoke in a rush of Italian so fast that I could not pick out a single word. The four of us shook hands with him and nodded, saying our names one at a time. I never caught his name, though my smile suggested otherwise.

"Our electricity. It is gone." Tim tried to support his words with awkward sign language.

"Is gone?" Annalisa said eyes widening. They ran to get their flashlights and followed us back upstairs to inspect the situation.

the heat wave

"How could that happen?" she asked.

"I have no idea!" we all said at once. No one wanted them to know about the Volkswagen parked in the bedroom.

The six of us, standing silently, eye to eye, took the elevator to the ground floor. They led us around the building to a closet in the back of one of the garages near the street. This was where all of the electrical boxes were located for the building. Peering inside, I saw a huge switch like the one that powered up Frankenstein. Tim brushed away the cobwebs and pushed it back into place. A loud click told us we were back in business.

Thanking them profusely, we followed them outside and stood in the dark.

"You must find out what happened in the morning. None of the other apartments lost power," insisted Annalisa.

"We will surely look into it," Tim said as Katie, Matt and I elbowed each other and suppressed our giggles.

"You will let us know?"

"Of course."

9   pasta sauce

Like the Red Army poised for attack, two dozen of Annalisa's garden tomatoes had been staring at me for four days from the kitchen window-sill. The intense heat was ripening them before my eyes.

I had never pretended to be a good cook. My friends understood this and always, God bless them, assigned me to bring the bread at every pot-luck occasion. But even I could not resist the compulsion to make home-made pasta sauce in an Italian kitchen.

I walked downstairs with a pad of paper and a pen and knocked at Annalisa's door. I stood for a minute and listened, smiling to myself at all of the commotion inside. This was a passionate household, filled with joyful noise from dawn till dusk. I knocked four times before I was heard. When the door opened, I was greeted by Annalisa, Zabo the family dog and the heady aroma of something cooking on the stove. I had come to the right place.

"*Ciao*, Annalisa."

"*Ciao*, Susan. Come in. Come in." I stepped into the marble foyer as four bodies zoomed past us laughing and screaming down the hall. I held up my pad and pen.

"Can you give me the recipe for tomato sauce?"

"Not this." She pushed away my pad of paper in disgust. "Easy. A baby can do it. Come." I followed her down a long narrow hallway in the opposite direction from the kids' roughhousing noises to the kitchen, which was clean but cluttered with all sorts of pots, pans and utensils. There was not enough counter space for a serious chef with a large family. Martha Stewart would have a field day here, offering all sorts of space saving remedies to accommodate and organize. Though it was only ten o'clock in the morning, a large black kettle of sauce was simmering away on the stove. Annalisa took the lid off the pot. My mouth watered as I peered inside at the chunky orangish concoction.

"Tomato?" I asked. She nodded.

"Is tomato,"—she gestured toward a counter that was piled with tomatoes—"with *formaggio* … cheese." She held up a wedge of Parmesan the size of a small animal.

"How do you make it?"

Annalisa began talking a mile a minute, with her hands keeping pace. From this whir of motion, I felt confident that I had picked up the basics.

"Blah, blah, blah, blah, tomatoes, blah, blah, blah, blah, water, blah, blah, blah, blah, chop, blah, blah, blah, blah, cook. Easy, yes?"

"A cinch." I smiled with confidence. This would be a no-brainer. She walked me to the door. "Thank you so much!"

"Is nothing. *Ciao!*"

"*Ciao.*"

"*Ciao, ciao, arrivederci.*"

Here we go again.

"*Ciao*, Annalisa. *Ciao, ciao.*"

"Okay, *Ciao.*" I left hoping I had said it enough times.

Back upstairs, I rolled up my sleeves and started washing all of the tomatoes. Tim walked in and poured himself a glass of water.

"What's all this about?"

"How does a little homemade pasta sauce grab you?"

"It grabs me just fine. Who's making it?" he teased.

"Funny."

"The kids and I are headed to the beach," he added, as Katie and Matt walked in with towels, bathing suits and relaxed faces. Everyone's good humor had returned now that our air conditioner was providing us with consistent sleep.

"Good, you can all look forward to a great meal when you return."

As they headed out the door, I sat down at the kitchen table and chopped up all of the tomatoes. Our new Ikea knife was very sharp and soon the mound of diced tomatoes included the tip of the middle finger from my left hand, the size of a large Rice Krispie. I quickly wrapped a paper towel around my wound, which would not stop bleeding as I searched frantically for the tip. I could not find it! It just blended right in with the pulp of the tomatoes.

As I stood for a moment applying direct pressure to my finger, I surveyed the situation. I couldn't just throw out two dozen tomatoes. How would I explain that? I would never live that one down. The piece wasn't that big. It wasn't like it was poison or anything. I decided to skim off the portion of the tomatoes I held suspect and threw it away. Any other germs would be killed during cooking. I threw everything into a big pot, added salt, pepper and a little olive oil and stirred it around just as Annalisa had showed me and turned on the heat. It was a beautiful sight. I felt the excitement of being a real chef for the first time in my life.

Like a first-time mother, I checked on my baby constantly. After about twenty minutes, I could already see that it bore little resemblance to Annalisa's sauce. It looked dry and tasted pulpy. I added a little more oil and a dash of water for good measure. By the end of the hour, the sauce had boiled down to a red mass a little larger than my fist. It was filled with little pieces of tomato skin, which had separated from the tomato during cooking. I didn't remember seeing any skin, tomato or human, in Annalisa's sauce. Obviously I had missed a few steps of her explanation.

Feeling deflated, I went ahead and boiled up a bunch of pasta because I knew everyone would be home soon for lunch. By the time they returned, the dining room table was set and a large salad made.

"Something smells good!" Matt exclaimed as they came through the door.

"Yeah, Mom," added Katie, "I'm starving."

"Matt, please pour the milk."

"Why do I always have to pour it? It's Katie's turn."

"I poured it last night."

"Just pour the milk, Matt." Tim took control as he lifted the lid of the saucepan on the stove to take a peek. He raised his eyebrow. "Interesting." I ignored him and handed Katie a huge bowl with enough pasta to feed ten people.

"Here, Katie, please put this on the table and have a seat." I scooped the sauce into a little bowl and carried it out. I set it next to the pasta and sat down.

"Is that it?" asked Matt. "That's all there is?"

"That's like enough for one person," added Katie.

Tim swallowed his laughter as I scooped pasta onto a plate. I balanced a small plop of the thick sauce on top like a meatball on a mountain.

"This is normal here." I tried to sound convincing as I made a plate for each person. "The pasta here is fresh, handmade. Much more important than the sauce."

"But it's so dry!" Matt complained.

"Here, drink more milk."

"What happened to your finger?" Katie suddenly exclaimed.

Tim picked at the tomato skins that speckled the noodles like red pepper flakes. "And what are these things?"

"Skin," I replied.

"Yours?" Matt asked.

"Don't be silly," I answered. "Tomato skin. I forgot to peel them. Now, *mangia*, eat!" There were a few minutes of silent chewing.

"Do they sell Ragu here?"

I sighed, looked at my throbbing finger wrapped in another piece of Tim's old T-shirt and said, "I hope so."

1 0 ❧ extreme marital therapy
part 1

I stood in the doorway and watched Tim as he organized the cabinets over the stove. He had always loved to line things up in exact rows. Back home, it did nothing but annoy me, but for some reason I now found it semi-endearing. And the fact that he could reach all of the top shelves with ease made it all the more convenient. He was deep in thought and didn't know I was watching. I wondered if he was thinking about the proper place for the two spices we had bought at the store the other day.

I felt a little twinge. That "Okay, I still think he's cute" feeling. It was a relief. These last two weeks had been surreal, a fragile time. I was hyperaware of every moment. Stepping outside the protective bubble of ingrained culture had left me vulnerable and invigorated, an unlikely combination that opened me up and drew me toward Tim rather than away. Our common goal of providing Katie and Matthew a sense of home as quickly as possible was causing us to lean on each other and climb the ladder of Maslow's hierarchy of needs together. These first few rungs were the things we had no problem agreeing on. Providing food and shelter and fulfilling the need to belong were at the heart of the matter now, not something we took for granted. Stage one of our Extreme Marital Therapy was turning out to be all about coming together to problem solve.

Tim caught a glimpse of me in the reflection of the kitchen window. He continued for a few minutes and just let me watch. Then he turned in my direction and said, "Hey."

"Looks good," I told him. "You moved the glasses to a different shelf."

"Yeah. I think this is better."

"Me too."

"And the snacks go better up here over the oven."

"And the cereal?"

"Right over here."

"Nice. Maybe the napkins and paper towels would work better under the sink." Tim thought for a moment, nodded his head and moved the packages to the open space below.

"That works."

Even this simple exchange would have been a minefield back home—each of us angry that the other was too controlling, always wanting everything his or her way. Here, however, I could put things in perspective and let him do what he was naturally good at without attaching deeper meaning. I had expected fights and fireworks these first few weeks, but was pleasantly surprised with our increasing ability to come together to get things done with our senses of humor somewhat intact. Being a realist, I was wary. This still felt like vacation. Time would tell if and how our relationship would evolve. Anything was possible at this point.

So far, Tim and I had tackled and accomplished a variety of tasks together while Katie and Matthew looked on with amusement, our family bonding with each other in the process. On Monday we had all gone to the Vodafone store and bought four triband cell phones that worked all over Europe. Who knew that phones came in differing bandwidths and why did we have to learn that in a forty-five-minute exchange of foreign words and sign language?

Then on Tuesday, after asking Annalisa where we could sign up for the Internet, we had gone back to the Vodafone store and worked with the same salesman, who had the patience of Job. It had taken another forty-five minutes to open an account with FastWeb and set up installation, which he assured us would happen within a few weeks.

"A few weeks?" Katie and Matt had cried.

On Wednesday, the four of us had ambled through the heat to the other side of town to Gentilotti—the appliance store where Tim had

51

gotten the air conditioner—to buy a TV and sign up for SKY Italia satellite service. It took forever to understand and fill out the paperwork. The saleswoman, Anna, also assured us that we could expect SKY to be up and running within a few weeks.

"A few weeks?" Katie and Matt cried again.

On Thursday, with the help of our landlord, Stefano, who knew everyone in town, we had opened a bank account at the UniCredit Banca. The branch manager, Giovanni, had crammed four chairs into his sleek office for us and painstakingly helped Tim and me fill out forms, understand systems and order checks. By the end of that hour and a half, the five of us were quite chummy. Giovanni had ended the meeting by complimenting our fearlessness.

"This is not ordinary. You are very brave family," Giovanni had said shyly.

It was now Friday, and after Tim was finished here in the kitchen we were all going to take the train to Ikea again for a few more items that we had forgotten the first time around. But we were in no hurry, as our days were without schedule now. It was luxurious to have time spread out before me like the wide-open sea. To have the emotional space to just sit for a few minutes in the kitchen and watch my husband, without all of the checklists running though my head about what needed to be done or where the kids needed to be next.

Tim took a deep breath, surveyed the cabinets with satisfaction and turned and stood before me. He gave me that great smile that said "what is this you-watching-me-thing all about?" Then he walked over and gave me a kiss. And then another one. I felt that twinge again. And I was glad.

1 1 ❧ the fire

Around 8:00 AM I was roused from a deep sleep by large hands that shook me back and forth with an urgency that my sixth sense picked up before I did.

"Hurry," Tim said and ran back out of the room.

"What?" I asked, knowing no one was there to answer. I threw my covers back and stumbled out after him in my P. J. Salvage pajamas. *This had better be important.* As I quickened my step, I smelled smoke. Katie and Tim were out on our side *terrazza*.

"Mom," Katie said, "there's a fire!" The mountain that our neighborhood backs up to was now sporting a brushfire at the ridgeline. It was about a half a mile away from us and big enough to fill the sky around it with white gray smoke. The flames licked the dry brush, bushes and scrub pines like a hungry dragon. The area around it was open land, but having lived in Southern California for ten years, I knew how quickly these fires could grow and become unstoppable, consuming everything in their path. All we needed were a few gusts of wind to send the dragon charging down the hill in our direction.

I raced back inside. "Wake up Matthew! We have to pack our things! Get the photos, important papers. Throw whatever you can carry into a bag!"

"Calm down," said Tim. "The fire's not that close."

"Yet!"

"Don't you think if it were dangerous there would at least be firefighters up there?" I searched the hillside for any signs of firefighting activity. Nothing.

"That's weird," I said, calming somewhat. Matt joined us in his blue gym shorts. His hair stuck up at all angles from sleep. "What's going on?"

"There's a fire, but no one seems to be worried about it," Katie said as we all walked back out to the *terrazza*.

"That looks like that one in Thousand Oaks a few years ago," said Matt. "Remember?" How could I forget? Matt and I had pulled our car over on Hillcrest Drive and watched with horror as flames shot high into the sky in the Santa Monica Mountains across the 101 Freeway. That fire had run all the way through the canyons and ended up miles away, near Pepperdine University, by the time the firefighters had gotten it under control.

53

"This one's a lot smaller," Tim assured Matt as he snuggled in close to us. We all just stood for a while and watched. "Take a look around," continued Tim. "We're the only people in sight who are watching this."

He was right. A quick scan of the neighborhood revealed nothing out of the ordinary. We could not see one other human being outside.

"Does Italy have a Twilight Zone?" said Matt.

"Maybe we're the first ones to see it," I offered.

"Oh great." Katie laughed. "And we can't speak Italian and have no idea how or where to report it."

"Somebody else knows about it. Look." Matt pointed to a nifty seaplane that was heading toward the flames. It had a long hose, like a tail, trailing behind it. We had seen plenty of those in California. It proceeded to drop its load of water over the burning area, something akin to a cupful on a house fire.

Intrigued, the four of us stood and watched the plane take a few trips to and from the sea, sucking up water through the hose and then spraying it on the fire.

"It'll take ten years to put out the fire at that pace," Tim said.

"If everyone else is okay with a blazing hilltop next to their homes, then we should be too. Right?" I asked.

"Even more so," Tim answered as the kids started to nod in agreement. "Isn't that why we're renting? So we don't have to worry about the big stuff anymore?"

"Who cares," I said, getting into the same frame of mind. "Let it all burn."

"Yeah," added Matt.

Keeping one eye on the fire and blackening sky, we ate breakfast and pretended that all was normal as we talked about how to spend the upcoming day.

"Isn't today market day?" Tim asked.

"Cool," said Katie.

"Let's hurry up!" I added. We had been looking forward to market day for a week, ever since Annalisa mentioned that Italy had traveling markets that go from city to city because department stores were few and far between. Every community had a market day, and ours was Tuesday, today.

Turning our backs to the fire, the four of us headed down the ancient steps. Katie and I walked slowly with our dictionaries open looking up the phrase "How much is it?"

"Here it is," Katie said. "*Quanto costa?*"

"*Quanto costa?*" Matt repeated.

So the four of us, acting silly, took turns saying *quanto costa* with all types of voice inflections to cover every mood and possibility as we continued down the steps. Soon enough, I felt I was an expert at it, though I had no vocabulary yet to handle Euro amounts. Since I could barely count to twenty at this point, I would have to rely on pointing and price tags for that.

At the bottom of the hill, a string of white tents—most with vans or trucks parked behind them—wrapped itself around a full city block. It looked like the circus had come to town. We all started at the beginning and walked, starry eyed, from tent to tent. There were handbags of every style, shape and color hanging from every possible inch of one tent's poles and canvas roof. In another, were tables stacked with men's shoes. Still another was a drugstore with toiletries, makeup, and deodorant on display. There were tents devoted to kitchens, rugs, tablecloths and underwear. Rainbows of scarves and shawls billowed in the wind. Jewelry for every occasion sparkled in the sun. It went on and on. I could buy virtually anything but furniture. The merchants, hawking their merchandise, were as colorful as their wares. A fat man called to me from behind his table filled with sewing notions. A tall man showed off his umbrellas. A human tattoo spoke in falsetto when he challenged Matthew to bargain with him for a yo-yo. And the fortune teller, with a gold front tooth and wearing a blue paisley head scarf promised great things would happen if we bought her knockoff perfume.

"I bet she's one of the Gypsies," said Matt as we hurried by her.

"Bet you're right," Katie agreed.

"Let's split up," said Tim. "Matt and I will meet you two in an hour."

Tim and Matt wandered over to a tent that sold watches as Katie and I wandered by a man asking for money, in a brown monk's outfit complete with sandals and a tonsure—the prerequisite bald spot surrounded by a ring of brown hair.

"Is he for real?" Katie asked.

"I don't know, but I give him credit for the authenticity of his look. Here, put a euro in the jar."

"I love all of this."

"Me too."

"Just stand a minute and listen. Close your eyes."

"Why do you always make me do this when we go somewhere new?"

"Just do it." We stood together in a sea of shoppers and listened to spirited haggling on all sides mixed with friendly conversations between friends and neighbors. I peeked before Katie opened her eyes and saw a huge smile on her face.

Katie linked her arm through mine and pulled me toward a tented area filled with skirts and cargo pants—European style. "Can we get something?"

"Why not?" Our American clothes and shorts didn't quite fit in here. No women over the age of ten wore shorts. Everyone wore pants, skirts or pretty sundresses. Feminine was in, and it was a welcome change. I patted my pocket to make sure my roll of euros was still there. We sorted through the racks and picked out a few things. After trying them on in a makeshift dressing room made of sheets and pins, we decided to buy two. I chose pumpkin-colored linen cargo pants and Katie selected a long tan cotton skirt.

"Where do we pay for these?" I asked out loud as I looked around for the owner of the tent.

"Over there." Katie pointed to a rugged, thirty-five-ish Bohemian-type blond merchant who was using his smoldering gray eyes to sell more than clothing to a young woman in the corner.

"Let me handle this one," I said as we headed toward him.

"Remember, Mom, *quanto costa*," Katie said.

"I know, I know. We practiced a million times."

With confidence, I walked right up to the merchant and cleared my throat. He turned from his conversation with the girl and bore his smoldering gray eyes into mine. Feeling suddenly weak at the knees and quite ready to buy as many items as he might suggest, I held up our two things and said loudly, "*Costa quando?*"

He looked at me with amusement. Katie's eyes widened and she began to giggle. I could feel the blood rushing to my face as I handed him the clothes. I had failed at my first attempt at communication. I was doomed.

"Susan, Katie!" Annalisa, laden with bags of all colors and sizes, suddenly appeared like an angel of mercy and helped me with the transaction. She then pointed up the hill and asked, "Did you notice the fire?"

"Oh, that?" I feigned nonchalance.

"Don't worry about it," she said. "Sometimes, these fires, they burn all the way down to the street. Is okay."

"I won't think another thing about it," I shouted over the noise of the seaplane zooming overhead. *Burns all the way down to the street?*

Tim and Matt caught up with us, and we compared purchases. They had found little trash cans for the bedrooms and lots of clothespins. Back up the hill we climbed, noticing that a special helicopter had joined forces with the seaplane. Still no sight of actual firefighters.

When we got home, I got a call from my parents back in the States to see if we were anywhere near the fires on the Italian Riviera that CNN was reporting.

"Yes, Mom, it's literally in our backyard. But we're fine. There's nothing to worry about."

12 ✻ buses part 1

"See, over there, that road that runs along the water? That's where the number fifteen runs. It'll take you all the way into the center of Nervi," I said to Katie as I pointed down from our terrace. "And this busy road closer to us? That's the route of the number seventeen bus that will take you in the opposite direction, all the way to the center of Genoa."

"I just don't get why we can't just buy a car. This is ridiculous," Katie answered less than thrilled with this impromptu lesson on buses. "So, every time I want to go somewhere, I either have to *walk*, take a *bus*, or take a *train*. What happens when it rains?"

"Well, I just heard on CNN that there's this new invention called an umbrella." I tried to joke but knew underneath that not owning a car was going to be a huge adjustment for all of us. "Look, the truth is that we don't have the money to buy a car or the wherewithal to get through all of the paper-work here. You're going to have to know how to find your way around."

"Not one person I know has to do this." Katie, tears in her eyes, folded her arms and plopped down into the Adirondack chair, her honey blonde hair flying in all directions. I sat in the one next to it. "I know I said I was excited to move here, but now that we're here … well, it's just hard." We had all been taking turns having these moments of truth, admitting our fear in bits and pieces to each other when it felt safe. Matt was down to just one shaking attack a day, and that usually occurred right before sleep.

"Once you get to know the system, you'll love it. I swear."

"I doubt it."

"You'll be able to go anywhere, anytime."

"Like I have so many places to go."

"You won't have to rely on our driving you. You'll have a sense of free-dom like you've never known."

"Whatever."

Buses here ran around the clock. They were, for the most part, clean and well maintained. I could chart a course from bus route to bus route to any destination in the entire country. Even if I never did it, I loved knowing that I could. Growing up just outside of New York City, I was no stranger to public transportation, and I was eager for the kids to become comfortable with it as well. It was a basic life skill that they never would have learned back home in Southern California.

In our area of LA, the only people who took the bus usually did not speak English. As a matter of fact, the buses were so *not* a part of our world that Katie insisted that she had never even seen a bus in our town— which, by the way, has terrific bus service. The bottom line was: Riding the bus in Thousand Oaks, California, marked you as a loser. Walking, for that matter, was considered odd unless you were dressed for exercise and moving briskly at a fervent pace.

"Let's just go try it today," I said with forced enthusiasm. "We can hop the number fifteen and get some gelato." My suggestion was greeted with an icy stare. "Come, on. We have nothing else to do. It'll be fun. We can wear our new clothes."

"Fine."

Twenty minutes later, we were trekking down the ancient steps in our new Italian outfits.

"Your skirt looks cute," I said, trying to keep things light.

"I know," Katie joked back. I was relieved to see that her mood was taking a turn for the better. "Your pants look cute too."

"I know."

We found the bus stop and waited along with a number of other people.

"Everyone looks normal," Katie whispered.

"Of course they do," I whispered back.

"No one's going to think I'm a loser," she whispered again.

"I told you," I said.

Finally we saw the bus approaching, so I took out a few euros (since I didn't know the fare) and got ready. The bus stopped in front of us and three doors opened, one in the front, one in the rear and one in the middle. We stepped through the front door by the driver and I said "*Quanto costa?*"

The driver did not even look at me. We tried to hand him money, but he waved us back, clearly bothered. Everyone else just got on and took a seat. Katie and I looked at each other and shrugged. We grabbed two seats in the back and exclaimed over the fact that the buses here were free! How great was that? Talk about your tax dollars at work. I felt a sudden surge of respect for a country that provided free transportation for its citizens.

During the short ride into town, we examined all of the people getting on and off, taking careful note of local fashions. There was a definite flair to the Italian look. Tighter fitting clothes, brighter colors and oversized sunglasses that looked modern and cutting-edge though we agreed they would make us look like bugs if we ever wore them. Katie noticed right away that the doors were strictly designated. People could only enter through the front and rear doors; the middle double doors were for exiting. So riders would constantly work their way toward the middle, as their stop got closer, jockeying for a position that would provide a quick exit.

The bus wound its way along the sea and then turned left toward the center of Nervi. We took turns pointing out little details that we were now just noticing.

"Look at that store over there, IperSoap. Is that a whole store that just sells soap?" I wondered.

"There's the gelato store that Sabrina said was the best one."

"I want to eat at every single one of these restaurants. Did you notice that they are all Italian?"

"Is that supposed to be funny?" Katie asked.

"No, seriously, there is not one place to buy any other kind of food."

Then a block full of upscale clothing shops caught our attention. "Let's get off and go through the stores," said Katie. She hit the buzzer to ask the driver to stop. We hopped off through the proper opening and made our way down the street.

"That was actually fun. So easy. And we didn't even have to worry about parking," Katie said with a big smile.

"That's what I've been trying to tell you. And I still can't believe it's free!"

"And everyone on the bus was … well, normal. It was cool to people watch."

"Just don't watch them too closely. Losers might not take the bus here, but weirdos might."

13 ✎ the dinner party

It was finally Thursday night. After two solid weeks with only each other, a deck of cards, a jigsaw puzzle and Scrabble, the four of us were thrilled at the prospect of a night out. I showered and got ready with a certain giddiness, as if I were preparing for dinner with the queen.

"Katie, what are you wearing?" I called as I walked down the hall to her room in my bathrobe.

"I don't know," she answered. I started to sift through Katie's closet, since we were now the same size.

"I think we should dress up," I said as I took out a cheerful yellow cotton dress.

"Dress up?" Katie pulled out a sleeveless tank and held it up to her in front of the mirror. "Why would we dress up to make pizza?"

"It never hurts to look nice."

"We can look nice in jeans." Katie pulled her favorite pair from the drawer.

"Dress."

"Jeans."

"Katie."

"Okay, let's make this easy,'" she said, a twinkle in her eye. She walked toward me with her hands behind her back and stood like a cowgirl ready to draw her weapon.

I drew in a deep breath and stared her in the eye. "Fine."

"One, two, three go!" She put her hand out in a sideways peace sign and I put mine out flat with my fingers spread.

"Scissors cuts paper," she said with a smile, "I win. I say jeans. Here, you can borrow my pink T-shirt."

As I headed back to my room, I shouted to Tim and Matt, "We're wearing jeans tonight." I thought I heard a muffled "duh" coming from Matt's room.

Later, in jeans and Old Navy flip-flops, I stood at our front door as Tim, Matt and Katie grilled me.

"How can you not remember when she said to come?"

"I don't know. It was either eight or eight thirty."

"Didn't you write it down?"

"No, I didn't write it down."

"You should have written it down."

"You never remember anything."

"Well I don't want to insult her by arriving late."

"But arriving too early might also be insulting."

"Well, I guess it's better to err on the side of earliness."

"Let's just go."

We opened the door and stampeded down the marble stairwell, our flip-flops echoing like hooves in the night air.

As soon as she opened her door, I knew I had made a mistake. With the back of her clingy green jersey dress yet to be zipped and her hands fumbling with dressy gold earrings, it was clear that she was not ready. Katie and I traded looks of alarm behind Tim's back as she ushered us through the kitchen and onto the terrace. A long, narrow table was elegantly set for twenty with cloth napkins folded expertly at each place. The blue seashells printed on the white linen tablecloth started to swim before my eyes. I had an awful feeling that the menu had changed.

"I thought we were making pizza?" I asked with forced casualness.

"Oh, I decided to cook you traditional Italian dinner! Here"—she turned showing me her zipper—"help me." I zipped her up as she continued. "I also invite people for you to meet," she said pointing to the first couple to arrive—dressed in a suit jacket and dress. I looked down the front of my faded Billy Blues to my feet. At least my toenails were painted. I made a conscious decision not to care.

Tim caught my eye and we laughed. Katie and Matthew went off with the other four children and we met the guests as they trickled in to meet the "Ugly Americans" who didn't even know how to dress properly for a party. The five other couples seemed very nice and eager to meet us. I had a hard time remembering all of their names, much less learning anything substantial about them. Tim and I walked around and mingled. I tried my best at small talk, but it basically consisted of other people doing all of the talking and me nodding and pretending I knew what was going on. From time to time, Tim and I would bump back into each other, relieved to be together again, a nice feeling that I tucked away in my pocket to think about later when I had time.

"This is hilarious."

"I was able to figure out that woman there is a teacher."

"Oh, I do remember talking to her for a while. We both agreed that the sky was blue and the sea was gray."

"Deep conversation."

"I feel like a kindergartener at the eighth-grade lunch table."

A short man in a navy suit headed toward us with an outstretched hand. "Good evening, I am Mauro Valbonesi. It is a pleasure to meet you," he said with a smile as we all shook hands.

"You speak English," I stated the obvious, feeling the relief spread through me like hot tea on a winter's day.

"I am a doctor. It is important that I speak English, as many of my conferences are only in English," he responded. "That is my wife standing over there in the red suit. She does not speak it as well. Don't talk to her." He laughed at his own joke and we joined in, happy to have someone to kid around with.

"What do you specialize in?" Tim asked.

"Blood. I am a hematologist," he answered, "and you, are you a basketball player?" This was a standard question in Tim's life along with How tall are you? and How's the weather up there? Tim answered the question quickly and then continued on into an abbreviated account of who we were and where we came from. I jumped in from time to time, adding

63

details or asking questions. Being able to communicate relaxed me and I started to enjoy myself. Dr. Valbonesi soon became our translator as other guests ventured near, so we followed him around like faithful hounds.

The whole party was standing in a clump at one end of the long table on the terrace. All of the hors d'oeuvres and drinks—pitchers of dark red wine with fruit floating in it, platters of small cubes of white cheese sporting fancy toothpicks, small bowls of olives and a few platters with different varieties of fresh focaccia—were sitting at the other end, but no one went near them.

"Are we allowed to eat that stuff?" whispered Tim.

"I don't know. Why isn't anyone else eating?"

"I'm starving."

"Me too."

"We'd better wait. There's probably some etiquette we don't know about."

Finally Annalisa's husband arrived in gray suit pants and a white dress shirt. He greeted everyone with a shy, universal hello and a wave to the crowd and then invited us all to the other end of the table. The entire clump migrated south together and everyone attacked the hors d'oeuvres in unison. There was no casual milling around and sampling a goodie here and there. Hands flew at lightning speed between platters and mouths. The food was eaten with intensity until the plates were clean. I wondered if anyone had had lunch.

I stood by Tim holding a glass of the fruity red wine that Annalisa's husband had just handed me along with a quiet string of syllables. He was gone before I could even get out a thank-you.

"Tim, did you catch his name yet?"

"No."

"I'm embarrassed to ask at this point."

"I know."

"Just keep your ears peeled."

The sun dipped below the horizon, and Elisabetta and Ester lit all of the candles that ran down the center of the tables. Some were long tapers in carved wooden candlesticks, and others were small tea lights in tiny glass bowls. The candlelight, reflected in the wineglasses and off the white dishes, beckoned us to come. We all sat, spouses together, on either side of the long table. I was relieved that Tim and I were positioned across from the doctor and his wife. Not only could he entertain us with local history and lore, he could explain what I would be eating.

The first course was *Torta Pasqualina*, a traditional two-crusted pie that is similar to a sweet onion quiche but lighter in density. Then a plate filled with stuffed, hard-boiled eggs was passed around. One bite told me that this was not your ordinary deviled egg at the Sunday barbecue. The yolks had been mixed with ground tuna and capers to produce a hearty flavor that was new and exciting. The third course was a platter on which were arranged thin slices of meat covered in a green parsley sauce.

"Sure I'd love a piece," I said as one was placed delicately on my plate. "This looks interesting."

"I'll take two," said Tim.

I cut the meat easily with my fork and took a taste. It was tender and delicious. Almost spongy.

"Umm. What is this?" I asked out loud.

"*Delizioso*, no?" answered the doctor. "It is *lingua*."

"Oh," I cut off another piece and held it up, balancing it on my fork. "Did you hear that, honey? It's *lingua*."

"Great," Tim said chewing away with gusto. "What kind of animal is a *lingua*?"

"I have no idea," I said.

The doctor started to laugh as he pointed to his tongue. "*Lingua, lingua*. It is tongue."

"Oh," I said as I began to chew very slowly. I looked over at Tim with alarm as I swallowed. "Here, you're enjoying this so much, why don't you finish mine."

"Yeah, thanks."

Next, we were served hollowed-out peppers in which lay fresh sardines and garlic, and then a variety of vegetables that had been stuffed with a mixture of breadcrumbs, Parmesan and pine nuts. My taste buds were dancing a jig with happiness.

It only took me these first few courses to see how this whole thing worked. The mother of the house sat at the head of the table. Each course, however, was served by the father. He would go to the kitchen, bring out a platter and then serve each guest with pride as if he were the one who had been slaving over the stove for the past two days. It irked me, and I kept looking at Annalisa to see if she thought he was stealing her thunder. Obviously unaware of my reaction, she just smiled back.

I was already full, but Mr. Annalisa got up once again and returned with course number six, some sort of baked fish fillet that was fresh and flaky. Then came large bowls of room temperature pasta filled with summer vegetables, oil and fresh herbs.

"This is heavenly," commented Tim.

"Speaking of heaven, check out the moon rising behind you," I said as I wound linguini around my fork. A milky half moon was climbing up the sky over the sea. Tim turned to look and then turned back to me with a smile so sincere that it caught me off guard. For a moment, the people around us, the laughter and words, the table before us melted away like the soft focus of a camera lens. Tim and I were sitting on the top of time, the past and future fallen away like rose petals in the wind. New faces, new flavors and a scent on the evening breeze that I had yet to name. I was having fun. Real, honest-to-goodness, fun. There was no place else in the world that I wanted to be.

He picked up his wine glass and motioned for me to do the same.

"No words," I said, afraid they would get in the way or ruin the moment.

"Okay."

"That was a word."

"So were those."

"Can we just do this?" We clinked our glasses and laughed.

Now I understood the transformative power of Hallie's advice to her older sister, Codi, in Barbara Kingsolver's *Animal Dreams* when she told her, "The very least you can do in your life is to figure out what you hope for. And the most you can do is live inside that hope. Not admire it from a distance but live right in it, under its roof."

As I started to move the rest of my pasta around the plate, I glanced down to the other end of the table to check on Matthew. A child with a limited palate, he had declined most of the courses, choosing instead to make a meal of the fresh bread. I saw him break a loaf in the middle and take a full half and put it on his plate. He was too far away for me to reprimand him. It didn't appear that anyone else had noticed, so I just left well enough alone. Soon, all of the children got up and went into the house. Matthew's loaf disappeared with him.

After the final course of roast beef, I excused myself to go check on Katie and Matt. I followed the narrow hallway to the back of the apartment and found all of the kids happily engaged. Katie was in Elisabetta and Ester's room looking at their music collection with them, and Matt was in Carlo's room playing a board game of some sort with Carlo and Andrei. No one had seen me peek into the rooms, so I decided to just slip away unnoticed. On the way back to the terrace, I passed by the bathroom near the kitchen and decided to make a quick visit. To my shock and surprise I saw the huge half loaf of bread bobbing up and down in the toilet! Like I didn't know how that got there! I looked around for a garbage can so I could quietly take care of the matter, but there was nothing to be found.

I sneaked into the kitchen and picked up the trash can. Just before I made it through the door, Annalisa came in. "What are you doing with the trash can?" she asked.

"Oh, *umm*, there's just a little something in the bathroom...." I stammered.

"What? Show me. I take care of it." She took charge. Oh no. *I have no choice but to show her the bread.*

"What is this?" she cried.

"Matthew ..."

"Why did he do this?" Her words were short and clipped.

"I don't know. I guess he was finished with the bread."

"Why would he do this?" she demanded again angrily. I was not sure how to respond.

"I'm sorry. Let me just fish that out of there." I reached my hand down and grabbed the pulpy mass. As I raised it from the water, it broke in two and half of it plopped back down with a big splash that shot up over the rim and onto the floor. Without making eye contact, I continued to pull out the pieces of shredded bread, using my fingers like a sieve. The whole extraction process was grotesque. I closed my eyes and conjured up a photo of myself sloshing my hands around in her toilet with a caption underneath that read "Don't try this at home."

"There we go. All done," I said with forced cheerfulness as I stood up, water dripping from my fingertips. Without a word, she turned on her heel and stomped back to the kitchen dragging the trashcan behind her. *Crap.*

After washing my hands, I decided to just lock the door and hang out while the scarlet receded from my face. Put a little time between the unsightly incident and whatever lame thing that was sure to come out of my mouth in a few minutes when I had to rejoin the party. Sitting on the edge of the tub I counted as far as possible in Italian. After struggling to fifteen, I took a deep breath and fixed my hair in the mirror.

I opened the door and headed back out to the terrace where all of the guests were chattering away and in fine spirits, talking and laughing, passing around the wine bottle. A slice of a dark chocolate torte had been put at my place in my absence. Thankfully, no one looked up at me as I slinked back into my seat. I turned to Annalisa and caught her eye.

"Annalisa, I am so sorry."

"Shush," she said as she handed me a glass of limoncello. "No more talk. Is okay."

The Ugly American had been forgiven.

14 — laundry

Laundry is as much a part of the unique beauty of Italy and its landscape as the cobblestoned alleyways and Renaissance architecture. When Tim and I first visited in May, before our decision to move here, I was mesmerized by the laundry artfully draped from window to window, its backdrop an ancient pastel colored building with shuttered windows and ornate cornices. Little glimpses into the domestic lives of those who live here. This family has a baby girl, this one lots of little boys, that one prefers pretty blue flowered sheets to this one's stark white. If I were a painter, I would have been compelled to sit right down and preserve the experience on canvas.

All of that was very charming and so Italian. Something I could enjoy from afar and appreciate as the visual poetry of a community halfway around the world. But when it came down to the decision of actually living here, I told Tim that I would have to draw the line on this laundry thing. I simply would *not* be interested in hanging sheets and towels, socks and underwear across the front of our building. I'm a dryer type of gal, plain and simple. A quick tumble in the dry heat with some fragrant fabric softener sheets and the clothes are done. Amen.

As luck would have it, the place we rented came with a full laundry room. Now this was something almost unheard of in Italy as most households have only a washing machine crammed somewhere in the kitchen or hallway. I could not believe our good fortune! Complete with a utility sink and ironing station, the room was even larger than the one we had in LA.

Tim was the first to try it out. He walked into the living room one morning carrying a full laundry basket. "What do you have there?" I asked.

"I tried out the washing machine. Works great." He held out the basket for me to see his clothes. "I'm going to hang them on the line."

"Is the dryer broken?"

"No, it's just nice out, that's all," he responded casually. *Okay, Mr. I grew-up-on-a-farm-in-Ohio, knock yourself out. I'm sticking with the dryer.*

"You have clothespins?" I asked.

"The ones I got at the market." He held them up with his left hand.

"So you've been planning this all along."

"No pressure." He said as he headed out the door. "Just feels right to me, that's all."

Later I decided to throw in a load of the kids' clothes. Tim was right; the washer did work great, but the dryer left much to be desired. It was, no surprise, small and not well vented. The clothes went around and around for close to an hour and were still wet. Because we had been warned that power was quite expensive here, I started to worry about our electric bill. Hands on hips, I walked into the living room.

"Tim, that dryer's completely useless." I held up one of Matthew's wet T-shirts. "I put this in an hour ago. Do you remember where we put Stefano's phone number? I want to get someone out here to fix it."

Tim just raised his eyebrows and nodded toward his freshly folded stack of clothes that smelled of salt air and sunshine. My eyes narrowed at the pile of clothespins that lay beside it. "Fine," I said, "but just until we get it fixed."

Reluctantly, I trudged up to the rooftop terrace with my basket of wet clothes. I stood at the top step for a moment to catch my breath as I took in the panorama. The azure sky met the sea on the horizon in an invisible line. Only the glistening of the sun on water revealed where the earth ended and the heavens began. It was a gorgeous day. Curiously, I felt my mood lighten as I made my way toward the two clotheslines that were strung across the opposite end of the rooftop.

Tearing open the bag of clothespins, I got to work. Suddenly I was six years old, hiding among the hanging sheets in my own backyard as my mother, always pretending to be surprised when she found me, checked to see if they were dry. The memory was unexpected. I felt a catch in my throat.

Shaking it off, I hung a pair of Matt's favorite Nike shorts, Katie's "I Love Lucy" T-shirt, well-worn pajamas and tiny boxers. In the time it took to position the article of clothing and pin it to the line, a snapshot of my child wearing it just the day before ran through my mind. A sweet slideshow only a mother could love.

Then I stopped, drawn suddenly by the deep resonance of church bells marking the hour from a nearby church, a sound that has sadly been eliminated from much of America. The ringing tugged at me deep inside. Again, for a moment, I was a child, dressed in my navy blue Sunday coat with tiny anchors on the gold buttons, walking with my family up the marble steps of Immaculate Conception Church.

I finished my chore and walked slowly back toward the stairs, oddly satisfied in some indescribable way. In those ten minutes I had played hide-and-seek with my mother, treasured my children, visited the church of my childhood and basked in the bright sun of the Italian Riviera. The dryer, I decided, would never hold a candle to that.

15 * the beach

Tim and I sat on the terrace and sipped our morning coffee. This had now become a simple, often uneventful, daily routine that we were enjoying together. Over the years we had stopped connecting in any meaningful way in the mornings. To beat the horrific Los Angeles traffic, Tim would be up and out of the house by 5:30, long before I needed to be out of bed. A groggy kiss good-bye was all we shared until a phone call later in the afternoon to see who was racing faster and thus having the more important day.

Tim was studying rudimentary Italian words in our current bible, *Italian for Idiots*, while I peered through the binoculars. I scanned up and down the coast and, more often than not, into the windows of the various apartments down the hillside. I felt like Jimmy Stewart in *Rear Window* but worried that I wouldn't know how to call for help in Italian if I happened to witness a murder.

"Tim."

"Huh?"

"See if you can look up the words for 'She's buried in the garden.'"

"What?"

Matt stuck his head out the door. "Can we go swimming?"

"It's kind of early," I said.

"I'll go," said Tim. "That sun's already blistering."

"Come on, Mom. Can you come too?"

"I don't know."

"You're the only one who hasn't been to the beach yet," he reminded me for the hundredth time. I looked from his cute little face with tilted silver glasses, out to the sea, and back at Tim.

"Okay."

"Okay?"

"Yup."

"Yesssssss!" Matt cried as he ran with glee to get ready. I called after him not to wake Katie. She had made it very clear that no one was to get her up early in the morning since she had no life yet.

I headed into my room and surveyed my suit choices. If there was one thing that Los Angeles had taught me, it was that bathing suits were more than suits. They were statements—loud and clear. In the land of body worship, you had to be toned, flabless and show as much breast implant as possible. You were never to be tan and your cover-up should match and appear just thrown on at the last minute .... "Oh, this old thing?"

Was forty-four too old here for this pink and green flowered bikini? What about this basic black one piece? Maybe that was too conservative. I didn't want to be branded as the American fuddy-duddy.

Matt knocked at the door. "Ready, Mom?"

"One minute!" Maybe this white tankini with the striped bottoms. Cute, athletic-cut top, high-cut legs. Showed some style, a little energy, sexy enough for starters.

"Mom, hurry up!" I could hear his foot tapping.

"Give me a minute, will you?" Matt was a chip off the old block when it came to impatience. It was another thing about Tim that rankled. I could feel my passive-aggressive nature start to kick in and made only a half hearted attempt to hurry. I lathered myself with total sun block from head to toe and ran around the room to make it dry faster. I threw on the suit and then started on my hair. Ponytail? No, not on someone my age. Down? No, too hot on my neck, no style—

"What are you doing in there?" He was starting to sound frantic, so I twisted it up into a sloppy-on-purpose bun and gave it a few spritzes of hair spray. I carefully selected the proper cover-up wrap. Something cotton and bright (need I say matching?) and my Old Navy flip-flops in just the right hue.

BANG! BANG! BANG! I opened the door.

"Finally." Matt rolled his eyes. "Now we're not going to get a spot."

"It's only nine thirty. There's a whole coastline, for goodness' sake."

We walked to the living room where, predictably, Tim stood rigid and impatient, his arms full of towels and sunscreen. Matt grabbed his boogie board and stomped out the door. *My, aren't we all in a fine mood?*

We marched in angry silence down the ancient steps. It was so hot and humid that I could feel sweat start to trickle down my back.

"Why does it always take you so long to get ready?" Tim said.

"Women take longer, that's why."

"It's the beach, not a fashion show."

"Yeah," grumbled Matt.

"Why can't you see things from my perspective once in a while? I mean, you don't even have hair for Pete's sake. I needed time to fix my hair. Brush it, pin it up."

"Whatever."

We stood at the bus stop and waited—what else—impatiently.

"Do you have the bus tickets?" Tim asked.

"Yes, I have the bus tickets," I replied immaturely.

"I still can't believe that you thought the buses were free." Okay, so the buses weren't free. Anyone could have made the same mistake. I mean, what kind of bus driver doesn't collect money? How was I supposed to know that I had to go to a *tobacco* shop and buy a book of tickets?

After being chewed out by concerned citizens on numerous occasions, I finally knew the drill. The trains and buses in this region used the same ticket. So you could buy a book of ten for about ten euro. Then, when you got on the bus you had to find this little machine set up in the aisle, which was invariably hidden behind an elderly man who wouldn't move over. Then, you put the end of the ticket into the machine, which stamped the date on it, thus validating the ticket.

The only weird thing about the whole system is that no one really checks to see if you are paying or not! It is set up on the basis of the honor system, which in America, would be renamed F-R-E-E. Thus, I constantly had this little conversation running in my mind about the fact that I could get away with not paying or I could be honest and pay. It was all very emotionally draining, and I just wished they would collect money when I got on so I wouldn't have to worry about moral choices every time I rode the bus. It was almost cruel.

"Here it comes." Matt pointed down the block at the approaching bus. "Can I do the tickets?" Though it was crowded and stuffy, we boarded the bus anyway. Close proximity to hot, sweaty bodies was exactly what we needed.

"Matt," I whispered as he pushed his way toward the yellow validation box, "watch your boogie board."

"What?" he said. As he turned toward me his board slapped a silver-haired woman with weary eyes, her arms filled with brown bags.

"Oops."

"Apologize."

"Sorry," he said as she fake smiled. As he turned back to insert the ticket, the board hit her again.

"Matt, watch what you're doing," Tim said in exasperation, though his eyes were smiling. The woman spewed a rush of words that couldn't have meant anything nice. After a few blocks we got off as Matt assured me that this was the route to the best beach in the area. We navigated through some tiny alleyways, and soon the sea came into view. There was no beach, only wall-to-wall bodies like bees on a honeycomb. Apparently, Italians started their beach days at sunrise.

The coastline in our area of the Italian Riviera was rugged and beautiful. It was quite narrow and composed of pebbles, stones, rocks, bigger rocks and boulders. People could swim wherever they wanted. Some small natural coves and inlets were proclaimed "beaches," and a few of them charged a fee for a lounge chair and some refreshments. A lifeguard was rare. If a person drowned, I doubted there were lawsuits about it.

Tim, Matt and I stood for a moment and searched for an open spot.

I could plainly see that beach culture here was not about image. Every woman from age four to a hundred and four was in a bikini. The majority of men wore Speedos. The choice of suit had nothing to do with body types. It had to do with being able to feel the luxurious heat of the sun on your skin. Flab abounded without apology.

Sitting close to us on the left, a blonde, middle-aged woman with skin tanned the color of chocolate poked her Tootsie Roll finger into her husband's stomach and pointed in our direction. I saw her eyes travel from me, to Tim, to Matt with his knobby knees and boogie board. She started to whisper to her husband, and I imagined her saying, "The albinos have come. You must shield your eyes from the sunlight that reflects from their skin."

"Don't they know that skin cancer claims lives every day? I haven't seen this much bronze skin since Gidget went Hawaiian."

"Seriously," Tim agreed.

"There's a spot." Matt pointed to an area out on a large boulder that looked less crowded. Of course it had to be twenty-five yards out into the water, and we would have to make our way over a man-made jetty the width of a balance beam to get there.

"Follow me," said Tim, "and watch your boogie board." We gingerly stepped between and around bodies. I found myself unexpectedly enchanted by the unpretentiousness of it all. People here looked human. Women looked like women. Their breasts were God given, their thin lips were just fine, and wrinkles were, well, wrinkles. People here were not painfully thin and not especially toned. No one cared. Your body was just your body, the vessel that held your spirit. And the spirit was what was most celebrated. I listened to the easy laughter and bits of conversation that rose like doves released in the salty air.

We made it to the boulder and nestled in among the other sunbathers. I laid out my towels and flopped down. It was not comfortable and I shifted about trying to make my body conform to the various crevices in the rock's surface. Finally, I gave up and pulled myself to a sitting position in time to see Matt and Tim jump from the rock into the water.

"Come on in!" Tim called to me.

"I don't know," I said.

"The water's perfect," Matt added, now hanging on to the boogie board for dear life. "Aren't you boiling?"

"Come on, Susan. Loosen up." That familiar look of disappointment was starting to cloud Tim's face. *I'm not much of a swimmer these days, and I forgot to bring a hairbrush, so if my hair gets wet—there I go again.*

"Okay. Here I come."

I stood and eased my way down the side of the slippery, mossy boulder. There was no graceful way to do it, and as I scooted along, I made a mental note to write to Old Navy to ask them to add tread to the bottom of next year's flip-flops. Finally I made it to the edge of the black rock. Poised to jump, I was suddenly overwhelmed with a desperation so real I could taste it like bile rising in my throat without warning. I wanted to be someone new. I wanted to be someone who didn't worry about age and hair and clothes and skin cancer. I wanted to join the ranks of those who didn't give a hoot about cellulite and age spots. I wanted to be the one who ran with abandon to be the first to jump into the water instead of the last. Trembling, I closed my eyes and tried hard to swallow the doubt that I could ever be that person. Taking a deep breath, I jumped as far out into the clear blue as I could. My first plunge into a sea I never thought I'd swim in. A sea that bordered a country I now called my home. A place where I just might find the courage to be just me.

16 ❧ permesso di soggiorno

It was 5:35 AM and the four of us were standing in a long line outside the police station, the *questura*, in downtown Genoa. The official decree was that you must present yourself at the *questura* to obtain a document, a *Permesso di Soggiorno*, which said that you had permission to stay in

Italy for three months. I was pretty sure that most visitors blew that off. However, since we had yet to obtain our residency visa, we wanted to follow all the rules so we didn't get ejected from the country after going through so much to get here. Besides, we did not have the body types that would enable us to physically blend in.

So the four of us stood, half asleep, not really sure of what to expect. Because why, in heaven's name, would they make people do this at 5:30 in the morning? What I was beginning to understand was that doing business here was usually as complicated and disorganized as possible.

I counted about sixty people in front of us in line. As time passed, scores of others arrived from every nationality in the world but ours. By seven o'clock, there must have been more than two hundred people. I wondered if everyone here had had an intense discussion with God at some point during the last few months. And if they had, I wondered why he was sending us all to Genoa. Suddenly a door opened and everyone straightened up as if Sister Mary Margaret had just scolded us. A mean-looking officer wearing a tight blue gray uniform and snappy black boots, stepped out with a roll of tickets—the kind you get at a carnival—and tore off one at a time to hand to each person in line. Everyone took his or her ticket and acted like they knew what was going on.

"Tim, ask the guy what we're supposed to do."

"He doesn't speak English."

"Why don't you write down the names of the documents we need on a piece of paper," Katie offered. "Then you can just show it to him."

"Good idea." Tim quickly tore off a piece of scrap paper from our folder and jotted down the names. When the officer handed him a ticket, Tim held up the paper as Katie, Matt and I gathered around in support. The officer gave an exasperated sigh, looked at us like we were morons and said curtly, "Nine o'clock."

He gave the rest of us our tickets and continued down the line. We stepped to the side in the state of confusion to which we had now grown accustomed.

"What does that mean?" asked Matt.

"I don't know. I guess we have to come back at nine o'clock," I answered.

"That means we have to wait around for two hours!" said Tim. "Like they can't just open the place right now and take care of us? What kind of system is this?"

"Let's just see what everyone else does."

"Why don't we follow them," said Matt, pointing to a suspicious clan of people from an undetermined country. The women were wearing peasant skirts and the men were not clean shaven. "I think they're Gypsies."

"They're not Gypsies." Katie groaned and rolled her eyes. "Why would Gypsies go to the trouble of getting a visa?"

"You never know."

We followed them anyway and ended up in a coffee shop nearby that was crowded with other ticket holders. Overhearing bits and pieces of conversations, I was able to figure out that they give out a set number of tickets (that's why you have to get there early) at seven o'clock. But then you have to wait until nine o'clock when the office actually opens for business. Everyone acted like this was completely normal. Why they would make us sit around for two hours was unclear and, I decided, mean-spirited.

"You know," Tim said chewing furiously on his fresh brioche, "by the looks of all the crowded coffee shops in the vicinity of the *questura*, I would bet you any amount of money that the owners and the policemen are acting in collusion. Probably even cousins or something."

Finally, at 8:30, Tim decided that we should be tricky and go back early. We entered the building and found the waiting room already packed to the gills. So much for being tricky. Rows and rows of people were clinging to folders and sweating. The place was old, run-down and about a hundred degrees inside.

"We must be in the wrong place. This is how they treat guests in their country?" I sensed Tim's impatience starting to rise.

"Remain calm. We have to do this."

Everyone in the room was already feverishly filling out forms for this or that. Suddenly a door opened at the far end of the room and I caught a glimpse of the same police officer who had handed out the tickets. The four of us, walking in unison, pushed our way through the crowd to ask for help.

"*Scusi*, sir... *umm. Quattro persone*," I pointed to the four of us, "*Permesso di Soggiorno?*" I held up Tim's scrap paper again. The police officer again looked at the four of us like we were morons, rolled his eyes and handed us four forms to fill out.

"Mom, I need some air," Katie said.

"Me too," said Matt.

"Okay, let's go out to the hallway and fill these in." Tim led the way.

By nine o'clock we were ready. We walked back into the waiting room and found a few seats. Soon, the *questura* began to process the applicants. Every time a red number flashed on the huge electronic board that hung on the wall of the waiting room, a magic door opened in the corner and people would disappear though it. It took so long for every number that I started to wonder what was going on behind that door.

"Katie? Matt?"

"Yeah?"

"No one's allowed behind that door without me or Dad."

"Fine."

"Fine."

Minutes and then hours ticked by. It was now eleven o'clock, and my good humor had long since left me. Tim and Matt were pacing outside. Katie and I were sitting with our heads in our hands. I was weak from fatigue, hunger and the heat.

"For goodness' sake, we have numbers sixty-four to sixty-seven. You'd think we'd be through by now." Katie complained.

"It's so hot in here."

"I know. The stench is getting to me. It smells like body odor and coffee breath."

"Why won't they open the windows?"

"It's the same thing on the buses. What is up with that?"

"I'm opening one." I bravely walked over and opened two windows, took a couple of deep breaths and turned smugly around and smiled to Katie, who was doing a silent cheer complete with invisible pom-poms. By the time I made it back to my seat, the windows had been slammed shut.

Twelve o'clock. Twelve fifteen. One thing we did know was that the office closed promptly at one o'clock for *intervallo*, the hours in the afternoon when all of the stores closed so people could go home for lunch and take a nap. If you had not been helped by then, you were out of luck. You had to come back the next day and do it all over again. They wouldn't hold your place in line. Tim trudged back into the room. Steam was starting to come out of his ears. There was no way we would come back tomorrow.

Finally we saw our number, and Tim jumped up and opened the magic door. We filed into a long, narrow room with about ten windows that resembled those of bank tellers. It was now obvious why this had taken so long. There were only three windows open. Tim went to one of the open ones and handed a woman our paperwork as she started to chatter away.

"No, no *italiano. Solo inglese.*" Tim said. She held up her finger to indicate that we should wait. She went to find a co-worker to help us. Twenty minutes and two hundred euros later, we were handed our documents.

As we left, I saw the woman hand another co-worker our papers to file. Behind them was a large wall with one cubical assigned to each letter of the alphabet. The co-worker stood and searched for our letter. She lost interest after about four seconds, and I saw her pitch our file onto an unmarked shelf along with about two thousand other pieces of paper. She might as well have just thrown it in the garbage can, which I had a feeling they probably did after one o'clock.

17 ✸ culture shock

I stood outside Katie's bedroom door and took a deep breath. "Katie, come on, honey. It's been almost twenty-four hours." There was no response. I knocked again. And again. Nothing. I opened the door and peered into the darkness.

She had the window shades down to block the midday sun. As my eyes adjusted, I could make out her tall, willowy frame curled up in bed. I walked over and lay down with her. I pulled her close to me and listened to her silence.

"I want to go home. We don't belong here. This is crazy. I miss my friends. I want my home back."

"I know." I responded as she started to cry again. "This is very hard." My words were so inadequate, and I felt tears starting to well up in my own eyes. I wondered again if we had made the right decision in asking her to do this at such a tender and difficult age.

"I hate *intervallo*. By the time I get up and get going all of the stores are closed and I have nothing to do. It's so stupid." *Intervallo* was now the invisible force that ruled our life.

"Well, you could try to get up earlier."

"I don't know who I am here." She was lost and floating in a huge sea without currents to guide her. I wanted more than anything to throw her a life jacket, but I couldn't find one.

How could I explain to her that we were here because many of the things she missed most were the same things that were slowly killing our marriage? How could I say that the yearly rhythms of holidays and daily routines and rituals were starting to become rote and empty? How could I tell her that all of the glitz, glamour and social expectations of LA that she found exciting and invigorating were stealing parts of my soul and making me question my worth? How could I break the news that coming here, a metaphorical jump off a cliff, was a lot safer than finding a real cliff in Malibu?

Quite simply, I couldn't. It was not her time to know any of this. We were both floating together but in waters thirty years apart. And we would continue to float until a new current picked us up.

I hugged her again and whispered, "You may not know who you are right now, but I do. You are a sweet and brave young woman. You have a big heart and a soul as pure as sunlight through the clouds. You will find your way. I promise."

18 the new school

The four of us sat in the living room, the morning sun beating through the glass. We had melted onto the L-shaped couch like long-forgotten rag dolls in an abandoned playroom. Limbs strewn, eyes closed. Our collective energy level was not even measurable. The newness of our situation had worn off. In this heat and humidity, everything was now an effort.

"This is pathetic," Tim said. "Let's go do something."

"That would mean we would have to walk down all of those steps," Katie responded. She and Matthew had yet to accept the fact that we had no other transportation than our feet.

"And then we would have to walk all the way back up," Matthew added with an edge to his voice.

"But we can't just sit here all day," I said.

"Yes, we can," he mumbled into his Game Boy Advance.

"It just doesn't feel right being bored in such a beautiful place." Tim said.

"If we had a TV we wouldn't be bored," mumbled Matt again.

It had been three weeks and they still hadn't come to connect the satellite TV or the Internet. Things took time around here. A lot of time. How could it not when people closed their businesses for half the day? Eating and resting seemed to take priority over making money. It was also near the end of "Holiday" time. Many stores in Genoa still sported little handwritten notices that the store was closed for family vacation. Other than swimming, there was not much to do.

"I know," offered Tim. "I think your new school opens its office today. Let's go check it out." That got their attention. They had not yet seen their school as it had been closed for the summer.

"Great plan, honey," I said as I jumped up off the couch. "But we'd better hurry so we get there before *intervallo*." Katie and Matt got spruced up in order to make a good impression. Matt even put on his nice navy blue shorts and a collared golf shirt.

We walked slowly down the ancient steps so Katie would not sweat and ruin her makeup and then stood at the bus stop for what seemed like an hour in the blistering sun. Finally a bus arrived, and it was packed with hot, sticky people. We pushed our way in, noticing that none of the bus windows were open.

"What do these people have against fresh air?" Tim whispered through clenched teeth.

"I can't breathe."

"It stinks in here."

"Breathe through your mouth."

"I'm just going to hold my breath altogether."

"Good luck."

The bus soon stopped at the school, and the four of us burst onto the sidewalk and filled our lungs with fresh sea air. The American School of Genoa was up a hill behind black iron gates.

"Great. More steps," Katie observed.

"So?" said Matt. "They're only steps."

Thirty cement stairs later we made it to the top and someone buzzed us in when we rang the bell. The black iron gate creaked as we pushed it open. Nobody said a word and our footsteps crunched in unison as we walked across the tiny white pebbles that filled the driveway.

The school was housed in an old yellow villa with large white shuttered windows. Because the school's population was increasing, there were also classrooms in some of the surrounding buildings that had once been stately villas but now had been divided up into apartments. There had been a welcoming courtyard with benches and shade trees when we enrolled the kids last May, but today it was completely filled with construction material.

"Is this it?" asked Matt.

"Do you like it?" I glanced at Tim and held up my crossed fingers in hopes Matt would say yes.

"I thought you said it was nice." Matt said.

"This place is a disaster area," added Katie. "School starts in two weeks."

"I hope they're working around the clock."

"I doubt it. Look around, we're the only ones here."

"Stop with the bad attitudes," said Tim. "Let's find the office."

"There's the sign over there."

I opened the front door to the main building and walked into a foyer. The walls were covered in children's artwork, school notices and student work in both English and Italian. I could see a kindergarten classroom down the hall, and the front two rooms had been converted into offices. A school with a homey feel.

"This part's nice," conceded Katie.

A dark haired woman with an agreeable face was busy at her desk in one of the offices. I knocked softly on the open door.

"*Buon giorno,*" said the woman.

"*Buon giorno, signora. Parla inglese?*"

"Yes, of course." She laughed at our obvious relief. "Come in, come in. I am Patrizia. You must be one of our new families," she said as she stood to shake Tim's hand.

"Yes, this is Katie and Matthew."

"Welcome to the American School of Genoa, Katie and Matthew. I hope you'll be very happy here." Suddenly timid, Katie and Matt just nodded.

"This is my first day back to work. As you can see"—she motioned around her office to stacks of brown boxes that needed to be opened and sorted through—"I am very busy."

"We won't take up your time. We were just wondering if the kids could meet their teachers."

"None of the teachers are here this week, but I can show you your class lists." She rummaged through a few folders and pulled out a sheet of paper.

"Matthew, you are in sixth grade?"

"Yes."

"Here are the names of your classmates. You will have nineteen total." She handed Matt the paper and he took it with a grin. "And, you, Katie … let me see. Ah yes, here we go. The tenth grade will have four students, including you of course."

"Four? Did you say four?"

"Yes, our high school is fairly new. There will be one other girl and two boys." Katie's face started to turn white.

"What is the enrollment in the entire high school?" Tim asked.

"Twenty-four. Everyone hangs out together. Don't worry, you'll have plenty of friends."

"How many other Americans are in the school?"

"Oh, about three."

"Three?" Tim and I looked at each other.

Patrizia explained that the majority of the students enrolled in the school were from sophisticated and global-thinking Italian families seeking bilingual education for their children. Other nationalities were in attendance as well and were generally connected in some way to the shipping business. I got the distinct feeling that the only thing American about this school would be its name.

"Our new director, Mrs. B, is in her office. Would you like to meet her?"

"Great!"

She made a quick phone call to announce our arrival and then led us back outside and across the courtyard. She apologized for the state of the campus and explained that they were making a lot of changes in their expansion. She seemed confident that it would all be finished by the first day of school. Patrizia pointed to a newly refurbished villa where Mrs. B waved to us from the door.

"You are in good hands now, so I must get back to work. I wish you luck, and I will see you two"—she pointed to Katie and Matt—"in a few weeks."

"See you then," Katie said.

Matt tugged at my arm. "Mom, she was nice."

Mrs. B greeted us enthusiastically with her proper Jane Hathaway British accent. She was petite with short brown hair and a happy smile that revealed white even teeth. Her graciousness inspired confidence, and I felt a surge of "this is all going to work out just fine" as we followed her up a stifling, hot, narrow stairwell toward her office on the second floor. She paused at the window at the top of the stairs and pointed to the waves crashing on the rocky shore across the street.

"Look at this mah-velous view. How does one study properly with such distraction?" She laughed.

"Looks just like the view I had from my school growing up in Ohio," Tim joked back. Instead of moving into her more spacious office, she continued to stand there and converse about the specifics of the school and its high expectations. Though beads of sweat started to make their way down my forehead, it did not occur to me to ask her to open the window. Behind me I felt Katie start to lean into my back. "Mom?" she said sounding funny. I turned and it took my brain a few seconds to register that she was not so much leaning on me as wobbling to and fro. Down she went. Fainted on the floor in a heap. We all stood around her, stunned. I knelt down and started to pat her cheek.

"Katie!" Tim yelled.

"Wake up," I added.

She opened her eyes and started to sit up. As she did, she started to vomit.

"Oh dear." Mrs. B ran to get some cold water and a towel.

"Tim, grab something!" The only thing available was a small box with construction debris. He thrust it under Katie's chin. When she finished, she looked up and started to laugh.

"What the heck?" Matt scoffed under his breath. "Good one."

"Are you sick?" I asked putting my hand on her clammy forehead.

"I think I just need some air," Katie said.

"Try to stand up." Tim helped her up as Mrs. B returned with a towel soaked in cold water. Katie wiped her face and leaned against the wall.

"Why don't we go outside," Mrs. B said.

"Good idea." We followed her back down the stairs and out the door.

"I'm fine." Katie was now beet red with embarrassment.

"Well, you don't seem to have a fever."

"It was too hot in there."

"The air conditioners are being fixed," said Mrs. B. "I must agree with you, it is quite close."

"She's never fainted before," I said. "But maybe we should head back home just in case she's coming down with something."

"Righto."

"Thank you for your time. We'll look forward to the first day of school."

"We'll have a terrific year together. Just brilliant. Here before we know it," she responded with a wink and a smile.

Heading back, I put my arm through Katie's and we ambled up the street a few yards behind Tim and Matt, toward the bus stop.

"You okay?"

Katie nodded, her expression a mixed bag of emotions.

"You sure? You'd tell me if you felt sick, right?"

"Really, Mum. It was just the heat. I'm jolly good." She giggled as the bus rattled past and the four of us ran like crazy to flag it down.

87

19 ❦ sibling rivalry

"Listen," Tim said as we both sat on the couch watching a fly buzz around the room.

"What?"

"It's happening again."

"I don't hear anything."

"Exactly."

Something had gone awry. Our home was too quiet, and it had been for several weeks. Like a teacher who watched her class with a raised eyebrow after they had suddenly become angelic, I was suspiciously taking note of the new civilized behavior of our children.

"I think they're back in Matt's room playing cards."

"Again?"

"Katie's teaching him every game she's ever known."

Tim and I weren't sure of what to make of it. It was a byproduct we weren't expecting. We had lived so long with slamming doors and arm punching that we thought this behavior was normal sibling rivalry. The name-calling, the "everyone is allowed in my room except you" pronouncements, the tattling … all gone. Katie and Matt had started to see each other through new eyes. For the first time in their lives they could actually relate to what the other was going through. Neither one made fun of the other when tears sprang to the other's eyes from frustration. Neither one laughed when the other started to physically tremble from fear and emotional overload. Neither one called the other a big baby when they needed to sit in my arms for a while. I even thought I had heard an "Are you okay?" slip from one of their mouths. We were afraid we would jinx it if we praised them.

"Whatever you do, don't disturb them."

"I'm not stupid."

Even if we were to pack up and go home tomorrow, this would have made it all worth it. They were becoming friends. They actually needed each other. I could see, with sudden clarity, the downfalls of all of the "stuff" we had surrounded our children with at home. Matt couldn't hide in his PlayStation. Katie couldn't insulate herself in a world of instant messages. I was not driving one to this sport and Tim driving the other to that sport. One to this person's house and the other to that one's. One to this school and the other to that school. Tim and I were not bending over backward to work out a driving schedule that insured they wouldn't spend any meaningful time together. We did not have the resources or wherewithal here to make decisions about each child's "uniqueness." I hadn't realized that that was a privileged way of life.

"I remember when my parents used to take us on our summer vacations," I said, feeling nostalgic. "They never rented houses with TVs. Though we complained, that was always the best part. Playing games, building forts in the woods, talking about stupid stuff, laughing at each other."

"Yeah, I know. Those days were golden."

"Do you think Katie and Matt will look back on these days and say that? That they were golden?"

"I don't know. I think it's too new yet."

All of a sudden there seemed to be no age differentiations or feelings of superiority because of this or that. They found themselves on a level playing field with no other comrades in sight. And it wasn't so bad. In fact, I rather suspected they were enjoying it. One day I witnessed a rare game of hide-and-seek. The next morning a Scrabble game where Katie even helped Matt cheat. Last week, Matt asked if we could buy, of all dreaded things, another jigsaw puzzle. I couldn't get out of the house fast enough to find one.

Life now was all about what they were sharing. About where they connected in the deepest and most important place of all. With their sibling. The one person who would travel with them through a lifetime of highs and lows, to laugh about the good old days together and make fun of their parents, to welcome each other's spouses and baptize each other's babies.

We sat in silence for a moment, the muted sound of a guitar floating up from the floor below. An accomplished classical guitarist, Annalisa's son, Carlo, practiced daily. Then we heard Elisabetta and Ester scream at each other, followed by a dog barking. Just a usual day.

Tim turned and looked me straight in the eye. *Uh-oh.*

"You doing okay?" he asked.

"I am. I'm trying to take it just one day at time. You?"

"Yeah, the same."

"No regrets?"

"Not so far."

"Me neither." I held out my hand and he took it. We sat that way for a long time in the quiet comfort of a peaceful house.

I knew in my heart that this magical time of harmony between Katie and Matt would be short-lived. That soon enough, they would make new friends and become involved in life here as well. But, I hoped the seed had been planted and their sense of shared battle would forge a deeper understanding of each other.

As for Tim and me, we were learning to pay more than lip service to what it meant to be a family. We were watching our children, and each other, rise to challenges and thus grow in unexpected ways, and it was filling our souls and teaching us to think outside "the American Way."

"We never used to sit in our living room back home. This is nice," I said.

"Scrabble?"

"I'll get the board."

20 ✿ the elevator

"Tim!" I yelled at the top of my lungs. He came bolting around the corner like he had been shot from a cannon. "What the—" He stopped short when he saw the serious look on my face.

"The kids are stuck in the elevator!" Slipping quickly into his flip-flops, Tim ran out the door to find the superintendent.

The very first day we moved in, the elevator was an immediate sore spot with Katie as she had convinced herself over the years that she had claustrophobia. But since we lived on the seventh floor, she still chose to ride up rather than walk because her exercisephobia was much more severe.

Now, Katie had called on her cell phone to say that she and Matt were stuck between the third and fourth floors of our apartment building. Hearing Matt's panicky voice squeaking in the background, I tried to calm them down. "You'll be fine," I said. "Just breathe deeply and relax. We'll be right there."

Grabbing my cell phone and keys, I headed down the outside stairs to the fourth floor. A sliver of light was shining through a small crack in the opening at the base of the elevator doors. If I lay down, I would be able to see the kids eye to eye through a crack. I prostrated myself on the cold, dusty marble and put my cheek on the floor.

"Hey you guys!"

"Mom, get us out of here!" Matt cried searching for the source of my voice.

"Calm down, I can see you. Look up here." They looked up and saw me. "Try that black knob at the bottom of the control panel." Katie pulled on the knob. Nothing happened. "Now push that red button." She pushed it and a deafening alarm bell rang through the building. "Stop! That's enough. I think someone heard us." Matt started to cry. Katie, surprisingly in control of herself, put her arm around him. He even let it stay there.

I tried to crack a joke to ease the tension. "Hey, Matt. So? It's only an elevator." Katie chuckled. Matt didn't. We heard muffled voices floating up through the elevator shaft. Tim was trying to explain the problem to a small crowd of neighbors who had heard the emergency bell. Urgent Italian responses signaled that help was on the way. Matt looked up with new alarm. "I have to go to the bathroom."

"Perfect," said Katie. "Well, you'd better hold it."

Suddenly the elevator made herky-jerky movements and inched upward. Then it made more herky-jerky movements and inched downward. Other frantic Italian noises drifted up from below.

"I'm going down to see what's happening," I said. "Meanwhile you two take a deep breath and repeat over and over to each other, 'God is with me, helping me. God is with me, helping me.'"

"What?"

"Mom, don't leave!"

"God is with me, helping me," I repeated. "Over and over."

I brushed the dust and dirt from my cheek and clothes and ran downstairs. On the second-floor landing an old wooden door to the side of the elevator was ajar. A few neighbors stood before the elevator staring with such intent that I wondered if they were sending collective paranormal energy to save my children. Joining the group, I motioned that I was the mother of the prisoners.

I glanced sideways through the wooden door and saw the silhouettes, in the musty dark room, of a very tall figure and a very short Italian shaped figure pulling with all of their might on a rope. *This can't be what I think it is. Can it?*

"Go back up and tell us when the elevator is even with the floor!" Tim shouted to me.

"Okay, Hercules."

I speed dialed Katie and explained the escape plan. As I made it back to the fourth floor, I could see that the bottom of the elevator was almost level with the floor. "Tim," I screamed through the shaft as Katie and Matt covered their ears and continued their chant, "three inches to go!" The elevator jiggled upward. "That's good!" I screamed again. I pictured them tying a huge knot in the elevator cable/rope to hold it in place.

Suddenly Tim appeared and pried open the doors with more superhuman strength. Katie and Matt flew out and into our arms.

"I have to go," said Matt as he ran up the stairs to the bathroom. Katie stood with us for a moment to collect herself.

"That was always one of my worst fears," she said. "And it really wasn't that bad. If I ever get stuck again, I know I could get out."

"That's how life is, Katie." Tim said as he turned and looked at me. "Face your fears and find your strength."

Tim went back downstairs to thank everyone as Katie and I went up to find Matt. Katie may have overcome one of her fears, but I suspected that Matt had discovered a new one. I had a feeling that he would be taking the stairs for a while.

21 ❋ sea glass

San Remo, a well-known town on the western edge of the Italian Riviera, was an old stomping ground of the European elite and boasted a grand old casino. It was also the destination of our first mini trip. Feeling adventurous, the four of us had packed one backpack each and headed west on the train to see what we could find. Because San Remo was the only name we recognized on the map, we got off there.

We set up our beach towels on the stony beach in San Remo, feeling duped because our Italy guidebook had promised white sand. Luckily, the water was calm and warm. Matthew swam and played in it for two hours straight. I loved to see him in these rare times of singular contentment. I watched as he lined up imaginary boats, torpedoed enemies and slew sea monsters. Without a single care, he was completely lost in his own imagination. I marveled that, at eleven, this state of innocence still reigned in his world. I wanted to lock him up in a little room so that adolescence could not find him and steal it away.

After a while, though, boredom overcame me. I stood and stretched, blocking Tim's and Katie's sun for a moment. They squinted up at me. "Think I'll go for a walk."

"Heart rock time?" asked Katie.

"I believe it is," I responded. She jumped up to join me. It was a tradition we had started long ago, a mother-daughter contest to see who could find a rock that was most naturally shaped like a heart. We had built quite a collection over the years.

"Good luck," Tim called after us as we started to scour the water's edge.

Matt looked up from the water, noticed that we had come to life and decided to join in. But predictably he couldn't control his male urge to try to skip every rock he picked up across the surface of the sea. He was good at it. Some of them would skip once and then plop to the bottom, but some would skip four, five, even six times before they sank.

"Don't waste the heart rocks on that," said Katie.

"I'm not. They wouldn't work, anyway," he responded, searching for his next specimen.

"Why wouldn't they?" I wondered out loud.

"Because hearts have too many angles and bumps. They won't surf the water and try to fly. They just give up and sink right away," he said.

A marriage was like that. A stone that leaves the hand with intense energy and floats over the ocean of reality until it arcs downward and hits the water, and there is a split second in which it either sinks or walks a way on the choppy surface until it lifts off again. In some marriages this happens once or twice until the final kerplunk, but in some it happens five, six, even seven or more times until a lifetime is spent. I think the ones that last a lifetime ask the Lord if they can walk with him for that split second on the water. They seek his wisdom and, with his grace, are able to catch the updraft of faith and sail again, buoyed with the hope that somewhere within the struggle lies the key to mature love.

Matt picked up a rock that vaguely looked like a heart and held it up. "Watch, I'll show you how this won't skip," he said and then whipped it as far as he could. It hit an old man in a blue Speedo standing knee deep in the water, who enthusiastically introduced us to some interesting Italian phrases and hand gestures. Katie quickly took her giggles down the beach.

"Matt," I said sternly, "apologize to that man."

"Sorry!" he yelled as he bent to pick up another rock.

"No, no," I corrected him, "your rock throwing is finished for the day." Of course he couldn't believe that I would be so unreasonable and started to stomp, fists clenched, back to the towel. His angry glare softened as a smooth piece of mossy sea glass caught his eye. He picked it up and held it toward the sun.

"Hey, Mom," he called, his anger already melted away, "what's this?" We talked about the sea glass and how it might have come to be here on this beach.

"Look!" he added excitedly as he pointed to the sand. Among the tiny stones and shells just beneath the gentle waves we spied other pieces just waiting for our fingers to pluck them from their sandy beds. Our search now shifted from heart rocks to sea glass.

Matt discovered specimens of every color and ran with excitement to show me each one. Again, he threw himself into this new project with abandon. His excitement and focus grew with the pile of glass, which I had been instructed to guard with my life. We decided it would become "our" collection just as the heart rocks were Katie's and mine. Now it would be "even." Visual confirmation that I loved him as much as I loved her.

I spied a piece of crystal clear glass in the pile. With its sharp edges and points, it was definitely not ready for the collection. It had not been pounded by enough waves or scarred by salt. It had not made its way through storms and rough waters, elbowed or beaten by its fellow rocks and stones.

I held it in my hand and searched for the best place to throw it so other beachcombers wouldn't cut their feet. As I looked around, I saw Katie showing her heart rock candidates to her dad down the shore a way, Matt running in a tizzy toward me with another handful of glass, and the backdrop of San Remo against a blue sky. I suddenly felt as if I were going to burst with contentment.

I decided, then, not to throw the piece of jagged glass back, but to keep it as a symbol of Matthew at this particular moment in time. How it

sea glass

resembled his little boy body, all skin and bones poking out every which way. How it symbolized the rough edges of his still-evolving personality and the clarity and purity with which he presented his emotions. I wanted to remember always, upon our return to America, the feeling of his innocence, his excitement and his ability to grant himself the space to live in a world of his own. I just couldn't love that little guy more.

I would bury the piece among the heart rocks in our collection to remind myself that we never would have made this memory if Tim and I hadn't chosen, again, to walk a way on the stormy sea with the Lord instead of sinking to the bottom where we were headed.

I handed Matt the baseball cap we were using for a pail, and seeing that it was almost full, he abruptly decided that we had enough and began to walk with it back to our towel. I turned in time to see him, out of the corner of my eye, stop and pluck something from the water's edge. He held it high for me to see that it was heart-shaped.

"Mom," he called, "this one's perfect!"

"Great find," I yelled back to him. "Put it in the cap."

Instead, he decided to sneak one last throw. The gray stone sailed gracefully over the waves, hit the water and sprang upward in a burst of droplets that caught the sun. Matt looked over at me in surprise, and we watched the rock skip three times before it sank.

"See?" I laughed. "They don't all sink." And he shrugged his shoulders, wiggled his butt and danced, capful of glass held high, all the way back to Tim.

22 & alassio

At 10:00 PM we were meandering down a crowded stone alleyway in Alassio, an enchanting coastal haven on the Italian Riviera close to San Remo. The thoroughfare was lined on both sides with shops and restaurants whose doorways were adorned with striped awnings or carved stonework. We had stumbled upon this village by chance early this morning on the way back home to Nervi and chose to spend the night in a hotel on the sea.

I felt very bold and daring since we had done this on a whim. Tim had spied this delightful town from the train window and we simply got off at the next stop. An event deemed so outrageous for our overplanned life that Matt and Katie didn't know whether to be excited or scared. It had been a charmed day on the beach packed with Italians on holiday and a lovely evening lit by a full moon.

Back at our hotel room, we got ready for bed and slid under the covers. Matt and Tim fell asleep without a hitch. I listened in the dark to their measured breathing and wondered why there was no sound from Katie at all.

Unfortunately, the bar on the first floor of our building was a hot spot. As the clock crawled toward midnight, the crowd and its noise increased.

"*Pssst*. Mom," Katie whispered. "You awake?"

"Yes."

"Want to go swimming?" she asked.

"Now?"

"Come on. It's so pretty out."

I rolled over and peered through the darkness. In the moonlight that cut a path to her bed, her youth was luminous.

"It'll be fun," she promised. Swimming was the last thing I felt like doing.

"Sure." *Did I say that?*

We silently threw on our suits, grabbed some towels and slipped out the door. The hotel was eerily silent as we made our way down the carpeted stairs.

We headed out through the front door and walked past the overflowing pub, trying to act nonchalant, as if it were perfectly normal for us to be prancing around in our bathing suits at this late hour. As the beaches here are all private, we searched for a spot where we could sneak in. We found a hole in the wire fence a few yards down and managed to wiggle through.

We tossed our towels on some stacked chaise lounges and stood at the water's edge. The sea was quiet and still, and its tiny waves barely licked our toes. Shards of light from the full moon floated and twinkled on the surface of the ink black water. Suddenly all I could hear was the music from *Jaws*.

"You go first," I said.

"No, you."

"It was your idea," I countered.

"You're thinking about *Jaws*, aren't you?" She laughed at me. Then admitted, "Me too."

"Let's go together," I suggested. Slowly we waded into the warm sea, checking only half jokingly for shark fins. The water stretched out over a sand bar and remained shallow so that by the time we were up to our necks we were some distance from the shore. Two ants that had strayed from the anthill.

"Look at that moon," I said.

"I can see the man's face," said Katie. "I think he is smiling upon us this very minute."

"He may even be casting a spell."

"I can feel it." Katie raised her face and hands toward the moonlight. She closed her eyes and twirled slowly in a circle, a mermaid who had surfaced to drink in the light from the heavens.

We floated, swam and talked for a long time about nothing and everything. I tried to remember the last time we drifted together in a space without boundaries. The last time we shared our feelings without restraint and laughed with abandon. All I could come up with was the little tea party she had invited me to in her room when she was four, and even that I had to share with ten stuffed animals.

"There's something about swimming at night," Katie began.

"I know."

"It feels magical."

"Peaceful."

"Look down the coast. We're the only ones in the water. I wonder why more people don't do this." I knew, but didn't tell her, that it was because not everyone had a fourteen-year-old daughter as beautiful as mine to suggest it when they were trying to sleep.

"Some nights are wasted on sleep."

23 ❧ carmelina

Tim found a tiny Catholic church about a five-minute walk from our door. This morning we were going—clutching our new St. Joseph missals—for the first time. My mother had had the foresight to give us the pocket-size books of church readings in English as a going-away present. Mass in Italian was a tad hard to follow.

We headed down some stairs that were hidden behind a big oak tree, then down an alleyway that wound behind buildings and through over-grown brush. We turned a corner and Tim pointed out the tiny com-pound, half hidden behind big iron gates. A pale yellow chapel and an adjoining villa beckoned from a shaded garden setting. Katie pointed to the name of the place etched in stone. "Villa Colombo."

A statue of Mary stood in an alcove to the right of the chapel's door with a crown of stars lit for the occasion and flowering plants at her feet. We peered into the chapel and walked in.

It was very old and quite small. There were ancient, severe-looking wooden pews, eight on each side. The altar was simple, but adorned with a starched white altar cloth and fresh flowers in an antique vase. Even this tiny chapel had its share of paintings and ornate gold etching around the ceiling.

A few people sat in the pews in quiet contemplation waiting for Mass to begin. Two nuns of Indian descent tended to the altar. An older woman with a lace veil covering her graying black hair welcomed people as they entered. She was so short that her twinkling eyes were level with Tim's belt buckle. She greeted the four of us enthusiastically and started to ramble away.

"No italiano," Tim tried to tell her, but this just made her ramble even faster. We all smiled and laughed so as not to hurt her feelings.

"Did anyone catch her name?" Katie whispered.

"Carmelina," answered Matt.

We chose a pew near one of the three narrow windows since it was quite hot even at this early hour. Soon, more people arrived and the chapel filled up. The priest appeared and Mass proceeded as usual. Everyone was catching glimpses of us out of the corners of their eyes. With our blonde hair and tall bodies, we were a curiosity, and our clothes were too casual compared to everyone else's. I stared intently at my blue missal and pretended not to notice.

Carmelina, clearly a bigwig here, marched up proudly to do the first reading. When she stood behind the podium, she was so short that all I could see was her forehead covered in lace bobbing up and down as she read. Matt elbowed me and we stifled our giggles since no one else seemed to think this was amusing.

At the end of Mass, one of the nuns got up and made some kind of announcement and everyone clapped. I looked at Tim and we shrugged our shoulders. As we all filed out of the chapel, we saw that everyone was headed toward the attached house/rectory, but we started toward the gate to go home. Whatever was happening, we certainly weren't a part of it. Suddenly Carmelina appeared and, with hands on her square hips, blocked our way. She motioned for us to turn around and follow the crowd.

"No, thank you, we don't belong there."

She put her finger to her mouth to shush me and continued to stand in our way.

After a moment, Tim motioned to Carmelina that we surrendered, and we fell in line with the others.

We were the last to enter the house. The entire community was crowded around a large dining room table that had been covered with food and refreshments of all sorts. The priest was the guest of honor and, as he gave a little speech, I surmised that he was retiring. Carmelina flitted about serving all of the guests and making sure everyone was cared for.

Matt and Tim checked out the food as Katie and I struck up a conversation with a man nearby. We found out that this was not a rectory, but a home for women who had nowhere to go. Carmelina must be one of those women. I watched her carry a silver tray of cream-cheese-stuffed tomatoes from person to person and wondered what heartache her life had held to get her to this point.

We worked our way through the crowd to the other end of the table where Matt and Tim were making a meal of some crackers. Along the way, we met many of the parishioners who were also our neighbors. Curious and fascinated by us, they made us feel welcome and shared with us the names of every single person they knew that lived in America in case we might know them.

"Can we leave now?" asked Matt when I finally made it over to him. "Other people are."

I waved to Tim, who was holding court over in the corner with a group of older women who were clutching their handbags and marveling at his height. I tilted my head toward the door and he nodded.

At the door we stopped to look for Carmelina. She was busy bustling around, but Tim managed to catch her eye.

"Everybody wave thank-you," Tim said, and the four of us put our hands in the air. Her big smile and the way she came over and shooed us out the door to go and enjoy the day needed no translation. Yes, there was something very special about her.

We made our way through the courtyard and out the gate. I glanced back over my shoulder in time to see Carmelina giving another person a big good-bye hug. Everyone was going home—except her. And she seemed happier than us all.

Maybe because she was home. *Maybe*, I thought, *it takes heartache on the long, often crooked road of life to realize that happiness is only found in the heart.*

24   first day of school

No sense trying to make light of it. This was a very big day. It was hard enough adjusting to a new grade level at home in America, but compound that with all else being foreign and it meant we had the makings of a nuclear explosion.

Katie went through about fourteen outfits. Matt dressed with his eyes closed. We all met at the breakfast table for a small bite and a pep rally.

"This is going to be an experience that you'll never forget," said Tim as he poured orange juice into four glasses. "You are going to meet students and teachers from all over the world."

"Pass the Cheerios." Matt was clearly excited and on board. Katie checked her eyeliner in the reflection of the toaster. I suspected that what mattered most to them was finding a friend to sit with at lunch.

My own stomach was churning from the taste of their fear. We finished breakfast, walked through the neighborhood and down the ancient steps and stood at the bus stop without a word. We boarded the crowded bus in silence and rode the few kilometers along the sea to school.

Entering the campus, I was happy to see that it looked very much like the first day of school anywhere. Parents and students milling around, greeting each other after a long summer. Shouts of joy, laughter, fresh hair cuts, new book bags, but not one word of English being spoken. Mrs. B waved to us from afar and pantomimed Katie fainting and Mrs. B being strong enough to hold her up if this were to happen again. I waved and fake laughed.

Tim scanned the campus for some direction. "Looks like the younger children are starting to line up on the playground over there."

Katie and I took Matt over to a line of spirited students who looked about his age. One boy with blond hair and freckles caught my attention with his easygoing laughter. "Excuse me, is this the sixth grade?"

"Sì…Yes, it is." He looked at Matthew. "You are new? What is your name?"

"Matthew."

"Matteo. You stand with me. I show you." Looking happy and relieved, Matt gave me the "you can go now" look. Katie and I headed over to a common area to figure out where she needed to be. I glanced over my shoulder and saw Matt, a head taller than all of his classmates, standing bravely at the back of the line. Our eyes locked, and we smiled at each other. Matt was turning out to be a resilient little guy.

"Oh no," Katie said under her breath.

"What?"

"Tell me this is not happening." She was frantic. I followed her gaze to where Tim was having an animated conversation with several students who we could only presume were all of Katie's prospective classmates. He waved to Katie to come over, but she headed in the opposite direction.

Having spent the last twenty years in corporate culture, Tim did not know that the rules of school culture were completely different. I should have at least told him the one main rule of thumb appropriate for all situations: Parents of children over twelve were never to be seen or heard.

I gave him my best big-eyed glare and neck snap to get the heck out of there. I looked back at Katie who was starting to cry and breathe very rapidly. I had her sit on some concrete steps away from the crowd.

In the background, on the playing field where the whole school was now lined up, Mrs. B started her welcome speech. She introduced all of the teachers and staff.

"Katie, just breathe deeply and slowly." I said through my clenched teeth so no one else could hear us. She held it together, barely.

"I wanted to meet them on my own," she said.

The classes started to make their way to the building, line by line. Katie continued to turn whiter and whiter. *Please, God, no fainting today.* As the students disappeared and the crowd thinned out, we just sat, wishing for the cloak of invisibility to fall on us.

Suddenly a group of five high school students passed by. Noticing Katie, they stopped. One girl with brown braids and clear blue eyes bent and looked Katie squarely in the eye.

"Hi," she said gently, "would you like to come with us?" Katie nodded as the girl held out her hand and helped Katie to her feet. She took a deep breath and started to walk forward on wobbly legs. Without looking back she headed off with them, taking a piece of me with her.

I stood and met Tim's gaze as he waited across the playground in the shadows, his face clouded with uncertainty. I could count on one hand the times I had seen him unsure of himself. Funny, how this glimpse of raw vulnerability made me love him more than the thousands of times I had watched him work a crowd, proud and confident. I walked over and took his hand.

"I thought I was helping," he said.

"Don't worry. We'll laugh about it someday." We started to amble down the driveway. "Besides, we have more important things to think about."

"Like what?" he asked.

"Like how we are going to spend the first day in twenty years that we are totally alone together with nothing to do and nowhere to be."

"I have a few good ideas." He laughed, and we quickened our pace so as not to waste a single second.

25 ✂ the run

The heat had finally broken and the weather was cool and clear. I put on my running gear, picked out a Bruce Springsteen CD for musical inspiration and strapped on my Tune Belt. After a few quick stretches, I kissed Tim good-bye and ran out the door.

I headed down the steps and made my way to the main street that runs along the coast. I turned on my music and started a slow jog to warm up. Bruce's unmistakable voice started to pound in my ears. After a couple of blocks I found my rhythm and settled into my run.

I navigated down the narrow sidewalks dodging people and mounds of dog doo. I zoomed past closed shops (nothing was open on Sundays) and around traffic. I entered my favorite alley and veered off down toward the port of Nervi. I slowed down just a bit as I jogged through. It was narrow, delightfully crooked and cast with shadows. The doors to the apartments above were ancient and heavy and the colors of the buildings a smeared pallet of oranges and reds. Predictably, laundry hung overhead. And the entire length of the alley was empty, always empty.

At the end of the alley, the path opened up onto the old port that was lined with a few restaurants and rows and rows of weather-worn fishing boats. Old men were sitting around shooting the breeze. At the far end of the port, a stone bridge crossed over the inlet and began the *passeggiata Anita Garibaldi*. This wide, red brick pathway clings to the cliffs above the sea and runs the entire length of the town. A perfect place to run. The place was packed with people, all dressed in their Sunday best. It seemed that I had happened upon some sort of town celebration! *These*, I said to myself, *are the little surprises that make traveling so exciting. Coming upon the unexpected.* I couldn't wait to see what it was.

I started to weave through the throngs of people. No one noticed that I was trying to exercise. They didn't move over for me. I dodged the strollers and the kids on their three-wheelers. I made my way around older couples walking arm in arm and thought about how cute they looked. *This must be one important day.*

Bruce started to sing to me about the "Tunnel of Love" as I exited on one of the paths from the *passeggiata* that veered up toward the center of town. I was sure that this was where the main celebration must be being held. Some sort of carnival or something.

Again, I had to weave and dodge through people everywhere. I slowed to a fast walk but made sure to keep my heart rate up. I didn't want to fall out of my fat-burning zone after all of this effort. Only one more block to go. *Okay. Here we are at the center.* I came to a dead halt and looked around, puzzled. Nothing. No booths, no tiny rides set up, not a thing out of place! *What the—?*

Then it dawned on me. These people were actually just out WALKING. Strolling even. Together. Nicely dressed. What was this?

I took off my headphones and fell in step behind a particularly large group and just watched and eavesdropped. I was immediately jealous. This entire extended family was out just enjoying each other. No one looked rushed or bored or angry. The grandparents had their arms interlocked. Their children (my age), each with their own families in tow, seemed to be teasing each other. The grandchildren looked content.

I didn't know that people did this anymore ... anywhere. The emphasis here seemed to be on heart ... not heart rate. Sundays were family days, pure and simple. And no one seemed annoyed by it.

I was suddenly sad for my country. That we have lost this simplicity. That families, like mine, are strewn all across the country and only see each other at reunions. That we treat Sunday like Wednesday, and the stores all remain open, giving us options and reasons to be away from home. That we think it is more important to cash in those Sunday coupons at Wal-Mart than to walk on a quiet street with the ones we love most. I thought about all of the families that have lost this sense of preciousness and have lost each other because of it.

After a few blocks, and a few stares, I realized I was an oddity here. I pretended that I was just fixing my headphones and halfheartedly started up my run again. Bruce continued to preach to me how "we lose each other, in that tunnel of love." And I once again fell into my rhythm, this time, more aware of my heart than my heart rate.

This just might be my last Sunday run for a long time.

26 ~ basket part 1

So far, Matthew's NBA career was on track. He had begun training at the proper age of two with his first Nerf basketball set that attached neatly to his crib. His indoctrination into the game had continued at a steady pace with appropriate gear, driveway basketball and drills in reading newspaper stats. Finally, in second grade, he had made the team along with all of the other hopefuls who tried out. Year after year, he honed his skills through an unending series of school teams, summer leagues and camps. He attended the prerequisite NBA games when he could and had even gotten ahold of one of Shaq's shoes that had been sprayed gold and affixed to a trophy stand which he displayed in his room.

So you can imagine our consternation when Tim and I made the decision to leave the States for a year, knowing Matthew would fall far behind, and thus leave his upcoming NBA rookie status in the lurch.

Upon our arrival in Nervi, I noticed a glaring lack of basketball hoops. Kids here don't even have driveways, much less a hoop affixed to a garage. After a little research Tim found that if we wanted basketball, we needed to live in Milan. Our little region just wasn't into it. Football (soccer) was king. Matt was doomed.

After school started I was elated to hear that one of the three other kids in Katie's class was referred to as "Basketball Alex." A quick call to his mother revealed that there was a league right there in town! Tim and I reported the good news to Matt.

"I don't want to play here."

"Why not?" Tim said. "You love this game."

"I don't know how to talk here. I don't know anyone."

"Basketball is a language all its own. And you already know it."

"No, it's too scary."

"Be ready right after school."

The next day, Tim arranged to go with Basketball Alex's mom, who would show them the gym and then would act as translator to help get Matt signed up. Off they went with Tim in a cheerful mood and Matthew perspiring and mumbling something about diarrhea. I felt a twinge of guilt and empathy for this little guy, being challenged to do something beyond what is required of most American eleven-year-olds.

A few hours later they returned with the good news. "Take a look at the newest member of the team," Tim announced as they walked through the door.

"Way to go, Matt."

Silence.

"Practice begins tomorrow night. It'll be every Tuesday and Thursday for the next four months, and the games will begin in January. Right, Matt?"

Silence. Tim and I exchanged raised eyebrows.

Matt walked, shoulders slumped, back toward his room. Without turning around, he said, "And by the way, it's not called basketball here. It's called basket."

27 ⚜ giglio and pierangela

A retired couple who went to our church, Giglio and Pierangela Reduzzi, invited us to come for tea. We spruced up a bit and wandered down to their apartment, just a block from us, at three o'clock on a Sunday afternoon. Giglio, his salt-and-pepper hair combed neatly in place, stood at his door, which was up a flight of white marble steps. He was all smiles and dressed nicely in dark pressed slacks and a pinstriped dress shirt. Pierangela, elegant with a beige silk scarf tucked in at the collar of a crisp white blouse, stood at his side with clasped hands. Her soft brown eyes matched the color of her hair, which was neatly pinned into a sophisticated updo. She giggled when Giglio pinched his nose between his thumb and index fingers and apologized that the hallway smelled of garlic. He pointed to the neighbor's door and gave a disgusted shrug.

"I am Giglio." He put his hand out to shake mine. "And this is Pierangela." Tim and I took turns shaking her hand. She spoke slowly and carefully and pronounced Tim's name with the Italian pronunciation of *Teem*.

Their apartment was typical of the region: a kitchen, bathroom, a few small bedrooms and a simple living room that opened up onto a spacious terrace. A narrow central hallway connected a few rooms on the left and right. The walls were white and decorated with paintings and photographs, many of which, Giglio explained, were his own original works.

"Please, let us sit in the living room," said Giglio showing us to a couch. Tim and I sat as Pierangela entered with a tray on which she had four minute glasses of limoncello. Pierangela handed one to each of us and then sat, perched on the edge of an armchair. We smiled at each other and sipped in silence, lips pursed like we were drinking from thimbles.

Everyone looked as awkward as I felt. Slowly, we found common ground when the topic turned to children.

"Paola, my daughter"—Giglio put his head in his hands and shook it dramatically back and forth as Pierangela giggled—"is spending all of my money. She asks for everything. She drops her two daughters off every day for us to feed them. And she"—he pointed to Pierangela—"never says no." Pierangela scurried over to a nearby bookshelf and grabbed all of the photos she could find. As I expected, the grandchildren were beautiful with their long brown curls and big brown eyes.

Giglio leaned over the arm of his dark green armchair and grabbed a small, slim book from the wall of bookshelves behind him. He handed it to me, explaining that politics was his passion, and he'd self-published this book of his political views in both Italian and English.

"That is so everyone can enjoy my opinion." He laughed. "Now, it is your turn. Why are you here?" Tim told them how we came to be living in Nervi, minus any relationship issues, and gave an abbreviated account of our backgrounds: that he was a big guy from a small town north of Dayton, Ohio, and I was a small gal from a big town outside of New York City.

Pierangela stood and clasped her hands together. "Please, come to the kitchen." The three of us followed her across the hall into the small, cream-colored 1950s-style kitchen where the white-linen covered table was set with china teacups and pastries from a patisserie that we were assured was the best in the neighborhood. Cozy around the table, we all relaxed a bit. Pierangela confessed that she was shy about her English, though she did speak it rather well.

"I have an idea," said Giglio as he stirred a spoon around in his tea. "How about if we teach you Italian, and you can help Pierangela with her English? We go to Nova Scotia every summer, and she cannot communicate with the neighbors."

Tim and I had been combing the area for an Italian tutor or a class of some sort but were finding the cost to be prohibitive. This would be perfect! I glanced at Tim for confirmation.

"We would love it," I said.

"How about twice a week for one hour?" Giglio asked.

"Tuesdays and Thursdays?"

"*Perfetto.*"

28 ❧ coffee shop

Taking the kids to school every day had taken on a new dimension. The four of us would all get off the bus and then head in different directions. The kids would climb up the steps to the campus, and Tim and I would head toward the coffee shop.

That part of town, in Quarto, intrigued us. We had decided that it must be the official meeting spot for retired Mafioso because it was always crowded with older men who talked to each other all day, every day. They sat on benches, stood on corners and walked along the sea.

"How much could they possibly have to talk about?" Tim asked.

"I wonder if they're reminiscing about the 'day Joey got gunned down' or 'how *The Godfather* was so Hollywood.'"

The coffee shop was the hub. Typically, these shops consisted of a bar/counter without stools. Behind the counter was an industrial-sized coffee/espresso machine and a glass cabinet filled with fresh brioches and focaccia. Sometimes there was a freezer case filled with the brilliant colors of gelato, and if the place was big enough, like this one, they might have a few tables and chairs in the back.

Tim ordered our usual, "*Due cappuccini, molto caldi, cacao.*" The guy who ran the place knew we were American, so he excused our accents and the fact that we ordered our coffees very hot, as they were usually served lukewarm. We also liked the added touch of cocoa powder sprinkled on the white foam. We took them to a table and sat down. Since we couldn't read the paper, we would read the crowd instead. The majority of people came in alone and stood at the bar. They would order an espresso as they lit their cigarettes. The owner would prepare the espresso in a cup the size of a golf ball and place it in front of them. Then the person would down the entire cup of espresso in one gulp, throw some money down on the counter and walk out the door.

That was the Italian version of going out for breakfast. Other than the cigarette part, I quickly grew to like it. It was cappuccino from heaven— rich and sweet. And the brioches would melt in my mouth if I got one early enough, when it was still warm from the oven. I found that I didn't miss stuffing myself in the morning. And it was nice to sip from a real cup rather than cardboard. To hear the clink of the porcelain against a matching saucer. I felt downright civilized drinking my coffee among the living rather than alone in my car. Even if I wanted it, hot drinks were not available "to go," and as a result there was a noticeable lack of litter outside from to-go packaging.

"So what should we do today?"

"Anything in mind?" Tim asked.

"We could get our books and read at the beach."

"No."

"We could go into Santa Margherita and get some of that great focaccia."

"No."

Once the kids started school and the basic chores of getting set up and settling in had been attended to, we found ourselves with large chunks of time with nothing attached to them. At first, it felt odd. Some days I would even feel guilty, like I wasn't accomplishing anything. That I was wasting the day. But that phase passed quickly when I realized that I was actually accomplishing all sorts of important things. They just weren't tangible.

Back home, I had measured my achievements by their visible results. A well-decorated room, a garden carefully planted so that something was blooming year round, a healthy meal that looked pretty on the plate, a themed party orchestrated to the last petit four, a killer forehand and a strong first serve. Everything was goal oriented. Envision, plan, execute, admire … repeat. Whatever time Tim and I spent together fell into some part of that cycle. If we were together, it was usually "to be together to get things done." I had forgotten that our goal had once been "to be together" without the "to get things done" part.

This new feeling of wandering through time enticed me with the element of surprise. I had forgotten how much fun it was and how it fed our relationship. Leo F. Buscaglia, who always wrote about the great power of love, warned years ago that "Love withers with predictability; its very essence is surprise and amazement."

"How about the train thing?" We had started hopping on the train and just getting off at random towns along the coast. We would explore them and invariably end up feasting at a little out-of-the way restaurant.

"Let's go north this time. It's nine thirty. So we'd better get moving if we want to catch the 9:42." Tim was already becoming the master scheduler. He would spend hours poring over maps and mass transit schedules. He had a mind for numbers.

I finished up the last of my coffee as Tim paid our bill. People nodded to us as we walked toward the door, letting us know that we were becoming regulars. Stepping out into the bright sunshine, I felt enthused at the thought of yet another full day completely free of obligation.

We walked past three older men in a heated discussion lined up in a row on a bench. They were all talking at once, hands flying and nostrils flaring. It reminded me of an American movie. I strained my ears to eavesdrop, but I couldn't make out a single sentence. It didn't really matter what they were saying because it was more fun just to wonder.

I caught the eye of a guy standing to the side who was well into his eighties. We exchanged a smile.

"Sorry to hear about Joey," I said, knowing he didn't understand a word. "And Marlon Brando is so Hollywood." He laughed and waved me on. He didn't care what I was saying either. He just got a kick out of the fact that two Americans were walking by. Just like out of an Italian movie.

29 ✨ basket part 2

It was my turn to take Matt to practice, and I was looking forward to it, because I was more than curious to see what the team was like.

"Matt, hurry up. What are you doing back there?" I was familiar with all of his usual stalling tactics, but he was starting to cut it too close.

He appeared in his Laker gear. "It took forever to find my shoes."

"That's funny, I put them on top of your bed right before you got home from school."

Silence.

I grabbed my red hooded sweatshirt and my purse and we headed out the door. He marched two steps ahead of me to make sure I knew he was still angry, his shoulder blades poking through the thin material of his jersey.

"Hey, save some of that speed for the court."

He slowed a bit without looking at me and soon we were side by side. I could see his eyes were wet with tears.

"It's so stupid. The team stinks."

"Doing something like this takes real guts."

"Like I have a choice." He wiped the lone tear that had spilled down his cheek.

The buses here were a little erratic, so we ended up waiting at the bus stop for ages. As time passed, it hit me that this scenario would be played out over and over in the next months—standing at the bus stop to go to practice … in the dark, in the rain, in the cold. I suddenly missed my car.

This would be a whole new level of commitment for me too. Finally the bus showed up along with two others right behind it.

We rode to the end of the line and then we walked another half mile with Matt leading the way. "Are you sure you know where you're going?" I kept asking every few feet.

"Yes, Mom, would you just trust me?" Sure enough, down a tiny alley there was a small compound hidden away. The door jingled as we walk inside to find a coffee shop/bar and an adjacent room filled with about forty old men playing cards. They all looked up at us at once like we had an announcement to make.

"Are you sure this is the right place?" I said under my breath as I gave a little wave to the fellas.

"It's in the back."

The place smelled old, like the YMCA where I used to take swim lessons as a child. It had the same dark mahogany paneling and white plaster ceilings. The wooden floors were pale and worn by a million footsteps of people looking for friends or a quick game. Matt led me through the room, down the hallway and outside onto a small patio that overlooked a bocce court. Older men lined the fences and rooted for the two teams—silently. After the play was made, the crowd relaxed and whispered. Our cue to move, Matt then led me down a sidewalk, past a soccer field and around a building to an old gym. I could hear through the windows that practice had begun.

"Matt, go on ahead. Hurry. They've already started." He hesitated.

"Go."

"Please don't leave."

"I won't."

He took two steps and then hesitated again.

"Do you think that you can sit right by the door of the gym so I can see you?"

"Are you kidding? There's no place else I'd rather sit. Now go get 'em, tiger." He gave me a nervous grin, and I watched him disappear around the bend. Matt still thought that courage and self-confidence were things you got from your mother's smile.

I plopped down by the door just as Matt ran in to join the others. I was the only parent there, and what I saw took me by surprise. I was not looking at a gym of seasoned young superstars, I was looking at ... well, for lack of a better word ... boys.

Nobody's clothes were logo driven. Short gym shorts, some T-shirts tucked into waistbands pulled up to the ribcage, socks of every color and height and gym shoes of every style except basketball, most looking worse for the wear. Peer pressure concerning clothes didn't seem to exist here. They were running up and down the court dribbling (if you could call it that) with exuberance and delight. No one was mocking anyone else, and they were downright giddy with the fun of it all.

Matt, in his cool duds and Nike Airs looked more than a little bewildered. The coach was yelling for order, and slowly, very slowly, the kids formed a group around him. He began to set up the practice, and Matt looked over at me shrugging his shoulders to tell me that he had no idea what the guy was saying. I gave him a thumbs-up.

The kids broke into two lines and then I witnessed mass chaos for the next hour. Matthew looked like Michael Jordan in comparison. There were a few players who were good, but obviously many of these boys were playing for the first time. Almost unheard of at this advanced age of eleven. Now the need for a four-month practice schedule prior to the season made perfect sense.

At eight, we headed back down the empty streets in the dark toward the center of town where we would get the bus. Matt was clearly bummed, his head down and his gym bag dragging on the ground behind him.

"They don't even know how to pass," he said.

"They'll learn how to pass, just like you did."

"Please don't make me play on this team."

"You can be the big shot this year. Maybe you can experience something that you haven't really had yet on a team."

"Like losing?" he asked.

"Like having fun," I said. "Now pick up your bag."

30 ❦ trofie e pesto

A few women stood in front of me in the *macelleria* (butcher shop). Staring at the case of meat, I felt one of those moments of complete mental shutdown coming on. They could last anywhere from a few seconds to a few hours. All of this living in a foreign country business was just plain hard sometimes.

Nothing in the case was labeled. To the right I recognized rabbit bodies without fur. Next to them, I saw chickens that still had their heads. I didn't understand why the heads had to be attached. To the left was a large slab of cow. Presumably, I was supposed to be able to recognize cuts of beef still attached to the side of the cow, name them in Italian, and ask for specific amounts in proper metric lingo. I felt as if I had entered a math word problem. I was never good at those, and I was just not up to this today.

Quietly I turned, walked out the door and stopped to lean against the wall of the building next door. Across the street I saw the pasta *fresca* shop (fresh pasta). Noodles, I could handle. I entered and was greeted by a happy pasta maker. I pointed to some *trofie*, a new squiggly little noodle we had been introduced to here and cupped my hands to indicate a certain amount. She wrapped it up and handed it to me.

Behind the counter she waited expectantly, a few strands of brown wavy hair had escaped her loose bun and were blowing around her face. I looked at her. She looked at me. I had no idea what she was waiting for. But I, on the other hand, was waiting for the bill, which I used as a cheat sheet to see what I owed because all of the words people said to me were still blurring together when a price was announced.

Another woman entered the shop. They greeted each other like siblings who had just discovered that the other existed while watching *Oprah*. Jealous tears welled up as I stood there, suddenly missing my girlfriends back in Los Angeles. Then the attention turned back to me. Four eyes now, instead of two, waited for my next move.

Fine. I'd buy something else. I pointed to some fresh marinara. The woman behind the counter looked at me like I was crazy. No, she shook her head, handed me a small container of fresh pesto, and pointed to the *trofie*. "*Solo pesto!*" she exclaimed while she and the other customer exchanged exasperated nods.

"Just kidding." I took the pesto and paid for the goods. As I walked back out into the sunshine, I looked at my watch. It had taken me over a half hour to buy two things.

I ambled slowly down the block. I still didn't have enough for dinner. I needed to get some fresh bread, salad makings—something else at least. But all I felt like doing was going home and curling up on the couch with a big carton of Breyers vanilla fudge swirl. That was one thing I really did miss. There was no Breyers in Italy. And people didn't buy big cartons of ice cream to gorge themselves on in private. If you were in the mood for gelato, you walked down to the shop and bought a scoop—like one scoop was ever enough.

I decided to reward myself by satisfying this craving at the gelato store down the street. I walked the two blocks and entered Columbo, our favorite coffee shop/gelateria in the neighborhood.

"*Buon giorno*," I said to the familiar face behind the counter.

"*Buon giorno, signora.*" Columbo was bright and cheery and had—we all decided—the best *stracciatella* (chocolate chip) in town. The guy behind the counter already knew what I was going to order. He pointed to it and laughed. I nodded and watched him scoop it out enthusiastically. He handed it to me and I sat outside at one of the black café tables to relax and savor every bite.

"Susan." I looked up to see Tim stepping off the bus outside the café. Dressed in workout clothes, he was returning from our new gym, The New Muscle Beach, which was located down the coast by the kids' school.

"Hey," I said as he pulled up a chair. "How was your workout?"

"Great. What are you having there? A little *stracciatella*?"

"It's been a tough morning."

"Looks like it." He grabbed my spoon and started to eat some of the gelato.

"Why don't you order some of your own if you're hungry?"

"I only want a taste. It's not like you never eat off my plate."

"Just keep it. I'll go get another one."

"Why are you getting so pissed off?"

"I'm not getting pissed off." Clearly I was. "One scoop's not enough for two people, that's all."

"Geez. I was in a great mood until I saw you."

"Thank you."

I ordered more gelato, this time asking for two scoops, just in case. I brought it back to the table and we ate in silence, pretending that the people passing by were so particularly fascinating that we had to watch them. Without warning, I could feel the tears welling up again.

"Are you crying?"

I nodded as I searched my pockets for a tissue.

"So why has this morning been so tough?" Tim asked gently.

"All of this overwhelms me sometimes," I said. An inordinate amount of tears began to flow down my cheeks. "The fish store smelled putrid…. And then the rabbits, their little legs all"—I blew my nose on the tiny paper napkin with a loud honk—"and I didn't even know the right sauce for *trofie*…" Another honk. "And those women—"

"Did they bother you? Say something mean?"

"I miss my friends." I took a deep breath and tried to straighten up. I was not in the habit of having emotional breakdowns in public.

Tim put his elbows on the table and leaned forward. "Well, I'm your friend."

"You're not my friend, you're my husband," I wailed before I could catch myself. I saw the hurt flicker in his sweet blue eyes and immediately regretted my words.

"Oh."

"I'm sorry. I didn't mean that the way it sounded. I'm just having a down day, and I'm used to being able to pick up the phone and joke it away with Karen or Gina or Diane. Of course you're my friend. A husband is way more than a friend." We sat there quiet, a long time. Tim picked at his empty paper gelato cup.

"I know you didn't mean it that way," he began, "and I miss my friends too. But I also think there's some truth to that. We both spent too much time turning to our friends instead of each other. Don't you think?"

"I suppose so." I pushed the remainder of my *stracciatella* toward him.

"Thanks."

"Does this mean you'll go shopping with me?"

"Some."

"Can you go with me right now and help me pick out something else for dinner?"

"Sure." We stood and Tim reached down and picked up the little grocery bag. As we walked across the street together, he looked inside and said, "*Trofie?* Great. I'm kinda tired of pesto, though. Can we get some marinara instead?"

"We're not allowed to."

119

31 ~ tb

Katie and I sat in the empty lobby of a private radiology clinic in Genoa waiting for a four o'clock appointment. Tim had gone to get Matt from school and then take him to basketball practice. It was our second visit to the doctor in two days and I was frightened but trying very hard not to show it. Katie had had X-rays taken the day before, after she casually informed me that she was coughing up blood and had been for some time. We were here, again, because a pulmonary specialist took one look at her chest X-rays and ordered an immediate array of blood work, CT scan and other related tests.

Giglio and Pierangela had helped us find this clinic. I had called them

tb

late yesterday morning in a panic. Italy had a socialized health care system, but the thought of walking into a foreign hospital to seek help was paralyzing. Giglio did a little research and then called me back with the name of this private office. Though citizens can get health care for free, you can get it faster—without all of the red tape—at one of these clinics, if you are willing to pay for it. He showed up at our door a little while later in the pouring rain in his fine tweed suit and drove us down to the center of Genoa in his forest green Chevy Neon. He stayed and translated for us, cracking little jokes from time to time to ease our tension. And he stood quietly at our side while we listened to what the specialist had to say.

"This small spot here," the doctor said as he pointed to a dark shadow the size of a dime, "looks to me like TB."

"TB?"

"I have been around a long time. This is nothing to fool around with."

"She just had a complete physical before we left America." I wondered if this had any connection with her recent fainting spell that day on campus. *Why did I let her talk me out of getting her checked then?*

He gave me a long speech about how TB germs were growing resistant and mutating into new versions of the illness. It seemed that TB had entered Italy from South America before, but not from North America. If Katie did have TB, it would be groundbreaking news for the Italian Center for Disease Control.

This had been one of my biggest fears in moving here—one of our children getting sick this far from home. Having to deal with medical emergencies was hard enough when we all spoke the same language. Not to mention the trust factor. Who knew how they worked things in the medical field in this part of the world?

So here we sat. Waiting. No Giglio this time to calm us with his fatherly manner. At four o'clock, the owner of the clinic came and stood before us in his white coat and slicked-back hair the color of coal.

"I am very sorry that it will be just a few more minutes." He was gone before we could respond. Visions of hospital beds and feeding tubes and nonstop coughing kept running through my mind. *Oh, calm down*, I kept telling myself. *For goodness' sake, it's the twenty-first century. They have medicine for this type of thing.*

"Mom, stop mumbling," Katie elbowed me.

A few more minutes went by and the specialist we had met with the day before came out and nodded. "I am very sorry for the delay! We are waiting for an anesthesiologist to arrive to help with the CT scan."

I looked sideways at Katie. We weren't used to doctors apologizing to us about being behind schedule.

"Katie, please come with me. I take your blood." He led her into a side office and closed the door.

I stood up and paced from one side of the room to the other. Why did they need an anesthesiologist? There was no way I was going to let these people put Katie to sleep. I could feel heat start to rise up my neck, and I ordered myself to relax. *God is with us, helping us. God is with us, helping us. And, God, by the way, none of this "taking the firstborn" stuff. You already have my full attention.*

Soon enough, the door opened and out walked Katie with a look about her that I couldn't name. The specialist followed her, gave me another curt nod of the head and zipped down the hallway. Katie sat back down and showed me her arm.

"He had me lay my bare arm across his desk, right on top of his paperwork and a stack of file folders. Then, he just threw the used needle in the trash can under the desk."

The heat was rising up my neck again.

"And he put the tubes of blood into his suit jacket pocket."

"His pocket?" I took a deep breath.

"He told me my blood looked bad. Anemic. And it hurt like crazy." Katie's face was getting red. *Since when does someone's blood look bad? This is how it happens*, I thought to myself. *This is how your child picks up a disease in a foreign country and dies. This is how your dream trip turns into a nightmare. God, you'd better be with us helping us. You'd better be here.*

Soon we were summoned to the back for the CT scan. The

anesthesiologist turned out to be a young woman with a black ponytail who calmed Katie down with some girl talk.

"Why does Katie need you here if she's just having a CT scan done?" I asked.

"In case she has a bad reaction and must be put to sleep."

"What kind of bad reaction?"

"Nothing is going to happen. She is a young girl. Her body is strong." She hooked Katie up to an IV drip.

"You will start to taste something metallic, and it will probably start to burn a little in your throat and mouth." I gave Katie's hand a squeeze and told her to relax, though I was shaking like a leaf.

I was ushered into the control room on wobbly legs. I felt weak but did my best to appear like a fighter, a lioness protecting her cub. The huge control panel sat below a large window so that we could all watch the procedure together. Another doctor arrived to observe. There were now three medical personnel and myself. They conferred animatedly in a rush of Italian. I wished I knew what they were saying. The specialist put the X-rays up on the light board on the wall and pointed out the area of concern. They all studied the dark circle with wrinkled brows and hands on chins.

Katie was ready. Lying on her back, she glanced at me through the glass one last time before she was inserted into the huge round piece of equipment. I gave her two thumbs-up followed by the okay signal, and then the top half of her disappeared into the machine.

The technician began the procedure. I was in the midst of turning my pockets inside out, looking for Matthew 6:25–34 when the specialist tapped me on the shoulder and offered me a plate filled with cookies.

"Hungry?" he asked politely.

"No, thanks."

He proceeded to chomp away as the technician took image after image. Everyone's eyes were glued to the screen. In between the clunking sounds of the machine, I could hear the doctors chewing on their cookies.

I stepped back so I could take in the entire scene. Here and there I heard murmurings from the bevy of doctors. I kept my eye on Katie's skinny legs sticking out of the machine like knitting needles from an oversized skein of yarn. If her knees started to knock, I wanted to be ready to take charge.

All of a sudden an alarm sounded and the machine clicked off.

"What's going on?" I asked, trying to keep my voice even. The technician turned around in his chair and informed us that Katie had moved and they had to recalibrate the machine. Everyone sat back to wait. The technician reached into his pocket and casually pulled out rolling papers and tobacco. He proceeded to roll a cigarette and light it! All of the doctors casually conversed as he puffed away.

No one seemed to think it was out of line to smoke while checking my daughter for lung disease. Soon the machine was reset, and the technician continued to work between drags. Finally he came to the area of question in her lung. Everyone jumped up and started to run back and forth between her X-rays and the CT image. Back and forth. Murmuring. Back and forth. Hands in the air. Murmuring. Back and forth. Loud sighs. Finally it was over and the specialist asked me to meet him in his office in a few minutes.

I collected Katie, who seemed to be holding up okay, and we found our way to his office. He was all smiles, so I immediately relaxed. He did not think it was TB after all. It seemed that Katie had an abnormal bone growth on her scapula that was showing up on the X-ray. She just had a little infection. I wanted to kiss him but hugged Katie instead. She was going to be fine! *Thank You, God, for helping us.*

The doctor fished around in his pocket and pulled out Katie's vials of blood. "If it is okay I would still like to follow through with the blood work."

"By all means," I told him. He put the vials back in his pocket.

"The girl in the lab at the hospital is my good friend," he added, "and I will immediately drive the blood over to her myself."

He prescribed a strong antibiotic and strict bed rest for a week. I handed him my Visa card to pay for everything. I had no idea what the cost would be and didn't care. Katie would be healthy again in no time. I signed the bill without looking.

3 2   italian dogs

By this point it was early evening and we were now on the number seventeen bus making our way home in the dark after the traumatic CT scan episode. Katie and I were punchy with relief that she did not have TB. I sat with my head back staring up at the ads that ran along the sides of the bus above the windows while Katie stared out the window and intently scanned the stores as the bus rumbled along.

"Mom, I remember seeing a pet store with puppies in the window in this part of town."

"That's nice."

"If I find it, can we stop?"

"Why would we want to do that?"

"There it is!" she yelled. "Let's just stop for a minute! Please?"

"Okay." I answered as she pushed the buzzer to stop the bus. It was not a particularly pretty part of the city with its old soot-darkened buildings and narrow streets. We backtracked a few blocks and found the tiny pet store. Indeed there were puppies in the window.

Italians loved dogs. I had never seen anything like it. Dogs were allowed everywhere. People took them on buses, into stores, hotels and classy restaurants. Basically they were treated like humans and got as much attention and love as children. This took some getting used to. But on the flip side, Italian dogs were very well behaved as a result of all the attention. They did not bother people, and they rarely barked and caused a scene.

We had left our dog, Carmel Corn, back in LA, and we all missed her. Katie and I had picked her up one day at the pound and brought her home. She was basically an outdoor dog with a comfy bed in the garage, a doggie door and the run of the property. She came in and "visited" us each day, but she lived outside. We didn't have to plan our life around her need to do her business or get exercise. She was totally self-sufficient. And we loved her.

She almost came with us on this journey until the family that bought our house called us and asked if they could take care of her while we were gone. Tim and I couldn't believe their kindness and knew that Carmel would be better off staying in her own home, so we left her there with little photos of us taped on the wall above her bed.

Katie and Matt had been relentless in their quest for a new puppy here. I knew that they were lonely and not quite settled, and a dog would fill up some of that void for them. But, a dog would also be a huge responsibility and would throw a wrench into our new footloose-and-fancy-free lifestyle. So, knowing—as every mother does—that any dog would become the mother's dog regardless of all the earnest promises by the rest of the family to walk it, I resisted all pleas. No dog.

My plan was to humor Katie and coo over the puppies with her for a few minutes before we went home. After all, she'd just had a very hard day. We entered the shop and peered into the large metal cage by the window. Inside were four puppies. Two were white Shih Tzus and two were black fur balls.

We waved to the elderly shop owner in the worn, blue plaid flannel shirt. The man shuffled over with his knowing smile and reached into the cage with sure hands. Moments later he put a tiny fluff ball into Katie's arms. The puppy's eyes were as black as his fur and his gaze as pitiful as Oliver Twist's when he asked for more soup. A little pink tongue darted out and tried to lick Katie all over.

"Can we?" Katie pleaded with those same Oliver Twist eyes.

"What kind of dog is this?" I asked. The man's wife had appeared from the back room and the couple was now hovering around us like grandparents showing off their favorite grandchild. Though they could speak no English, I was able to deduce that he was a *barboncino* (miniature poodle), and would only grow to about ten pounds or so. He didn't shed and the breed was quite smart. Only he and his sister were left from a litter of six.

Katie and I just stood and stared at each other. Before I knew it, I whipped out my Visa card. I knew I shouldn't be doing this. But some otherworldly force had taken over. Again. As the man completed the transaction, Katie and I agreed that this was meant to be.

"For some reason the stars aligned just right so that I, this girl from California, would walk into a tiny store in Genoa and get this perfect puppy," Katie philosophized as she held the puppy to her face and gave him a big kiss.

"*Amore mio*. My love." She whispered to him as I basked in the glow of her first truly happy moment since we had arrived in July.

I knew we were just talking ourselves into doing something we shouldn't. Something that went against all logic. *But why should we start being logical now? Logic is not what brought us here.* We picked out a royal blue collar, a leash and a small bag of food. Katie put the puppy inside her jacket and close to her heart. We bade farewell to the owner and his wife, who were happy to see their baby in the arms of caring people.

After a short walk to the bus stop, we stood in the cold October air and thought of ways to surprise Matthew and Tim with the new member of the family. The puppy's little head stuck out of Katie's jacket for a second and then disappeared. We shared another giggle, and somewhere inside I knew this was a good thing. We would bring home a new friend for Carmel Corn. An Italian friend. A dog that would end up bilingual and love us through this whole adventure. Another letting go of "how things should be" and opening up a little wider the door that read Caution to the Winds.

33 ⁓ buses part 2

I stood alone at the bus stop trying to lift myself from a foul mood. I had awoken that morning from a dream that had reopened old wounds and I knew that any innocent word from Tim would send me sideways into some sort of fight. I had decided to head into Genoa for the morning and walk around by myself to let off steam and work though some feelings.

Before children, we had been a "work hard, play hard" kind of couple. But as our marriage evolved and our responsibilities grew, we settled into roles that had been subconsciously defined by our own separate experiences of growing up in traditional homes. Before we knew it, we had two children and a huge mortgage. I quit my teaching career and stayed home while Tim went out every day to earn a living. Basically, we had started to play house like a couple of six-year-olds who didn't understand the depth of the rules.

Both of us felt that the other person just didn't get how hard it was. I resented that the "play hard" part of the equation had disappeared for me, The Mom, who was at home with the kids, but stayed fully intact for Tim, The Dad, who had all the freedom he wanted once he left the house in the morning.

Tim, on the other hand, felt that I was not supportive of his demanding career and that I didn't have to get up and face the monsters every day on the freeway and in the office. I had a cushy life in the suburbs, what right did I have to complain? Nor did I understand that socializing was a big part of the radio business. He had to be out often at night. Drinks and dinner were part of closing the deal. *Right.*

Our trust in each other eroded like a sand dune in the wind. In the end, I wanted more freedom and he didn't want to give up any of his. Stalemate. Game over.

Now that we had erased the mortgage, the job, the long commute and the cushy life in the suburbs, and sent the kids to school every day, I knew that this long chapter of resentment could end. But I would have to stop letting the past color the future. Easier said than done. I figured a brisk walk through a splendid city on an autumn day would be a good way to put me back on the path to letting go and looking forward. I could even hear Dr. Phil commanding me from the TV to "stand up and walk out of my history."

I took a deep, cleansing breath, checked my watch and wondered where all of the other riders were. Usually this bus stop was full. *Hmm.* I looked to my left and saw a bus headed my way. I took out my book of tickets and walked toward the curb. I held out my hand to signal for the driver to stop, but he didn't even slow down! He zoomed by me without even so much as a glance in my direction. *Jerk.*

I went back and took my seat again since it was going to be at least another ten to fifteen minutes until the next bus came along. *So irritating.* I looked to the right and saw another bus coming in the opposite direction. The bus stop on the other side of the street was empty. As the bus zoomed by at top speed I noticed that there was no one aboard. *Something's strange here.*

This whole bus situation was confusing. I was learning something new about it all the time. Last week, poor Katie and Matt were thrown from a bus in the pouring rain and issued a thirty-five-euro fine. They even had bus tickets on them! Okay, so they weren't validated. But Matt had explained between sobs that that was because the old man blocking the machine was overweight and wouldn't move over even when Katie politely asked him.

It turned out that someone *was* watching to see if we were paying. Anyone could have made the same mistake. How were we supposed to know that there were uniformed secret agents who boarded the buses periodically, blocked the exits like they were James Bond, and checked to see that everyone had a validated ticket? Was this something left over from the days of Mussolini?

A few people walked by and eyed me suspiciously. An older woman in a black overcoat with a white scarf tied around her unruly auburn hair came up and blasted a string of sentences my way. I couldn't discern even a single word. So I just nodded and said thank you. She clomped away, clearly annoyed with me.

Finally, another bus came into view. I stepped out again and flagged him down. Again he just accelerated and left me in a cloud of exhaust. *Another jerk.*

An elderly gentleman in a plaid suit coat and gently worn green corduroys spied me from across the road. I watched him hobble toward me with the look of a father wanting to impart wisdom to his daughter. Soon he was standing before me.

"*Gli autobus,*" he said, "*sono in sciopero.*"

"Oh," I answered feeling stupid.

"*Lei dovrà camminare.*"

I was able to make out the words *bus on strike* and *walk.*

"*Grazie,*" I said with a tired sigh. *You mean to tell me that these guys show up for work and drive their routes all day long and just don't pick anyone up? That's outright cruelty. Why show up at all if you're on strike? How do they expect me to work through my old anger if I have to add this to the top of the pile?*

The kind man waved me on, and I decided to walk toward downtown Nervi instead. I pulled my jacket up to block the cool breeze that was starting to blow in from the sea and got a move on. As I marched toward town another bus barreled past. *Jerk.*

34 ✻ school meeting

Something BIG was going down at school. Katie was all atwitter about it, though Matthew, naturally, was oblivious. All parents had been summoned to a MANDATORY MEETING in the school cafeteria. Winning the coin toss, Tim got to stay home with Matt, so Katie and I made plans to go with our new friend, Veronica, who also had two children in the school.

School politics here was in a state of flux. The balance of power was being tested. Basically, it appeared that the families wanted to control and run the place. I suspected that Mrs. B was not too happy about that.

"Mom, all I know is that kids are saying that a lot of the families don't want the high school anymore. It takes up too much of the school's money and there aren't enough students to support it," Katie explained. "My whole class is planning a sit-in tonight in favor of keeping the high school."

"All four of you?"

Mrs. B answered to a largely Italian school board. She believed strongly in the current "keep the high school" vision of the international school. The school board was, apparently, very powerful, and I guess there was great dissension among the members as to the proper direction for the school.

After being quite involved in school activities for most of my adult life, I had no intention of getting drawn into any of this. I was officially on a break. The schools our children attended in Los Angeles required that the parents do forty plus hours of volunteer work as part of the tuition requirement. So after classroom teaching and more than four thousand hours of volunteering over the years, I was just plumb tuckered out. The following words had been declared taboo in our house: *magazine drive, gift wrap, cookie dough, jog-a-thon, Tupperware, silent auction, casino night, school festival, yard duty, Scrip, fundraiser, PTO, PTA, hot lunch envelope, fashion show, room mother, assistant to the room mother, assistant to the room mother's assistant.*

I didn't want to know who hated whom, who thought so and so was showy and had a big mouth. Who used to be best friends until … Who was overly strict with their kids or who let theirs hang from the chandeliers with six-packs of beer tucked under their arms. I just didn't want to know.

Over the past several days, strange notices and covert letters had started coming home with the kids. They were written by rogue members of the school board on both sides of the issue to "set the story straight." Unfortunately, none of the letters came home in English. So nothing was set straight for us. I had pieced together the meeting tonight was mandatory because there would be a vote as to who would be named to the new school board and, thus, would have power over the BIG DECISION.

All I cared about was making sure there was a high school for Katie to attend. I would go and cast a vote. I had no idea for whom, but I would figure that out when I got there.

Around 6:30 PM, Veronica picked us up in her car and off we went.

"This meeting could take hours, you know," Veronica said as she turned right onto the coast road. "Thomas has worked in this country many years. He said that any discussion that includes large numbers of Italians could last well into the wee hours of the morning."

"Oh, please. I'm sure he's exaggerating." Veronica and I had already made secret plans to be at a wine bar within the hour with a glass of Chianti in hand. "How long can a vote last?"

We drove in her black SUV along the water toward the school as the sunset cut the sky into ribbons of ginger and gray. Easy laughter filled the car as we took turns sharing funny stories about the first awkward weeks of school. I glanced sideways at Katie and Veronica, their skin golden from the waning sun reflected off the sea. I was, suddenly, hyperaware of my sense of delight in meeting this new friend. I had been graced with the exquisite gift of another kindred spirit to enrich my days and expand my world.

Someone had introduced me to Veronica on campus during the first week of school when the few of us who spoke English frantically searched for allies. She was a pretty blonde from Sweden whose compact body was too small for her vibrant spirit. It oozed out everywhere. A former health club executive who now gave seminars on body language for a living, she had moved to Genoa a month ago with her husband, Thomas, and two children, twelve-year-old Jennifer and nine-year-old Emil. They had decided to make Italy their home because Thomas had been working here for years and the commute was making family life impossible.

Veronica and Thomas had stumbled upon a villa to purchase in the mountains and were very excited about it. Their children were not. As a matter of fact, they hated their new school.

"It's terrible," Veronica had lamented to me one day over coffee. "Every day, Emil wakes up with the stomachache and then the intestinal issues. He stays in the bathroom until we are almost late. Then all the way to school he cries. Last night he locked himself in his room and would not come out. He kept yelling through the door"—Veronica cupped her hands around her mouth and pretended to scream—"Where is my *real* mother? You're not my *real* mother because my *real* mother would never make me go to that school. Send me my *real* mother right now!"

So Veronica spent her days sitting on a bench in the courtyard on campus with a book in one hand and a Kleenex in the other so that Emil could catch a glimpse of her through the day. If not, he would implode.

We laughed about it, but it wasn't really funny. "What about your daughter?"

"Jennifer's silent with anger, but she's lucky since there is another Swedish girl in her class to share the torture."

We arrived at the school promptly at 6:50. The meeting was to begin at 7:00.

"Good luck," I teased as Katie gathered her things, "Don't get arrested."

"Funny."

"Meet us afterward at that restaurant across the street."

Katie ran off to find her friends and organize their protest while I followed Veronica across the courtyard and into the cafeteria. It was packed, and the tension in the air was so thick we had to hack our way through it to find a seat. Mrs. B and the board were sitting behind a table in the front of the room with narrowed eyes and clenched jaws. It was all very official. People were dressed in business attire. I spent a lot of time checking out the Italian moms and their nice handbags. I wondered if it was true that ingesting more olive oil would get me a complexion as beautiful as theirs.

A line of high school students paraded in and sat together in the back of the room. I caught Katie's eye and gave her a nod. I wondered if anyone but me knew that it was a sit-in.

Some unknown person slipped me a folded piece of paper. I was instructed to keep it hidden. Any sight of it could cost me. What, I don't know, but the look in the woman's eye told me not to make fun of it. I opened it and got a glimpse of the five names I should vote for—the ones who wanted to keep the high school. I made a mental note, furtively glanced from side to side and expertly slid it over to Veronica. Such drama. We were getting a kick out of it.

Finally, the meeting began. Mrs. B and the head of the board gave separate welcome speeches. Then people started raising their hands. One by one various individuals got up and gave fervent minispeeches in Italian, arms waving, fists pumping the air. People in the audience likewise reacted with great emotion. Angry murmuring, nodding heads. I wished I knew what they were saying. In all, eleven people stood and spoke. Suddenly there was a long silence, so I leaned over to an Italian woman next to me.

"Is this when we vote?" I asked her.

She gave me a quizzical look. "No, not yet."

"What were they talking about?"

"That was just a discussion on whether or not the order of agenda items five and six should be flip-flopped."

"We spent an hour on that?"

She nodded and shrugged like this was all normal. I couldn't even look at Veronica because I knew we would laugh. And that would not be good because these people were all dead serious.

Then the next grave topic was raised. Should people have to wait until the entire evening was over to vote or could they vote early if they had to leave for some reason (*like going to the wine bar across the street*)? About eight people got up and gave a little howdoyoudo about that subject. Another forty minutes went by and we all voted on that. Luckily the vote fell in our favor. We were getting thirstier by the minute.

Finally, the real meeting actually started. Various board members and those up for election started to give their speeches. I watched the clock as it ticked past 9:45. People around us were agitated, reacting violently to some speakers and cheering on others. *The energy in this room could light up New York City at midnight,* I thought. Veronica was fascinated, furiously taking notes on body language for her next seminar. Katie, Basketball Alex and two other students were waving handmade Save Our School signs in the back corner.

Suddenly one man charged the stage in a wave of emotion that held me spellbound. Thoroughly disheveled—his dirty brown hair a tad too long, his blue suit jacket pulling at the buttons and his wide striped tie loosely knotted and pushed over to the side—he carried a huge stack of

133

handouts that he raised and slammed to the table with a blaze of heated words. A huge blue blood vessel pulsed at his temple.

What could possibly be that bad?

As he ranted and raved, Veronica looked over and whispered, "I told you we could be here until two in the morning."

"Or we could leave now," I said, nodding toward the parking lot.

"Move on three," she whispered. I signaled to Katie that we were leaving as Veronica softly counted.

We got up and strode forward, eyes straight ahead as a hush fell across the room. The two blondes had pulled their ejection lever and were barreling toward the door. We handed our votes to Mrs. B and bolted outside, dissolving into giggles. Within minutes we were sitting at a cozy café table, our wine being placed before us.

I held up my glass to toast hers. "Here's to the first and last PTO meeting we will ever attend in Italy."

"Here's to the vote going our way so we won't have to homeschool the kids," she replied.

We clinked our glasses together with the standard toast of the country. "*Cin, cin.*"

Two hours and two glasses of wine later, Katie burst through the door, wide-eyed and breathless. "They finally voted."

"Well?" Veronica and I said in unison.

"They decided to revisit the issue at the next board meeting."

35 ❧ italian lessons

The door buzzer rang promptly at eleven o'clock as it did every Tuesday and Thursday morning now. Giglio and Pierangela were always on time to the second. Tim buzzed them in and we heard the elevator click on as they came up to the seventh floor. A knock on the door and I opened it to their smiling faces. "*Permesso?*" Giglio said. The custom was to ask for permission to enter your home.

"*Buon giorno*, Giglio. *Buon giorno*, Pierangela. *Come state?*" I said. Giglio, handsome in his herringbone suit coat, entered with a newspaper under his arm. Pierangela, in her slim-cut camel skirt and white blouse, was the picture of elegance, her silk scarf the same shade of brown as her Louis Vuitton bag.

"*Bene, bene,*" said Giglio. "*E voi?*"

"*Molto bene,*" I said as I took Giglio's suit coat to hang in the closet.

"Her Italian," he said to Tim, laughing "is better than yours."

"Except that those are the only six words she knows."

"Then we had better get to work," Giglio said as we all headed into the dining area and sat around the rectangular glass table.

Tim and I glanced at each other. We had not studied hard enough, and we knew it. Giglio was a taskmaster and wondered what our problem was. We had been going over the same material for three lessons.

"Pierangela,"—he put both hands in the air—"where is it?" She looked through the manila folder that she had brought and pulled out an over-sized piece of white paper. She carefully unfolded it to reveal a cheat sheet to end all cheat sheets. She had diligently handwritten an entire page of Italian grammar. I had never seen so many endings and tenses in my life. The words blurred on the paper.

Tim started to read from the sheet, "First person singular—*o*, second person singular—*i*, third person singular—*a*, first per—"

"Susan, you must say them also," reprimanded Giglio, "Now let's try again. Your head today, it is in the clouds." He snapped his fingers.

He was right. I had been walking around in a haze of depression for two days. It had descended upon me Sunday night while I was standing at the kitchen sink and washing the dishes. The dappled light of the setting sun through the trees outside had looked, for an instant, like the tall, lacy birches outside my kitchen window in California. My heart had skipped a beat at the thought of some other woman standing there, watching them now. Then a bee flew in the window and stung my soapy hand, unleashing a torrent of tears that I hadn't realized were there. Because I was not one to fuss over something as minor as a bee sting, Tim, Katie and Matt had all stared at me with eyes that asked questions I wasn't prepared to answer. One by one, they left the kitchen and I continued to fall apart as I dried each dish until it squeaked against the towel.

"Sorry. Okay, I'm back. Here we go." I sat up straight in my chair and refocused.

"*Camminare*, to walk …"

Pierangela smiled and nodded as I said the correct endings. Tim joined in and slowly, very slowly, we started to pronounce the words correctly in unison. Giglio threw his hands up in the air, rejoicing. "*Mamma mia*. There is hope still."

"Is there?" I asked him. "Is there really?"

"There is always hope, in any language." He didn't know that he was speaking to my deepest fear.

Pierangela caught my eye with a motherly glance. I looked away quickly so she could not look down to my soul. I wanted to ask her if the sheer tenacity of staying together for life was really worth it. Were they happy? Was it all just about going through the rhythms of housekeeping while your heart stood on the windowsill looking to the horizon?

That day at the sink, I realized I was mourning the slow death of my American Dream. The one I had always known would be my destiny. The perfect family. The beautiful house. The picture-perfect holidays. Fulfilling jobs. Now I had begun the painstaking chore of designing a new prototype. It was still a blank page. The fear that I had made a huge mistake paralyzed me. In a rare moment of complete clarity, I saw myself as I was. A frightened woman with nothing to call my own except for a closet full of clothes and a fragile family that wasn't exactly sure what it was doing.

Tim and I were slowly mending our fences and beginning to enjoy simple moments of life together again, but something inside of me was still holding back. I was having a difficult time breaking off with my longtime friends Anger and Distance. For years they had encouraged me to revisit issues over and over until I was stuck, like a tire spinning in the mud with no hope of forward movement. The thought of living without these loving enablers left me feeling vulnerable and alone.

As I focused on the more simple lesson before me—Italian verb conjugation—the hour flew by, and soon Pierangela's phone rang. "It is her again." Giglio sighed with false mockery. Their daughter, Paola, wanted to know what was being served for lunch. She was on her way over with the two girls. Pierangela hung up the phone with a smile. We were used to this signal that always ended our sessions.

"You must memorize these endings for next time so that we can move ahead."

"Yes, we promise." Tim and I both nodded earnestly.

"Learning to communicate here will take much work." *We know.*

Tim helped Giglio on with his jacket, and we all exchanged the now-comfortable double kiss. *Grazie, ciao, arrivederci* … and they were gone. I closed the door and breathed a sigh of relief.

"Whew. Got through another one." We laughed at ourselves.

Then Tim went off to make lunch and I found something, anything, to do elsewhere.

36 halloween

We awoke to torrential rain. The kind I was sure was being sent from a very angry God. I had no idea what he was mad about, but he had picked a very inconvenient day to throw a fit: Halloween.

"I guess it's all going to be canceled," Matt moaned between bites of cereal.

"I'm afraid so, honey."

"Now what are we going to do?" All of the spooky festivities that had been planned at school were going to be held outdoors. We had all been looking forward to them for weeks. There would be no carnival today.

Halloween was a family favorite. There was nothing like the juvenile delight of decorating the house with scary ghosts and monsters. Fake spiderwebs and bloody rubber limbs sticking out of drawers were a given. And we had to have bowls of black and orange M&M's and candy corn or it was just not right.

Italy didn't do Halloween. They recognized it as an American thing, but they didn't really get it. I stopped trying to explain it to people because it lost a lot in the translation, and I could see them deciding not to be friends with me before I even finished.

The few pumpkins I did find in the store were actually sold for people to eat. There was evidence that the holiday was starting to seep its way into the national consciousness in that a few of the stores carried one or two witches or face masks for expats like us. But since they charged a bloody arm and a leg for everything we had decided that we could make do without all of the scary décor this year, especially since the school was going to go all out with a festival to give the students a real Halloween experience.

But now that it had been canceled …

"We can't just *not* have a Halloween," said Katie as she joined us with her toast and orange juice.

"What will we do, run around our own apartment in costumes and yell 'trick-or-treat' at each other from behind closed bedroom doors?" Tim said as he wandered in and stood by Matthew.

"Look, why don't you guys go on to school. Dad and I will figure something out."

"We're going to be drenched by the time we get there."

"Can't we call a cab?"

"Raincoats and umbrellas are a lot cheaper. Throw an extra pair of jeans in your backpack to change into when you get there."

"This is so stupid."

After they left, I called Veronica, who was in a snit because she had spent fifty euros on creating costumes for her children and now knew it was wasted money. The three of us put our heads together and decided that we would just have to have our own Halloween party. Veronica promised to bring a pumpkin to carve and a bottle of wine. I told her that we would take care of the decorations and would get some scary movies.

Tim and I and Zucca—we had named our new puppy *Zucca*, pronounced ZOO-ka, which means squash or pumpkin, in honor of our having bought him around Halloween—all made our way through the downpour and found the *cartoleria*, the paper goods shop. We shook off the rain and searched the tiny store for anything black and orange.

Tim held up a Jason mask in one hand and a few two-inch witches on long broomsticks in the other.

I grabbed some orange-pumpkin-and-black-cat confetti and then looked to see if I could find anything bone or skull related. Tim held up some fake eyeballs.

"How about these?"

"How much?"

"Seven euros each." We decided we could live without those.

On the way home we stopped at the grocery store. We searched the aisles but couldn't find any waist-high mountains of bagged candy. No caramel apple kits. No candles shaped like fingers. We settled for a few bags of M&M's and reminded each other to make sure that Matthew shared them instead of hiding them as he had been known to do.

Late that afternoon, as the deluge continued as if Noah were coming to town, our five guests, Veronica, her two children and two dogs, arrived. They were cranky, soaking wet and not in the mood to pretend they were scared of anything. After a change of clothes, we decided to unwind with the first scary movie. Tim plugged in the DVD and all of the kids got comfy. Matthew started to pass the M&M's around, and Veronica and I went to the kitchen to get to work on the jack-o'-lantern.

I noticed right away that she was pretty darned handy with the big carving knife, which of course reminded me of the Jason mask, so I backed off and gave her free reign. I stood with my glass of pinot grigio and offered a few slicing suggestions and soon enough we had a perfect pumpkin that didn't look the least bit Italian or Swedish or anything but American. Something inside me relaxed a little.

Veronica proudly carried it into the living room and placed it in the middle of the coffee table that Tim had lined with tea lights and sprinkled with the pumpkin-and-black-cat confetti. The whole room glowed eerily from the light of the candles, the scary movie and the bruised gray light from the clouds outside the windows.

A sudden clap of thunder and a streak of lightning split the sky and made us all jump and scream, thus completing the perfect Halloween moment.

"That was a good one!" yelled Matt.

The doorbell rang and in walked Cinzia, a woman we had met in the neighborhood, and her two-year-old son, Nicola, who was dressed like a clown. Then Thomas arrived with grocery bags full of food. The mood turned festive, while outside the storm raged on. As night fell, the candles and the jack-o'-lantern grew brighter and threw spooky shadows everywhere. Tim and I shared a smile from across the room. Halloween was turning out just fine.

We had all we needed. A pumpkin, a little candlelight, candy and a group of friends to share a scream or two. God threw in the thunder and lightning.

"What happened to the last bag of M&M's?" I heard someone say. "Matthew?" Tim, Katie and I said in unison as we all turned to look at his devilish grin. Staring at the TV screen, he pretended not to hear us.

37 ✂ haircut

Italians do not do blond the way California does blond. In Los Angeles it was often difficult to figure out who was a natural blond and who wasn't. Here, they dyed hair in a chunky weave, or "mesh," with colors that ranged from white to orange. When you laid that over the base color of dark brown or black, you ended up with a softer, more feminine version of, let's say ... Tony the Tiger.

For the past few weeks I had been politely asking people with tiger hair what salon they used. This way I had crossed off my list all of the ones they named. I was able to narrow it down to a few choices and finally picked one with the help of a blindfold and made an appointment with Maurizio. A young guy of medium height and build with a shock of black curly hair called to me from one of the chairs.

"Susan?"

"Maurizio?"

"*Si, si.* Come on now." His manner was comfortable as if we had already met. I walked over, sat in the black leather chair and he draped me with a black plastic cape. He twirled the chair around so I faced the mirror. Standing behind me, he started to pick up big clumps of my hair and examine them. I opened the magazine and pointed to a picture of a cute little model.

"*Non parlo italiano*" I said.

"Is okay," he assured me as he grabbed the magazine for a closer look. "I speak a little English."

"Make me look like her." I laughed. He did not respond to the joke, so I just let it go. "I want two colors of blonde in my hair, like this girl. A weave and then a good cut."

He rubbed his chin, deep in thought, as he examined me from every angle with one raised eyebrow.

"*Hmm*...yes, double mesh." He said. "Okay."

"I want it to look natural. Like I was born that way. No big chunks."

"*Naturale, si.* I understand." Our eyes met in the mirror as he nodded, giving me confidence that he understood. After mixing up a few colors, he lined them up on a silver tray beside me and went to work. He took his time with every strand, slathering on one color and then the next. We chitchatted the best we could, and about an hour later I had a head full of foil. He escorted me over to a chair and handed me some magazines.

I grabbed my purse and took out the book, *The Unsolved Problems of Italy*, which Giglio had written. He was waiting for me to read it, so I had brought it with me, knowing I would have time while I waited for the

141

color to set. I was afraid the people in the salon would take offense to the title, so I hid it inside one of the magazines and started to read.

I didn't know a thing about Italy's government or its unsolved problems. Nor did I wish to. But I wanted to be supportive of my new friend and give him feedback the next time we saw each other.

Maurizio came over periodically to check the color. Each time I would smile up at him and say, "Natural." To which he would reply, "Don't worry!"

"The back part. It is ready," he finally announced. "Come sit at the sink."

I walked over, sat and put my head back so he could rinse it. As he took off some of the foil and started to wash that part of my hair, he glanced at the magazine in my lap. With my head tilted backward in the sink, I was unaware of the fact that the book, with its bright red and green cover, was peeking out from the magazine.

"What are you reading?" he asked casually as I sat up straight. *Oh no!* I glanced down and saw that the magazine had slipped all the way to the floor leaving the book exposed with my finger holding my place.

"Just some book my neighbor wrote." I tried to play it off like it was nothing, but he reached for it.

"*The Unsolved Problems of Italy.*" He announced to the full salon. People turned to look at me. He made some snide remark in Italian and handed me back the book. He turned on his heel and went back to his other customer.

Great. Now he thinks I'm some obnoxious American know-it-all who thinks she can fix Italy. I felt heat start to rise up my neck and into my cheeks and slunk down a little further into my chair.

Why did I even bring the stupid book with me? To save face, I took a deep breath, opened it up and continued to read, though the words were now just a blur on the page. I was acutely aware of all of the other women casting looks my way.

I continued to pretend I was reading, making a big show out of licking my fingertip and turning the pages. I let out a few sighs and *hmms* to appear extra thoughtful.

"America has way more unsolved problems than you guys," I announced to anyone who was listening. "Come on. This place is great. Italy does an amazing job. Your food is out of this world! Seriously, we even left California and moved here because of all of the unsolved problems we were having."

Everyone ignored me. Not that I blamed them.

Time passed. Maurizio only checked on me once without so much as a grunt in my direction. He continued to help all of his other customers and I started to wonder if he was ignoring me on purpose. This was the problem with a language barrier. It was a virtual breeding ground for paranoia. I never really knew what was going on at the deeper level. I told myself to stop imagining things. A weave took a long time anywhere. Why would he care what book I was reading? Getting my hair done had never been so stressful.

Finally, he came back, and now he was Mr. All Business, with pursed lips and expert hands. He took off all of the foil in complete silence and washed my hair with clawed fingers that infuriated my scalp. I walked over and sat at his station and explained about the cut I wanted. He twirled me around so that my back was to the mirror. I thought this was odd, but I certainly wasn't in any position to comment. He went to work like an artist cutting with only a barber's razor. He took forever and treated each strand of hair like I was Rapunzel down from the tower for my first haircut. He blew it dry and announced that it was finished. I was afraid to look. He wheeled the chair around with a final flourish so that I faced the mirror.

"What do you think?" he asked.

I studied my tiger-striped hair, felt sick in the pit of my stomach and replied like my good friend Tony, "It's *grrreeeaaat!*"

143

haircut

38 ❧ the vespa

Vespa owners were not what I would have called stellar drivers. They were reckless and maniacal. It seemed they were allowed to go anywhere, squeeze between any moving or stationary objects and travel at any speed they wished. They reminded me of oversized mosquitoes darting here and there through crowds of people.

But with the narrow streets, lack of parking spaces and the cost of gasoline, they made sense. Everyone drove these small motorcycles around here. Still, I was not crazy about the idea when Tim bought two Vespas from Thomas, a sleek black two-seater and a smaller cream-colored one.

"I promise this will be fun," said Tim.

"Compared to what?"

"You've been on motorcycles before."

"But we don't have licenses for these."

"It'll be fine."

"I'm nervous." He ignored me and handed me a black helmet. "The most daring thing I've done in the past few years is drive to the supermarket without my seat belt on."

"This should fit."

"It looks too big."

"Susan."

"What?"

"What's with all the excuses?"

"We don't even have insurance for these things. I might crash."

"I'm not only talking about the Vespas. You've been really quiet for days, like you're only half there."

The empty white walls of the garage, or "box" as they call it here, began to close in on me like a trick room in a haunted mansion. I searched for my escape route.

"Hey," his voice softened. "Look at me." I met his eyes, but the intensity caused me to look away. "Why is that so hard for you? You only hold my gaze if we're joking around or if the kids are involved."

"I don't know. It never used to be hard." I propped the helmet against my hip and forced myself to look into his eyes.

"You're slipping away from me again."

"I *uhm* …"

"These last few months have been remarkable. We've been doing crazy things together like we used to. It's like we're dating again. This is why we're here, right? Are you having fun too? Or am I seeing this all wrong?"

"Yes, I'm having fun, but you know me, Miss Overanalyzer." A lump was rising in my throat. "What if this whole 'fun' experiment doesn't work? What if we're fooling ourselves, spending what little savings we have traipsing around a country that apparently has all sorts of unsolved problems, and end up in financial ruin? Where will we live? What will happen to our children? I mean, really, look at my hair. It's a perfect example of my having talked myself into trusting another person and then regretting it."

"If this is going to work. If *we* are going to work, then you're going to have to let go a little more. Stop putting so much pressure on everything. If we want things to be different between us, *we* have to be different. Just get on the bike and ride it. It's as simple as that."

"Then why doesn't it feel simple?" A tear escaped from my right eye and trickled down my cheek. He took his thumb and gently wiped it away.

"I gave up as much as you did to be here. And I have no idea how this year will end. But right now I am having a ball and I know you are too. And if we can be having this much fun after all of the crap we've been through and all of the awful things we've said to each other over the years, that proves our feelings for each other are still there. You can't deny that."

Well, he has a point.

Tim turned and pointed toward the Vespas. "Do you want to take the cream-colored one or do you want to ride with me?"

I studied the two Vespas for a moment, and it occurred to me that we had been riding through life separately for a long time. It would be most

145

comfortable for me to jump on the cream-colored one that was just my size and plod along below the speed limit, eyes fixed to the pavement to avoid all bumps. He could drive the black one as recklessly as he wanted, speeding around curves and disregarding traffic rules. Then we could come back home and pretend we had had fun together, when in reality our experiences would have been as different as night and day.

Tim was right, if we wanted our relationship to change, we had to be different. I would have to trust him to drive safely and he would have to make decisions with my well-being in mind. We would have to work as a team.

I turned and looked Tim straight in the eye, daring him to be the first to look away. When he didn't, I said, "I'll ride with you if you promise not to hurt me."

"I promise."

Uneasily, I put on the helmet, buckled the strap under my chin and climbed aboard. Off we went down a winding and crooked alley. Tim laughed and yelled over the grinding engine, "Stop squeezing the air out of my lungs." Around a very sharp curve I leaned all the way to the right while he leaned all the way to the left. A pair of broken scissors zooming down the highway of life.

We turned on to the main street that ran along the sea. The last of the afterglow of dusk sat low on the horizon, red yarn floating on gray water. I snuggled closely behind Tim to shield myself from a cold November wind that whipped us. We were so close that every time he accelerated, our helmets clunked together sending me into nervous giggles.

In spite of myself, I took a deep breath and relaxed. This *was* fun. Exhilarating even. After a few miles, I peeled myself off Tim's back and looked around. Stars were beginning to pop out. The moon was rising down the coast over Portofino. It even felt good to be cold. I thought of my friend, Grace, who had said to me before I left, "I envy you. You're going to feel alive every day."

We zipped along with no destination in mind. And yes, Grace, I felt alive. And it felt good. Somewhere in all of this craziness, Tim and I were realizing that it was better to make life "all about the ride." Predetermined destinations had turned out to be false truths that locked us into an unhappy life and stale routines that gave birth to boredom and guilt feelings about having so much and being so unfulfilled.

We continued on, content in the falling darkness now, leaning the same direction as we navigated the unexpected curves and bends in these Italian roads. As with any pair of broken scissors, a skillful hand can get the blades to act together and cut a straight edge, can tighten the bolt that connects them and shine them up good as new. I imagined I just might know whose hand was trying to fix us. I looked to the heavens, searched the stars and quietly thanked him.

39 ✂ acqui terme

The four of us stood with Veronica, Thomas and Emil on the expansive porch of a lodge that sat high on a hill next to its own vineyard in Alessandria. We had arrived just before sunset on our way back home after spending a cool November day driving through Piemonte, a wine region about ninety minutes north of Genoa. Like a quilt that has been strewn across a big lumpy bed, the vineyards on the rolling hills created a patchwork of hues determined by the grape varietals.

The owner, Veronica's friend Björn, a tall handsome blond from Sweden, was proudly finishing up the grand tour. He had bought the place as a ramshackle old farmhouse and refurbished it with his own hands. Over the years he had added a few dormitory-style outbuildings, transforming it into a serene and tranquil haven for business groups, or those just in search of a weekend away from the city. He named it *La Madonna*.

Another blonde, a woman with chin-length hair and probing blue eyes, came through the door to join us.

"Annika!" Veronica rushed to give her a hug and then introduced us. Annika was a yoga instructor who periodically brought groups of women down from Sweden for spa trips. The group had flown home yesterday, but she had decided to stay a few extra days by herself to relax. When Annika had invited Veronica to come for a visit, Veronica had, in turn, asked us if we wanted to come along for the ride.

"Annika," I said, "I understand that you had quite a crowd here this week."

"Yes, many women, many needs." She put her hand on Veronica's arm. "I am hoping that Veronica comes to join me next time. I would love her to do her seminar on body language. It is fantastic."

"Oh, please," murmured Veronica, though her smile told me that the compliment was appreciated.

"You must share a glass of wine with us before you leave," insisted Björn with a twinkle in his eye. "Now that I think of it, why are you leaving? If you would like, I will call my friends in town and find you some rooms. I would offer you some, but I have another group arriving in about an hour."

We all looked at each other and shrugged our shoulders.

"It *is* Saturday."

"We can buy a toothbrush."

"Jennifer's at a friend's house. I can call her mother to see if she can spend the night." Veronica pulled out her cell phone.

"It is decided then." Björn strode across the porch and disappeared into the house.

Katie pulled out her camera to take a few shots of the fading sunset as Tim grabbed my hand and pulled me to the far edge of the porch where a hammock was waiting for a weary traveler.

"I don't think the hammock will hold both of us," I said.

"I just want to stand here with you for a minute. It feels so peaceful." We stood in the stillness, arms entwined, as the twilight faded to dusk.

A glass-paned side door opened and a woman, dressed in black leggings and a wraparound black tunic, appeared and stood before us straight and regal like a ballet dancer. A dark scarf was wrapped tightly around her head accentuating her wide smile and black almond eyes. She looked exotic, like a princess from Morocco or Tasmania. There was something about her that made me intensely curious as to who she was and how she had come to be here. But there was also something about her that made me know that I was forbidden to ask.

"Follow me," she said as she turned on her black slippered heel and headed back indoors. We all followed her into a kitchen where two cooks were busy chopping and stirring. She lit a candle and opened a hidden door beside the pantry.

She motioned to us with her hand as she took a step downward. The flame danced and threw shadows on the old stairwell. I felt like Nancy Drew on her way to solve a mystery. We followed Thomas, Veronica and Emil down the primitive steps and into a hand-hewn cave. It was hundreds of years old, the wine and root cellar of this restored villa.

It had a good-size main room and a smaller cave down a short hallway that Matthew and Emil immediately claimed as their play space. The Moroccan princess found a switch that illuminated a dim bulb in the far corner, instructed us to sit around a heavy, round oak table at the bottom of the steps and lit the three beeswax candles in an antique silver candelabra that she took from a shelf. She placed it just off-center on the table.

The rough, hand-hewn wall was cool to the touch and I imagined a farmer and his son with mallets and chisels working away trying to finish in time to store food for the winter.

"Look over there," Tim pointed to a wall lined with wine racks, some of the bottles caked with dirt and time.

"Some of them are over a hundred years old, not drinkable anymore, of course," said Annika as she came down the steps carrying a tray of crystal wine glasses in one hand and a bottle of wine in the other.

Veronica took the tray and set it on the table. Annika poured white wine into the glasses as the Moroccan princess went back upstairs to whip up a few snacks. The rest of us sat in complete bliss, enjoying the "cool factor" of the moment.

Tim raised his glass. "To Annika, for inviting us to share this evening." We softly clinked our glasses together, adding other silly toasts about the day we had just spent together.

Here we were, laughing and teasing around a table in an ancient wine cellar while Matthew and Emil happily played "Let's pretend this is a medieval dungeon" a few feet away. A group of fast friends who had only met a few short weeks ago.

Veronica poured a small flute of champagne and handed it to Katie, who looked over at me with questioning eyes.

"Come on, Mom," teased Veronica. "She's old enough by European standards."

"Fine. But only one."

As Katie reached for the glass, we heard a commotion overhead.

"What the heck was that?" Katie asked looking at the ceiling.

"The next group has arrived," explained Annika. "Swedish cardiologists. They are most likely sitting down to a gourmet meal in the dining room."

Suddenly the door opened at the top of the stairs with a bang and Björn descended with a guitar in one hand and a songbook in the other.

"Would you like to hear a few tunes?"

"Of course!" We egged him on as if he were Bob Dylan. He opened up his songbook and chose American songs. He belted out "Hey Jude" and "Rocky Raccoon" and then started into Paul Simon's "50 Ways to Leave Your Lover." Before I knew it, I was singing solo about going off to "look for America" as he strummed along beside me. I had never sung a solo in my life … and with good reason. But the wine had given me courage.

The song was interrupted when one of the doctors shuffled quietly down the steps. Slight and blond, he stood shyly before us in his khakis and blue button-down shirt.

Tim invited him to pull up a chair and scooted his own a few inches to the right. Annika filled another glass and set it before him.

He fit right into the group as we all quietly began to sway to Björn's next rendition of Van Morrison's "Moondance," and soon the doctor was calling out suggestions along with everyone else. After a while, he stood and cleared his throat.

"I would like to sing for you a song," he said in broken English.

Björn held out his guitar, but the doctor shook his head.

"I will sing it a cappella." He cleared his throat again. "It is a Hawaiian love song." He started to sing, low and sweet and clear.

I studied the chiseled face of the doctor and knew that this was a man who had held life and death in his very hands. I glanced down the hallway to see Matthew and Emil all aglow in their part of the cave as they pretended to be prisoners of the king. Suddenly I could see us from all angles and I realized our new way of living the "unexpected" was like finding the fountain of youth for my parched and tired soul. Like drops of water on a dried-out sponge, I could feel myself slowly coming back to life. It was what I had been seeking for a long time, without knowing it. The enchantment, the mystery, the happenstance, the pure exhilaration of meeting people from the other side of the world who just wanted to share an evening, a glass of wine and a few songs. I realized at that moment that I had been blaming Tim for this lost part of my soul. Thinking that it was his fault that I didn't feel a sense of delight about life anymore. It wasn't his fault at all. It was mine for not choosing to include adventure on my To Do list.

I looked around the room, sensing that God had a hand in my sudden realization. The air around me felt rich and layered, like a prayer. Again pieces of Matthew 6:25–34 floated through my head. *Seek first his kingdom … and all these things will be given to you…*

God, you knew what I needed before I did. I'm beginning to feel the power in what you said. I'm trying to follow your lead. It hasn't been easy, by the way.

And then, just as quickly, he was gone and the song ended with cheers and clapping. I grabbed Tim's hand and pulled him close. "I love this night, and I love you."

"I love you too." And we kissed, to Katie's embarrassment, in the flickering light of the antique candelabra.

I have heard it said that at the end of our lives the questions we must answer for ourselves number only two: Did I live fully? Did I love well?

I felt we had finally begun to live fully. The love part? Well, I was working on that.

40 ⚬ buses part 3

The buses were on strike again. It seemed nothing had been solved during the last strike. Suddenly I understood the logic behind the buses and trains accepting the same tickets. There's a fifty-fifty chance that at least one form of transportation will not be running on any given day.

41 ⚬ the birthday party

I heard the key in the door and nudged Tim. "She's here. Pretend you're asleep."

"I was."

"Sorry."

I turned over in bed and lay on my back. I pulled the big fluffy white duvet cover with the red piping up under my chin. It was quite late. Katie had gone out for the evening by herself. It had not been easy to let her go. She had come to us about a week before and pleaded her case during dinner.

"I was invited to a party!"

"Great. Whose party?"

"Two girls in the eleventh grade are having their birthday party together. The whole high school's invited."

"The whole school?"

"That's only twenty-four people, Mom," Matt added, trying to get some action in this conversation.

"So whose house?" I asked.

"It's going to be at a restaurant down in Genoa."

Tim and I exchanged glances over a gulp of water while Katie watched our every facial movement.

"Can I go? Can I please, please, please go?"

"How are you going to get there?" Tim asked.

"Bus."

"At night?"

"It'll drop me off right in front of the restaurant. All the kids take the bus at night."

"You're not taking the bus alone."

Public transportation was fine during daylight hours, but neither Tim nor I wanted to send our nubile fifteen-year-old into the cruel night. Alone. On a bus. Into a big city.

"The kids keep inviting me places, but I never go. They're starting to think I'm antisocial."

"I know." I said. "We can take a taxi down there with you." Katie closed her eyes, shook her head slowly. Exhaled.

"Do you know anyone in the neighborhood that you can go with?" Tim asked.

"No."

"Do you have any friends yet that you could spend the night with who live down there?"

"No."

"Katie, even if you were safe on the bus, which is a stretch when you're talking about a fifteen-year-old alone during prime attack hours, it would have to drop you off way down at the bottom of our hill after midnight."

"You could just walk down and meet the bus."

"We'll think about it."

I knew Katie was right. I wanted her to go. She was a teenager, for goodness' sake. The real issue here, which had nothing to do with life abroad, was letting go. The handing over of the reins.

If we had a car, then we could still be in control. We could drive her within a block of the restaurant and watch until she was safely inside. Then we could pick her up the second she was ready. That would leave zero time for any errant child molesters, flashers, pimps, child abductors, pornographers, drug pushers, homeless psychos, thieves, or murderers to get to her. Of course that also left zero time for any chance innocent and lovely human interaction to occur either, but who cared about that?

It had been a stressful few days with all of the staring and waiting going on. The nonanswer that hung in the air between us. Katie patiently and politely waited for us to give in, say okay. And really, we both knew that we would in the end, but the dragging out of the answer just bought us a few more days of the fantasy that we could always protect our daughter. And the even bigger fantasy that she even wanted us to anymore.

At the eleventh hour, we had a stroke of luck. Marissa, Basketball Alex's mother, said that she would be happy to pick Katie up and bring her home.

So this evening, Katie, after an exhaustive search of both of our closets, found the right jeans and T-shirt combination and I walked her downstairs to the car where Basketball Alex and Marissa sat waiting, Marissa's bubbly personality in sharp contrast to her son's brooding demeanor. With barely a nod of acknowledgement from Alex, Katie climbed into the backseat and away they drove as I stood waving long after they had rounded the corner.

"Here she comes." We both quickly feigned deep sleep positions.

Katie's footsteps softly made their way to our room. A loud whisper.

"I know you guys are awake."

"Okay, fine." We all giggled as she sat on the end of the bed.

"How was it?"

"It was so incredibly amazing."

"We all went to dinner and sat around this big table, about twenty of us. And everyone was so comfortable around each other. It was the first time that I could sit back and say, 'Wow, there's nowhere I'd rather be right now.'"

"That's so great."

"Then the most amazing thing happened. After dinner, we all walked to the coffee bar down the street. As the night wound down, we decided it was time to sing 'Happy Birthday.' I've come to learn that Italians aren't big cake people, and okay—don't freak out—but they brought out a round of drinks instead of cake. We all started to sing 'Happy Birthday' but got about five seconds into it and broke out in laughter because half the table had started to sing in English and the other in Italian. We settled on Italian first, then we broke out in English. Then, because one of the girls whose birthday it was—Malin—was Swedish, her brother—Fredrik— stood up and sang to her in their native language. Then, Stav stood up and sang it in Hebrew. Followed by Angelo in Korean and Rami in Lebanese. Then, Neha in Indian and Eugi in French and Spanish, and Phillip in Danish. It was surreal. It showed me how amazing these people are and how blessed I am to be here."

Imagine if we had not let her go.

42 — extreme marital therapy part 2

Tim stood near the shower and picked up the bar of Dove soap that had been happily resting on the side of the tub. I was brushing my teeth. He looked at the soap. He looked at me. He looked back at the soap and then proceeded to put it up high on a window ledge that was close to the ceiling. He looked at me again to make sure I was noticing.

"Put the soap up here from now on. This way it won't get hit by water and it will last longer. We have to watch every penny," he announced like he was Alan Greenspan giving helpful hints on how to weather the economy. It was a good thing that my mouth was full of toothpaste as I had another good idea about where he could put the soap.

We had officially entered the second stage of our new life. We seemed to have mastered the art of "Hanging Out Together," but we were still far from perfect in the "Effective Communication While Hanging Out Together" category. But there was progress.

We had fallen into a routine that was comfortable for both of us. Coffee together every morning, see the kids off to school, gym, market, lunch, sex, nap, read, nap, laundry, more sex, nap, kids come home from school, homework, dinner, bed. And thrown into that mix, from time to time, was sightseeing and eating at restaurants.

We were remarkably compatible. Tim was very good at organizing things, making rules and lists, and generally steering daily life along in the right direction. He was excellent at *being in charge*.

I was very good at nodding and acting like all of the little things he cared about (like damp soap) also mattered to me. I usually agreed with his logic, as there was certainly nothing wrong about it, but I was more of the big picture sort of gal. I often just let the details evolve and work themselves out as I went.

I'm more like the "Let's watch our money by not buying things like extravagant Prada shoes and accessories" kind of person. Not the president of the Save the Soap Foundation type.

I rinsed my mouth and put away the toothbrush. I made a big show of carefully pushing errant toothpaste back into the tube and screwing on the top. I shook the water out of my toothbrush and placed it near the windowsill to air dry. Clearly Tim was not amused.

"I was just trying to be careful about our money."

"I know. I was just teasing you."

"We have no income. All of the money is going out. It's just a weird feeling, that's all."

"This is nothing new, Tim. We knew what we were getting into. I have never been a spendthrift, and I have no reason to start now. But I am not going to sit and worry if the soap is perspiring on a hot day. We can afford soap."

"It was just a simple suggestion. Why are you getting so worked up about it?"

"Me? You were the one who couldn't handle a little teasing about it."

Tim started to towel off with vigor. I left the room. Neither one of us was really mad. It was just a little frustrating. In my mind's eye I saw us bantering like funny couples in a sitcom. Where men and women can argue and throw inane insults around with no repercussions. In reality, everyone can do this except for married couples. Girlfriends do it. Guys do it all the time. Co-workers do it. But married people? Nope. No, siree. No. No. And I wanted to know why. Why can't we banter in such a way that ends in fun and frivolity?

When we were dating, teasing was all about joy and laughter. Once we got married, it was apparently about something else entirely. I think it's a control issue. Doesn't everything eventually boil down to that?

Phase two of our Extreme Marital Therapy was about being forced to watch our own dynamics as if we were in a fish bowl. I started to realize that some of my nodding and fake agreeing was really thinly veiled passive aggressive behavior since I knew while I was nodding that I would immediately forget whatever he had just told me or asked me to do. I simply wouldn't do it. It wasn't malicious. I just didn't buy into the idea. I knew as well as I was standing there that I would not always put the soap up top where he wanted it. It's just soap to me. But to him, it was not just soap. It was *a good idea*.

And everyone wants recognition for *a good idea*.

So I was learning to just go with the *good idea*. Because, really, that was what supporting each other boiled down to. I support your good ideas and you support mine. Even if it was something as minor as where to put the soap.

I went back into the bathroom and gave him my best hand-on-the-hip stance. "What?" asked Tim.

"You're right. I should be more supportive when you have a good idea. I'll put the soap up where the water won't hit it."

"Thank you."

"I have a good idea too."

Silence.

"Don't you want to hear it?"

"Yeah."

"We can use the money we save from the soap thing to buy tickets to get into those museums I've been telling you about. Won't that be fun?"

Silence.

"Did you hear me?"

43 ❧ thanksgiving

"Here, use this knife. It's sharper."

"Mom, where are the oven mitts?"

"Do you think this bowl's big enough to hold all of those potatoes?"

"No, carve it this way, against the grain."

"You just put your thumb through the crust. Be careful!"

"You're spilling ice cubes on the floor."

"Matt, get the dogs out of here!"

Thomas was carving up his first turkey, Veronica was putting the sweet potatoes in a serving dish, Tim was filling the water glasses, and I was trying to make gravy. Katie, Jennifer and Bettina, Basketball Alex's sister, were putting the homemade apple pies in the oven. Matt was running around the apartment with the three dogs, two of which belong to Emil, and Emil was sneaking up near Tim and throwing him "the finger," a new bit of sign language he had picked up at the American school. Everyone was shouting at once. Yet it was all joyful noise.

It was a regular Thursday (*giovedì*) with its regular Thursday rhythms going on outside. Nobody but the nine of us knew it was Thanksgiving. But we had been up early cooking away.

The preparation for our celebration had started weeks ago when I asked my friend Lynne, who had visited from Boston and since left, to bring some traditional Thanksgiving ingredients that I couldn't find here.

"You want me to bring what?" she had yelled over the phone.

"Yams, brown sugar, marshmallows, Pepperidge Farm Stuffing mix and turkey napkins. They don't sell that stuff here."

"In my suitcase?"

Tim found a butcher, Aldo, who made a yearly trek up to the mountains to an organic turkey farm for a few expatriates in the area. He put in our order and we were delivered a turkey that had been roaming free just a few days before.

Around four o'clock our guests arrived. None of them had ever experienced Thanksgiving.

Veronica was the first to ask, "So what is Thanksgiving anyway?"

"Well, it's a day we set aside to give thanks for all of our blessings."

"Isn't there something about Indians?"

"Well, the first Thanksgiving was a meal shared by the Indians and the early settlers in America. You know, Plymouth, Squanto, Pilgrims."

"So is there curry involved?"

"That's a different kind of Indian."

"Who were these, how do you call them … Pilgrims?"

"Veronica, here, have a glass of wine already. We'll discuss this all later."

For the next few hours we laughed and played cards. Every once in a while Tim and I would catch a glimpse of Emil giving Tim the finger again. He would do it in a very slow and measured fashion. First he would ball up his hand into a fist. Then he would pop out his thumb. Then he would push down on his thumb with his other hand like a lever and up would pop his middle finger. The only peculiar thing is that he wouldn't laugh. His big blue eyes would stare down Tim in a challenge. Of course all of this was done out of Veronica's and Thomas' line of vision.

Soon we were ready to eat. "Okay, everybody. Grab something to carry to the table and take your seat!" We set all of the bowls and platters on the table that Katie and Matt had decorated with yellow and brown burlap from the market and colorful leaves and foliage cut from the trees outside. With everyone gathered around, it made a beautiful sight.

"This is lovely," said Veronica.

"The food smells great," added Bettina. "Alex is going to regret missing this."

"Thank you for having us here to share your Thanksgiving." Thomas' brown eyes were warm and sincere.

"I think we all feel lucky to be here," added Tim as Matthew lit the candles.

Katie had downloaded and printed out a variety of Native American blessings and general quotes expressing thanks, which she had then mounted on separate pieces of construction paper. The idea was to go around the table and each person would read the one at his or her place setting. Katie started with a quote from Ben Franklin and then Jennifer read something from Mother Teresa in Swedish-laced English. Bettina followed with a poem and Matt read a few verses from Scripture. When it was Emil's turn, he promptly burst into tears at the thought of having to decipher and read English out loud.

"It's okay, Emil, you don't have to," Tim gave him his best reassuring voice. Emil hid his head in his mother's lap as we moved on to the next reader. Finally it was Tim's turn. He instructed us to hold hands as he began to read "Hold On," a Pueblo Indian prayer:

Hold on to what is good,
Even if it's a handful of earth.
Hold on to what you believe,
Even if it's a tree that stands by itself.
Hold on to what you must do,
Even if it's a long way from here.
Hold on to your life,
Even if it's easier to let go.
Hold on to my hand,
Even if someday I'll be gone away from you.

As Tim read, I closed my eyes and imagined sending a thousand balloons filled with gratitude up to heaven and then asked God to bless each and every one of us and keep us in his care. Then I opened my eyes, sat back and enjoyed this Norman Rockwell moment: a table filled with food, the love of family and friends, Tim proudly saying the blessing and Emil quietly pulling his thumb and giving us all the finger.

44 ❦ trains part 1

The four of us stood on the platform waiting for the train to Rome. Jack and Ronit, our good friends from Paris, were there for Ronit's birthday and we planned to surprise her.

"Mom, I have to go to the bathroom," Matthew said looking at the clock.

"Can't it wait?"

"Hurry up," said Tim. "Train will be here in a minute." Matt looked at us. We looked at him. The four of us did a group sympathy grimace, and he disappeared behind the building. Using the restroom in most of these train stations ranks up there with one of the most unpleasant experiences a human being can have.

The last time I visited the ladies' room here, it took me a day to get over it. It was small and square with a once white porcelain floor and a little hole that stared up from the center like an evil eye. There was nothing to hold on to, and all I could think of while I was in there was that Italian grandmas must have thighs of steel after having had to squat like that for generations.

It would be a five-hour ride to Rome, so getting good seats was crucial. People started to trickle into the station and form groups here and there. Having done this several times now, we had fine-tuned the art of boarding.

In general, I'd say that Americans are polite or, at the very least, aware of manners. Hold the door for someone, wait your turn in line, please and thank you. Watch out for those nearby and see if there is something you can do to help. I'm talking the basics here.

When I first started taking these trains, I assumed that the first people to arrive on the platform would be noticed as the "head of the line" and be able to board first in an orderly fashion. They were not. The concept of forming a line did not exist here. And forget the orderly fashion part.

Elderly people did not get preferential treatment. At first I would instruct the kids to stand aside and let the elderly on first, even give them a hand or a little boost up onto the high steps of the train. But we were thanked with suspicious glares like we were trying to steal their purses or pick their pockets. And then we would all be stuck scrambling on at the end and we'd rarely find four seats together.

So we had had to reassess the process. We knew that the crowd formed in loosely-knit groups along the platform roughly the same distances apart as the train doors would be. The hope was that when the train came to a complete halt, you would luck out and have a door directly in front of you. A signal light down the track a bit would change from red to yellow as the train started its approach at a point still far from the station. Then a little bell would start to ring and people would plan their entry. Suitcases were picked up, scarves tightened and cigarettes put out. All in phony nonchalance. Everyone knew what the goal was. Be the first one on the train at all costs.

The train would come into sight and start to slow. As it came to a stop, the informal groupings would move as one unit toward the anticipated stopping point of a door. God forbid the train stopped and you were stuck in the middle of the car, equidistant from two doors. That was the least desirable position.

With a hiss, the doors would open and the rush would be on. A mass of humanity pushing its way into the small opening. It was every man for himself. I was astounded at the nerve and strength of the old ladies who pushed their way in front of us. Legs of steel. And then, of course, I would be reminded of their many years of squatting in those bathrooms and I would have to visualize them.

Even though the whole process was downright ugly and Darwinian, no one got angry, because none of it was considered bad manners. It was just the way it was done.

Today, to make matters more interesting, we would be boarding a long-distance train. These trains looked different inside. Rather than rows of seats, they had these nifty compartments for six with a door that closed. The goal was to get on and secure an entire compartment for our family so we could spread out and enjoy some privacy.

I was not worried. We had this process down to a science. We were a well-oiled, train-boarding machine. The yellow signal light turned on and the tiny bell started to ring to signal the coming of the train. Matthew was nowhere to be seen.

"Where's Matt?"

"Better go get him."

Matthew raced around the corner and ran over to us. He looked at us. We looked at him and we all shared another group grimace.

"Okay, everybody, here it comes."

"Grab your stuff."

"Where's Zucca?"

"Got him."

"Old ladies at three o'clock."

"Check. I'll run the elbow block."

As the train chugged into view and started to slow, we moved as one and followed the door with precision.

"Dad gets on first. He's the biggest."

"Matt, you stay with Dad."

"Check."

"Find an empty compartment and spread your stuff around."

"Check."

"Mom, old ladies now at one o'clock!" Katie whispered through clenched teeth.

"Oops." I shifted my shoulder and physically wedged myself in front of them. They were familiar with my tactic and responded with a maneuver of their own. Admirable.

The doors of the train hissed as they opened.

"Go, Tim, go!" Tim expertly charged full steam ahead. His six-foot-eight frame cut the crowd like Gulliver slicing through the Lilliputians. Katie and I saw him and Matt disappear inside as we struggled against the tide. We didn't want to lose Zucca, so we were a bit slower. Knowing that Tim and Matt would scout out a compartment for us took some of the pressure off.

The old lady with the black suit and gray quilted jacket stomped squarely on my foot and then onto the step right before me wedging her knockoff Louis Vuitton bag between us. Another fine technique and she knew it. I conceded defeat and let her friend board next.

I heaved my bag up the steps. I saw the two women fumbling around in the open space near the bathroom. I blocked them in with my bags for a moment, pretending I didn't notice them pinned against the far wall. I slowly looked to the left and then the right. Katie hopped on behind me and caught Tim's eye from the far end of the car. He waved us on frantically.

"Hurry, Mom. I see them. They found one!"

We pushed our way through the crowded corridor to the compartment. With a sigh of relief Matt slammed the door and pulled the drapes. Katie put down Zucca and we all took off our puffy down jackets and stowed our gear. We sat in four of the six seats and put the dog and our stuff in the other two to make the compartment look uninviting to other passengers.

A deep breath and high-fives all around. Another fine execution. Suddenly the door jiggled and was pulled open. Two old ladies poked their heads in and asked if the seats were taken. I would recognize that gray quilted jacket anywhere.

I looked her straight in the eye and said, "Sì." Her eyes narrowed as she surveyed the cabin. Mine narrowed in return as I pulled off my shoe and started to knead the spot she had crunched. A smile of recognition came to her face, a slight nod, and she was off.

I had a feeling we would meet again.

45 ❧ why americans love italian restaurants part 1

"I don't think this taxi driver has any idea where he is," whispered Katie.

"*Sh.* He probably speaks English," I whispered back. Ronit and I shared raised eyebrows. Wandering was not a good sign. We, along with Zucca, were all crammed into the back of a taxi driven by a seasoned cabbie who had traversed the alleyways of Rome for two decades. He was trying to find a supposedly exquisite restaurant that specialized in truffles where we were to celebrate Ronit's birthday. I was curious about truffles, as I had never had any before. But I was more curious to see if we would ever even get to the place.

Ronit's good friend, David, who was well traveled and in another taxi that had long since disappeared, had assured us that this was an exclusive and gourmet "find" well hidden from the ordinary riffraff.

"Zucca, sit still."

"Katie, hold the dog tighter."

"I'm trying."

"Let me hold him," said Matt.

"I said I've got him," hissed Katie.

"I think we're getting closer," whispered Ronit.

"My foot's falling asleep."

"I feel carsick."

After thirty minutes we came to a screeching halt at the end of a dark alley.

"Get out here," said the cabbie gruffly.

"Here? I don't see a restaurant. I don't even see lights," I said, not knowing how much he understood.

The cabbie pointed down the spooky street and then to a One Way sign that was pointing in the other direction. "I can not go in that way. You must walk."

"I just watched you go all sorts of directions down one-way streets for the last thirty minutes," I muttered under my breath as Ronit shushed me and paid the fare.

I think he was just done with us. We all piled out and stood as he disappeared down the street in the exact direction that he said he couldn't go. The alley was quiet and eerie, an unlikely place to find a fancy restaurant.

"Come," said Ronit. "It will be fine. Act like you know what you are doing." Zucca tugged on his leash while we made our way silently though a neighborhood so ancient that I felt we should be wearing togas. As we rounded a shadowed corner, I was thrilled to see the rest of our group illuminated beneath a gas street lamp.

"See, I told you it was okay," said Ronit and we all breathed a sigh of relief. The restaurant was a tiny little storefront and our group of ten had to wait outside while they prepared a table for us. I peeked through the front door and saw maroon walls, white linen, candlelight and couples in love.

"Katie, let's take Zucca for another walk around the block so he'll get tired," I suggested in hopes he would sleep under the table inside. I still felt a little strange about bringing a dog into a fine restaurant.

By the time we returned, everyone had been seated inside. Katie and I stood outdoors for a moment to settle Zucca and plan our entry.

"We have to keep him quiet in there. We don't want to ruin Ronit's birthday."

We walked in. The place was so tiny that our table for ten took up the full rear third of the restaurant. The other tables were cozy and private with parties of two who all eyed Zucca as we walked past. I said a prayer to the Patron Saint of Puppies, whoever that might be, for Zucca to behave himself.

We sat at the end of the table by Matthew and tied Zucca's leash to Katie's chair. Katie made it short so he couldn't wander and immediately started to hand him *grissini* (breadsticks) by the handful to keep him busy.

A matronly waitress in a plain, zippered-front black dress with a white apron came to the table and started to describe the night's offerings. All of Jack and Ronit's friends were boisterous and funny. A lot of friendly repartee passed back and forth. The waitress started to write down people's orders on her big white pad. Another, identically dressed waitress came to fill our water glasses and open bottles of wine. Zucca, stimulated by all of the festive energy, alternated between tugging at the white linen tablecloth from underneath and sticking his furry black head up onto Katie's lap in efforts to jump onto her chair. His leash stopped any forward movement, but each jump pulled on Katie's chair causing a sharp noise.

Squeak.

Squeak.

Yelp.

Squeak.

"Mom!" Matt and I exchanged looks of alarm and amusement across the table. As the waitress made her way to us, Katie, Matt and I all tried to lock eyes with her to distract her from the movement going on below. Matt moved his chair around to pretend that the squeaking was coming from him.

"So, *uhm*, what are the different colors of truffles again?" I saw Zucca peek his head out. His black curly fur was silhouetted against the white cloth near Katie's left leg. The waitress looked down and exclaimed, "*Cucciolo!*" (puppy!) Darn it. We're in trouble now. As she bent down and petted Zucca, I looked at Tim who was sitting at the opposite end of the table. He shrugged. There was nothing he could do to help us. We were on our own. The waitress took our orders and then unleashed an unintelligible string of Italian.

She haughtily disappeared behind swinging black doors. Katie quickly leaned down to tighten the leash. Suddenly there was a shriek and all sorts of commotion in the kitchen. I could hear energetic murmurings and scuffling.

"Katie, I have a terrible feeling that we'll have to take Zucca back to the hotel."

The swinging doors flew open and all five of the cooks burst into the dining room. The head chef, a portly older woman with salt-and-pepper hair pulled into a loose knot, led the way with a pewter tray in her hand. She came to an abrupt halt in front of us and looked to our waitress with the countenance of a queen.

"Dove?" (Where?)

The waitress pointed to Katie. I gritted my teeth and started to gather my purse, but the chef broke into a huge grin and knelt at Katie's feet. When she laid down the tray, I saw that it was filled with water for Zucca. Then she started to lavish all sorts of love on him.

"Oh, il mio barboncino! Come è bello. Amore mio." (My little poodle! It is so beautiful. My love.)

"È maschio o femmina?" (Male or female?)

"Maschio."

"Come si chiama?" (What is his name?)

"Zucca."

"Zucca?!"

Katie giggled and explained that we had bought him near Halloween. Matthew was all smiles like the proud father.

The chef then straightened up with a huge smile on her face. She stood for a long moment with her flour-covered hands on her wide hips and just stared at Zucca. Then she gave one last contented exhale like she was saying good night to her new baby grandson and quickly disappeared back into the kitchen.

I loved this country.

46 ⁓ the pope

It was just before noon on Sunday, and we were in St. Peter's Square. The four of us stood close to stay warm. Yesterday, a taxi driver informed us that the pope always came to his window at this time each week. Though we were headed back to Genoa on the afternoon train, we could not resist such an opportunity. If we missed our train, so be it.

I had never seen the pope, and I knew only the basics: that he was from Poland, that he was widely traveled, that he was brilliant and spoke the word of God in many languages. And from the varied comments I had overheard during this long weekend in Rome, he was truly and deeply beloved in this country.

At 11:45 AM, the square was more than half empty. We had fifteen minutes to kill, and I could see that the kids were antsy. "Matthew, why don't you take Zucca around for a little walk."

Matt happily took the leash and sauntered away.

"I think I'll check out those tables over there," Katie pointed to a small area where people were selling religious articles.

"See if you can find Grandma a nice medal or something for Christmas," I said as I handed her some money. Tim and I, dwarfed by the massive scale of the basilica, turned in slow circles, studying every detail of the colonnades.

"I wish we could stay here a few more days." I sighed. "I love this feeling of wonder."

"Yeah, I know what you mean," Tim agreed as he looked me in the eye. "It's intoxicating." He put his arm around me and we stood together in our awe. This was new, my ability to share something real and have Tim actually listen and respond with feelings of his own. A year ago, my comment would have been greeted by a man with faraway eyes who would have grumbled a response about what he had to do that day.

Almost imperceptibly, the piazza filled with people. Their coming was so quiet and reverent that it did not intrude on our private reflection. Katie and Matt made their way back to us and we huddled together as a soft mist started to fall from the sky. Umbrellas popped open above the ever-increasing sea of heads. A study in pointillism.

A murmur from the crowd alerted us. I looked up to the papal apartment of the Apostolic Palace and saw that the shutters of one window

169

had been thrown open. A priest leaned out and gently unrolled a long purple velvet drape on which was sewn the papal seal.

I glanced over my shoulder and saw that the square was now completely full. Thousands of people had come to see the pope and receive his blessing. All eyes were fixed on the window.

Waiting.

Suddenly he was there. Long and respectful applause greeted him as he waved his welcome. John Paul II started his blessing "Nel nome del padre ..." We all looked at each other and, without a word, instinctively joined arms to pull our family close. A single unit before God. Even Zucca sensed that he had better behave.

It did not matter that I couldn't understand the words. I felt the power of the Holy Spirit seep into my pores, causing my worries to fall like pennies from my hands to bounce along the cobblestones until they disappeared into the cracks. Only a profound calm remained.

He read a few prayers to a crowd so silent that I turned to see if it was still there. Thousands of faces turned upward. Thousands of hands clasped in prayer. Thousands of hearts yearning at once. It was deeply moving. World peace could only come from this. All hearts seeking God at once.

And family peace can only come from the same. All hearts seeking each other's at once. I looked up at the pope and then back again at the three other faces of my family, serious and focused.

After about twenty minutes, he gave a final blessing and was gone. The crowd slowly dispersed. The four of us walked wordlessly with our backpacks, in single file, with the rest of the crowd down Via Della Conciliazione. After a few blocks I turned to get one more glimpse of St. Peter's Basilica and the multitude that was silently receding into the streets and alleyways like a wave from the shore.

Zucca pulled on his leash and barked as Tim flagged a taxi. "Hurry up, everybody. Get in. Let's not miss the train."

"*Il treno,*" Tim told the driver as we arranged ourselves in the backseat.

"*Si, sì.*"

The taxi moved slowly through the throngs of pilgrims, the driver relaxed and obviously used to the weekly occurrence.

"*Il Papa. È magnifico, eh?*"

"*Si.*" We all replied in unison as we nodded our heads.

"Mom?"

"Yes, Matt?"

"Can we come back here again?" His glasses were still moist from the rain.

"Someday, honey. God willing."

47 ❦ busalla

As I trudged up the mountainside, I saw that my shoes were picking up clumps of mud and not letting them go. I was not exactly dressed for this impromptu hike, and I had no gloves. I periodically stopped to scrape the gloppy soles of my shoes against the grass so I wouldn't slide as I climbed. It was quite cold, and the air filled my lungs in icy puffs. It had been a while since I had been in weather cold enough to see my breath. I exhaled hard so I could watch the vapor slip away on the breeze.

When I reached the top of the property line I stood and took in the view of this mountainous area just north of Genoa. Veils of mist shrouded the peaks in the distance. The wind through the pines and the trickle of some hidden stream were the only sounds. I thought of the little sleep machine with programmed nature noises my children used to have on their bedside tables to lull them to sleep. It disgusted me, all of a sudden, that I had let myself become the kind of person who thought that was a suitable substitute.

The only building in sight was the remarkable villa that stood proudly below me. It was the house that Veronica and Thomas were hoping to buy, and they had brought us here to see it. After the obligatory espresso in the kitchen served by the present owner, we had been left to explore the place as we wished.

Veronica was thrilled beyond measure. I could see why. The villa was large and sprawling with a pool, stable and its own outdoor pizza oven. The owner didn't know the exact acreage, but it could certainly accommodate a small village. High above Busalla, it was private and rural. This was the reason they had come to Italy. To live in peace, raise horses and enjoy the simple treasures of the Italian countryside.

While the rest of the group toured the various parts of the villa, I had been lured to this ridge of pine trees. It was only a week until Christmas and, in my mind's eye, I could see these pine branches lining the various bookshelves in our home and gracing the doorways. There were few pines close to the sea where we lived, so I knew that this would be my only chance to procure them—for free.

We had all been missing our Christmas decorations. It didn't feel right. I also missed that we wouldn't have our annual decorating day, when we would take all of the boxes down from the attic and carefully unpack them. I missed seeing Matthew unwrap the reindeer and saying, "Hey, Mom, remember these? How about if we put them on the mantle again." And Katie hanging up the woven wall hanging she had made in art class in the second grade.

We had bought a few things at Ikea to decorate our tiny Charlie-Brown-size tree (the norm for this part of Italy) and a lot of candles. But that was it. The apartment felt a little empty. It smelled like sea air, not pine and cinnamon.

I walked over to the first tree and surveyed the branches. They were thicker than I had thought and very rough. I had nothing to cut them with so I looked for a sharp rock like I was Pocahontas or something, but there were none to be found. I was going to have to do this with my bare hands. I rubbed them together to warm them up and then I grabbed one of the thinner branches and tried to snap it in half. Of course, it just bent. I tried again and again, and soon I was left staring at a tree with unsightly limbs, like arthritic fingers scratching at the air. This was not going well.

I noticed that there were many types of pines around. I opted for a new species and squished toward it in my muddy shoes. I heard my name wafting up from below and people wondering what had happened to me. I felt a little stupid and hoped they couldn't see me up here bending these poor trees into Picasso sketches. How could I explain myself? I ducked farther into the woods and chose my next victim.

The branches of this one snapped off easily, and I was greatly relieved. I snapped away until I had a huge pile on the ground and bloody hands sticky with sap. I scooped it all up in my arms and started back. It was bulky, prickly and uncomfortable. The needles poked me all over. But I breathed in the musky fragrance and knew that I hadn't sprayed it from a can or opened a bag of potpourri. I was Laura Ingalls Wilder for a moment heading back to my little house on the prairie with Christmas decorations on loan from God himself.

As I loaded it all into the trunk of Thomas' car, Tim and Matt walked by.

"Check out all the great pine boughs I got to decorate for Christmas!" I said with enthusiasm pointing to the greenery.

"Nice. Have you seen Thomas?" They were matter-of-fact and quickly on to other things, but I was strangely buoyed by the experience. How real it felt to do this with my own hands. How real all of this felt now that I couldn't just open a box and depend on last year's memories to pull us through and add meaning to the season. This would be the first Christmas that didn't begin and end with a trip to the attic.

It didn't mean this was going to be perfect. Christmases away from home never are. But it would be forever marked in its uniqueness. Set apart from the blur of regular holiday memories.

As we all piled into the car and headed back down the winding driveway, I sneaked one last look up the hill and secretly smiled at the sight of the Picasso tree. I was sure that tree was in pain and utterly furious. Ready to hurl pinecones or secrete large amounts of sap. Something. When Veronica moved in, I would tell her to watch out and steer clear of it when next year rolled around.

48 halfway to each other

"Morning, Mom," Katie said as I walked into the kitchen. She sat at the table reviewing her Social Studies homework.

"Test today?" I kissed the top of her blonde head as I walked over to Tim, who was busy stirring pancake batter, and gave him a hug from behind.

Matt arrived fresh from the shower and took his place by Katie. "We have to leave in ten minutes."

"Good morning to you too," said Tim as he poured the batter onto a hot griddle.

"Hey, Mom," said Katie as I sat down with my coffee, "can we go Christmas shopping after school? Remember how much fun we had last time?"

"Sure."

"I'll go," said Tim as he reached into the fridge for the orange juice.

"That's okay. Mom and I kind of have this routine we do every year."

"Oh."

Katie closed her book and picked up Zucca. He put his little snout on the edge of the table and sniffed for crumbs.

"Not at the table, Katie," I said.

"He's fine where he is," Tim said. I looked at him sideways over the rim of my coffee cup.

"Since when do we allow dogs at the table?"

"Lighten up."

"Lighten up? What's with you this morning?" I stared at Katie until she put Zucca back on the floor. She and Matt looked back and forth between Tim and me as tension filled the room. What was this all about? My immediate reaction was to suppress my anger at his challenge and pretend that all was well. Like my mother, I had become an artful smoother-over whenever a hint of conflict appeared.

Tim flipped the pancakes to reveal their blackened underbellies. Matt, Katie and I glanced at each other as I slid them a few euros under the table so they could stop at the bakery on the way to the bus stop.

Tim plopped two plates of black pancakes down in front of the kids.

"Yummy." Katie suppressed giggles and poured herself a glass of juice.

"If you like hockey pucks," Matt mumbled as he cut the pancake with his fork. Though the outside was burned, the inside was still runny. Matt rolled his eyes as he took a bite. Tim had started getting up every morning and cooking breakfast. This was all new since he had always been gone by the time we had gotten up for school at home. Katie and Matt loved that he was doing this for them, but they didn't love his cooking. No one wanted to hurt his feelings by telling him that he cooked everything too quickly at too high a temperature.

Katie sliced her pancakes into little squares and pushed them around on her plate to make it look like she was eating. Tim poured more batter in the pan. "Anyone want more?"

"No, gotta run," they said in unison as they gathered their books and headed out the door. "See you around four."

"Then I'll finish it up."

Tim brought his breakfast over and sat across from me at the table. He poured syrup all over his plate and began an elaborate and vigorous display of "how to cut pancakes to show you are angry."

"Not hungry this morning?"

"Just coffee," I muttered.

"Katie barely ate a thing!"

"I know. What a waste of food." One of Tim's pet peeves was wasted food. I couldn't help but rub it in. "That's like two and a half pancakes. We could have frozen those and had them tomorrow."

"Maybe I'll get them up earlier so they have more time to eat."

"Good idea." I slurped my coffee as he took bite after bite, scraping the fork extra hard against his teeth each time. The silence stretched into minutes as I weighed my choices: (A) I could bring up the Zucca comment and start what would surely be an argument over who knows what, (B) get up and do the dishes in silence, or (C) spin my wheels with Anger and Distance out in the living room with another cup of coffee and a side dish of uproarious sarcasm.

These were the situations I hated. Little moments that created canyons between us. And the crazy thing was that I had no idea, really, what was going on. Why did this morning start so differently from all the others when we had shared burned pancakes with runny insides? Recently, I had started comparing marriage to the negative of a photograph. I remembered, as a young girl, holding one up to the light and marveling at how the image had a secret dark side. I had become acutely aware of the negative spaces of our relationship, finding that the words unspoken and deeds left undone were equally as destructive as the fighting. For years I had been able to fill my days with the positive and obvious images of chores, school, events and parties and such, but the negative images, the empty moments like this one, were the ones that slowly wrapped their fingers around my throat and suffocated me. I was not about to let that happen again.

Ask and it will be given to you. Seek and ye shall find. "Okay, God, I am asking you to help me change this pattern. Help me create a choice D that will help us communicate."

The new me put down my coffee cup and took a deep breath.

"What's going on with you this morning?"

"Me? What about you?"

"Why would you challenge me in front of the kids? Why would you change the dog rule for no reason?"

"Because you are always telling everyone what to do."

"I was reminding her that we have a rule about Zucca at the table."

"Same thing."

"No, it's not."

"Now you're telling me what I should think." Great. This was why I avoided conflict. Our conversations were like arrows shot in the dark. They never quite hit their mark. *Take another deep breath. March forward. Use the technique you learned in therapy last year.*

"Honey, when you challenge me in front of the kids, I feel diminished. Like you're telling the family that my opinion is less important than yours."

"Let me tell you what makes me feel diminished."

"Go ahead."

"The way you and the kids are like a club that I'm not always a part of. You guys have all of these looks behind my back and chuckles and secret understandings. How do you think that feels?" *Bingo.*

"Not very good."

"No. And I get up early every morning to cook breakfast and make the start of their day something special. That's the gratitude I get."

"We're not some club holding clandestine meetings behind your back, we're just three people who have spent a lot of time alone together. That's what intimacy looks like, sometimes. I'm not saying it was polite."

"Spent a lot of time together when? Like when I was working my ass off to support you all?" I could see him lacing up his boxing gloves. *Here we go.*

"Yes, like then. And other times."

"You lived a darned nice life as a result of my blood and sweat. I didn't hear complaints about that. Ever."

"Look, I am *not* going to rehash all of this again. That's all gone now, remember? All I can tell you is that you won't connect deeply with your kids unless you are there with them in the deep moments. And those moments don't occur at sitcom family times like the dinner table when you get to sit at the head like the dad on *Wonder Years*, or when you make it to their ball games, or stare like a zombie at the TV every night. They happen in the silent spaces. The unexpected dark times of their little lives. Like when they climb into the car after a tough day at school when no one passed them the ball at recess, or in the bathroom in the morning when you can't get their hair fixed just the way all the other girls have it, or in aisle seven of the grocery store when they finally work up the nerve to tell you that you are embarrassing them beyond words because your jeans are out of style."

Tim dumped his plate in the sink and left the kitchen. The canyon between us was officially larger than when we started. *Why do I always say too much?* I exhaled, let my head drop forward and laid my cheek down on the heavy wooden table. When it was obvious that Tim was not coming back to finish the conversation, I got up and started doing the dishes.

"*Lord, I am seeking, but I don't feel like I am finding much.*"

"*Keep seeking. You people give up too soon. You're both halfway to each other in this conversation.*"

"*Why does this always have to be so hard? He doesn't want to talk to me. He doesn't care what I think.*"

"*Go to him.*"

"*It won't do any good.*" I busied myself rinsing the dishes, putting away the food and wiping the counter with the sponge. As I dried my hands with the dish towel, I sensed that he was still there.

"*Go already!*"

"*Fine.*"

I found Tim on the rooftop, his forearms resting on the wrought iron fencing which wrapped around the perimeter. The morning's laundry hanging on the clothesline behind him flapped in the frigid winter wind. I pulled my sweater close and stood beside him, my hair like Medusa's in a storm. We stared forward to the horizon where the slate sea met clouds like curdled milk.

"I don't want to be the one they only come to for money. I want some of the good stuff, too, you know?"

"Yeah, I know."

"I'm not angry at you. I just … I just don't know how to change that. I have to work."

"You're already changing it. Cooking for them? That'll turn into all sorts of inside jokes to share. You'll see. They love it."

"You'll stop sneaking them money under the table?"

I nodded.

"Susan," Tim turned and faced me, "I know things have not exactly gone smoothly for us over the years."

"Stop. Let's not dig up anything else right now."

"I am sorry for everything I did or didn't do that hurt you. That hurt us or the kids. I don't know—"

I put my frozen fingers to his lips. "I'm sorry too. We hurt each other. But those two people? Those mixed-up, lost, stupid, unhappy people? They're gone now. They are." I searched his tear-filled eyes. "Aren't they?"

"Come here," Tim said as he pulled me close and warmed me in the wintry air as hot tears began to drip down my cheeks. "I hope," he whispered, "that I never see them again."

We stood for a long time watching a lone sailor brave his way in the choppy water along the coast. Wherever he was going, I hoped it was worth the trip.

"Tim, why don't you take them Christmas shopping today."

"You sure?"

"And try turning down the flame under the pancakes. Let them cook longer."

179

49 ✻ why americans love italian restaurants part 2

"*Ciao*, Tim!"

"*Ciao*, Susan!"

"*Ciao*, Katie!"

"*Ciao*, Matthew!"

"*Ciao, ciao, ciao. Buona sera. Ciao!*"

Egizio, his wife Christina, his sons Simone and Daniele, his daughter Maddelena, and Giuseppina, the elegant blonde mother-in-law who worked the cash register, all hollered their greetings at the same time. The whole restaurant turned to catch a glimpse of the tall family that haunted this pizza joint. My smile made my cheeks hurt.

We had just entered Egizio's, the famous pizzeria that sat high up in our neighborhood, literally two hundred feet from our front door. If you didn't know it was there, you'd never find it amid the scores of high-rise apartments. But, obviously, everyone in Genoa knew where it was. It was always packed.

Simone, glasses tilted and brown hair disheveled like a scientist at work, cheerfully marched us to our table, passed out menus and took our drink orders while chatting a few minutes about his day. Over the last few months I had learned that he loved fast cars and was trying to start a T-shirt company. He was also dying to come to America but was too afraid to fly.

Pretty Maddelena, a petite blonde, arrived moments later with plates of homemade Genovese hors d'oeuvres and salads that Giuseppina made each morning for special customers. We looked over to her, perched at the cash register, and waved a thank-you. She beamed. Simone returned with our drinks and a platter of bresaola. He showed us how to eat it covered with arugula, shaved Parmesan cheese, olive oil and lemon juice. We enthusiastically sampled everything as we browsed the menus for our favorite pizzas.

I loved this restaurant. It was filled with wooden tables, family memorabilia and the air of hard work and family pride. We had come here, starving and numb, the very first night we moved in. Stefano and Sabrina had said that the pizza here was outstanding. I can remember sitting in the corner and trying to make sense of the menu. We knew the word *pizza* but there were so many types and combinations of toppings that were riddled with words we had never seen. We were so tired and it was very stressful. It must have looked like we were trying to decipher the Rosetta stone. Simone had come to our rescue that night and, with his broken English, helped us wade through such words as *quattro stagioni* (four seasons), *melanzana* (eggplant), *cipolla* (onion), *carciofo* (artichoke) … and the dreaded *acciughe* (anchovies). In the end we had all ordered plain cheese just to be safe.

We also learned that night, by watching those around us, that Italians used a knife and fork to eat their pizzas. Picking it up with your hands was barbaric. Akin to something like holding a filet mignon in your fist and gnawing on it at Morton's Steakhouse.

But now, months later, we were experts and knew all of the combinations by heart. We had all settled into our favorites. Matthew always ordered cheese and würstel (cut-up hot dogs), Katie loved the margherita, I loved the one covered with fresh tomatoes and arugula, and Tim favored the ones with lots of meat.

"Matthew!"

I heard Egizio's voice and turned to greet him as he approached in his white apron. His sweet face and gentle manner made us feel at home. He was the same age as us, but he looked a little older from hard work, and he always remarked about how tired he was. His near-black eyes, kind and tender, were always ringed with dark circles. I often wondered if he should get his iron checked.

"Come." He motioned for Matthew to follow him. Matthew's face lit up and we all knew where he was going. Egizio smiled and winked at us as he followed Matthew down some narrow steps.

Christina, shy and serious, arrived with a tray filled with drinks. We exchanged smiles as she quietly placed each glass on the table.

"I'll be right back," I said to Katie and Tim, holding up our camera.

"Good idea," Tim answered as I headed down the narrow stairs where Matt had disappeared. The temperature in the stairwell rose with each step downward. Soon I was standing at the bottom, where an old stone oven was blazing. Egizio, his collar-length black hair falling around his face, was throwing in a few more chunks of wood as Matthew, now in a white apron and baker's hat, was scooping the pizza he had just made onto a big wooden paddle. He put the paddle into the open oven and deposited the pizza close to the embers. I snapped a photo as Matthew grinned from ear to ear.

"He is expert!" Egizio exclaimed with a smile and two hands thrown in the air. "Another!" He ordered Matt to get to work on another small mound of dough. Matt gently kneaded it and stretched it as though he had been doing it for years.

"Matthew. Look up. Say 'cheese pizza.' " I snapped a few more photos as he piled on the ingredients and readied the pizza on the paddle. He put this one into the oven and took out the other, beaming with pride as he slid it onto a large round plate. Egizio handed the plate to Matt and motioned for him to take it up to our table.

"Okay?" Egizio asked as he waved him on.

"Okay!" said Matt.

We headed back up the steps and Matt proudly placed his creation before Tim and Katie. Flushed from the heat of the oven and his own pride, Matt took his seat.

We complimented him on his talent, gorging ourselves as the other pizzas arrived and the place filled with more customers. It was busy like this every night. Voted one of the ten best pizzerias in all of Italy, Egizio's had perfected a paper-thin crust that was unlike any we have tasted elsewhere. When we asked for the secret he told us that it was a family recipe that had been handed down to him, a combination of a few different types of flour, a few secret ingredients and good water. People here swore that the quality of the water was always the key.

At the end of the dinner, Simone came and stood at the table.

"Digestive?"

"Sure, why not?" He returned within minutes with two glasses and the latest infused grappa that they were experimenting with. This particular bottle had crab apples floating in it.

"This," he kissed his fingertips, "is terrific and refreshing." He filled our tiny liqueur glasses and then left the entire bottle on the table.

This was another custom I loved. You could never do this in America, as the entire table would most likely take complete advantage of the fact that no one was there to watch you pour it. Like a bottle set before eighth graders whose camp counselor just stepped out of the tent, the bottle would be empty within minutes and no one would fess up to having drunk more than a mouthful. But here, you feel trusted. The bottle might sit on your table for an hour and no one measured.

I took a sip and it was downright vile. I saw Egizio and Simone making their way toward our table, and since I didn't want to hurt their feelings,

I forced it down with a smile and a cough. I could feel my own digestive juices putting up a fight as it burned its way down my throat.

"You like?" Egizio was proud of this new flavor.

"Very good," Tim said. Katie and Matt giggled.

Tim and I sat and shot the breeze with Egizio and Simone until the other family members came, hands in the air, to complain that they were doing all of the work. Egizio and Simone got up with much drama and just-for-fun familial discord.

"Egizio," Tim called after him. "*Conto?*"

Egizio whipped out a pad of paper and made up our check. "Five euros," he announced as he slapped the paper down, his eyes mischievous.

Tim peeled off a five, laid it on top of the bill and then handed fifty more to a smiling Giuseppina as we chuckled out the door.

50 ⚜ buses part 4

The buses were on strike again. Apparently nothing had been resolved during the last two strikes. I figured Tim and I would have to take the train into Genoa to finish our Christmas shopping. Maybe we'd actually buy some of the items on our list. The last few times we got sidetracked and ended up eating fresh grilled calamari. And, of course, then we had to wash that down with a bottle of white wine.

51 ⚜ the three christmas stars

Matthew lit the last tea light, the tiny flame reflecting in his glasses. There must have been at least forty of them strategically placed around the apartment amid the cut pine from Busalla and baby poinsettias that Tim had coaxed from the florist. I wasn't sure which was more luminous, the glow of the candles or Matthew's happiness. Christmas Eve had officially begun.

Our little Christmas tree stood in the middle of the living room proud of its new woven straw ornaments and red ribbons. Katie carried in platters of exotic hors d'oeuvres that included the glögg (hot, spiced wine punch), smoked reindeer heart and pickled herring I had picked up on my early December trip to Stockholm with Veronica. Tim stood at the stereo, choosing just the right music to put into the CD player. This was our favorite night of the year, and we all worked hard to make it special.

"I think we're ready," announced Matt.

"You know what, I'm just going to run to the bathroom first," I said as I headed down the hall to my bedroom.

"What do you think about Bing Crosby?" I heard Tim and Katie start to debate about which CD to put in.

Truthfully, I just needed a moment to myself. I was feeling out of sorts. It didn't worry me, though, as I had grown used to this predictable episode. I sat on the bed in the dark, took a deep breath and gazed out our sliding glass door toward the ink black sea. The night air beckoned me, so I slipped quietly outside and stood on the *terrazza*. It was cold, like it was supposed to be on the night of Christ's birth.

A hush had fallen across the countryside. There was little traffic noise, and for once, I didn't hear the train. Even Annalisa's apartment was silent, a rare occurrence.

Twinkling lights seemed to shine in every window from Genoa to Portofino. Off shore there were a few ships anchored whose captains had decorated with green and red lights.

The moonless sky was strikingly clear and strewn with stars. Right overhead was Orion. I mentally connected the dots of his belt. It was my little routine, wishing on these three stars, which took me back, all the way back to my brothers' bedroom.

The eight of us had shared a four-bedroom house. Since I was the only girl, I had my own room, which doubled as the guest room. When my grandparents came to visit, my dad would drag the black iron rollaway cot from the closet and set it up in my brothers' room. The cot fit between the foot of their twin beds and the old metal radiator where I could warm my feet through the blanket on cold nights.

I used to love those occasions, since bedtime in their room was infinitely more entertaining than solitary confinement in my own. Dirty socks thrown in the dark and silly stories would send us into fits of giggles that we expertly muffled with our pillows. After a few rounds of my father's booming "If I have to come up there …" shouted from the living room below, we would settle down and drift off to sleep in happy contentment.

The head of the cot was positioned right below a window on the side of the room. In the tranquil moments before sleep, I would look up to the small strip of sky that peeked down at me between our house and the neighbor's. In the wintertime there would always be three stars lined up exactly in a row. I didn't know anything about astronomy or constellations at that age; I only knew that it happened around Christmas. Like the three kings making their way across the sand.

They became my three Christmas stars, one of those childhood things that I would make up and keep to myself since I knew that sharing it would only invite teasing and ridicule from my five brothers. And, my three Christmas stars were always linked to the arrival of my grandparents bearing armloads of presents that we would all immediately start shaking and feeling for hints of the contents. For a week or so, our home would be full to bursting. And so would my heart.

As a child I felt this holiday from the inside out. Like a burning candle inside a lantern, the spirit filled me with the heat of excitement and the light of love. I simply glowed. As an adult, however, it was like someone had taken the candle out of me and placed it in some other holder on the far side of the room, its flame—throwing both light and shadow— much too far away to cast much warmth.

I thought that a Christmas Eve in this beautiful setting might somehow fill that void, but it didn't. I felt stupid to admit it, but I missed being eight years old and standing at the window waiting for Gramps' blue Thunderbird to turn into the driveway. I missed having to line up in height order in front of the fireplace in our new holiday outfits for the yearly photo. I missed sitting around the tree with my family and having my little brother methodically turn off every lamp in the house so the big colored lights on the tree would work their magic in the room. I could almost taste the ribbon candy that would always appear in the Santa Glass with the red felt Santa hat that was so hard to replace correctly before anyone could catch you sneaking yet another piece.

The deep, rich voice of Nat King Cole broke my reverie. "Oh Holy Night," my favorite holiday song, floated from our apartment and drifted out in all directions on the still air. Because Italians didn't have Christmas music, I knew it was coming from our living room. Tim's way of telling me that they were waiting.

I took one last look at my three stars and knew that it was, indeed, a holy night. Any night that called family members together, whether through memory or ritual, to renew their sense of joy and connectedness was a holy night. To announce to the world that we had chosen to be together on this holiday because we were a family, and that our laughter and celebration were all about love. Jesus could have appeared on the planet at any time and any place as a full grown man. But he didn't. He chose to be born into an ordinary family as evidence of its place in the hierarchy of life's most precious entities.

So I silently made the same three wishes upon my same three stars as I had done each year since our children were born. I prayed for all grandparents who drove many miles bearing gifts. I prayed for all parents who held the power of Christmas in their words and the choices they made to create this holiday for their children. I prayed that all children, regardless of their circumstance, felt God's peace and joy in a place so deep that they, too, would miss being eight years old for the rest of their lives.

I slipped back inside and flushed the toilet a few times for good measure to be sure that the whole house heard and wouldn't guess that I was faking the whole thing. I headed back to the living room and arrived to tapping toes and folded arms.

"Finally," said Matthew.

"Can't a mother have ten minutes to herself once in a while?"

"Not on Christmas Eve," he countered.

"Come on, first game. I'm dealing out the cards." Tim, as usual, got the ball rolling.

"Well, I hope you feel better anyway." Of course, Matt couldn't leave well enough alone.

I took my place at the table with our steaming mugs of glögg and took in my three treasured faces in the candlelight. "Yes, Matt, I feel much better now."

52 ❧ innsbruck

December 26. Starry, starry, bitingly cold night. We were strolling through Old Town Innsbruck looking for a restaurant where we could warm our bodies and fill our stomachs. We had arisen before dawn that morning, grabbed our quota of one backpack each, some food for Zucca, and tromped down the hill to the bus stop in the dark so that we could make it to the Genoa Brignole train station for the earliest departure. The kids had two weeks off from school and we didn't want to waste a minute.

A full day on the train took us north to this former Olympic village in Austria, where the ski jump still towered above the town. We were all wrapped in down jackets, like a rainbow of Michelin men bumping our way down the street. Our mission now was to find some hats and warmer gloves. We would never survive this snowy wonderland without the proper gear.

The streets were dotted with people. Who knew whether they were tourists or just townspeople out for a bit of air? As promised by Fodor,

Innsbruck was quaint and adorable with its old stone abundantly adorned with handmade pine garland. I found myself humming "Edelweiss." "Blossom of snow may you bloom and grow...."

"There's a shop with scarves in the window." Katie pointed to a little gift store on the right.

Matt, with Zucca in his arms, pushed open the door to the tinkle of a cow bell. The tiny colorful store was filled with trinkets and gifts.

"Tim, I think these would fit you." I said holding up a pair of authentic lederhosen. "You wouldn't have to worry about the length." Tim took them from my hand and positioned them as if he was wearing them.

"Do people actually wear those things?"

"Only if you have a granddaughter named Heidi."

"Here are the hats," Katie called from the corner where she was already trying one on before a mirror.

Matthew and Tim chose the first two hats they picked up without even trying them on.

"I'll take a blue one."

"I want gray."

Katie and I took much longer, ruminating over every stitch and detail. We finally left the store, wearing our choices of a fuzzy cream cap for me and a navy/white ski hat with ear flaps for her, and joined Tim and Matt who were waiting for us down the street, arms folded and noses red like cherries. Most shops had closed and a hush had fallen with the dusk. The snow crunched under our feet as we turned a corner. A merrily lit Christmas tree decorated a deserted square, like a Christmas card come to life.

"Listen," said Tim as he stopped suddenly.

"Where's that coming from?" The sounds of Christmas music played by violin, cello, flute and other instruments floated around us.

Like children following the Pied Piper, we followed the notes through a maze of cobblestones to another square surrounded by tall narrow snow-covered buildings. Large wrought iron balconies clung to the top floors. On two opposing balconies sat chamber groups engaged in the most delicate "battle of the bands." One played a stanza or two and then the other would continue the song.

People were gathered in silent groups. Their faces, reflected in the glow of Dickensian streetlights, turned upward toward the musicians. A few decorated booths were set up to dole out hot drinks, but their operators were also still and reverent. The scene was dreamlike. "Hark! The Herald Angels Sing" had never sounded more beautiful. Even Zucca remained still and content in Matthew's arms. The song ended and there was muffled applause through mittens and gloves. No one moved.

A lone violin began "Silent Night" and the simple purity of it brought a tear to my soul. Tim caught my eye. I grabbed his hand and we silently acknowledged the intense beauty of this experience. Back and forth the groups played as they took turns narrating the Christmas story through an arrangement so exquisite that words would have ruined it.

I could not get over the constant soul food I was being fed during this year abroad. Like manna from heaven, unexpected gifts like this were becoming regular occurrences. Magic had disappeared during all of those years of my controlled over-planning, because I was in charge. And I knew, now, that I was not a magician.

We had lived in Europe for six months by this point. And the funny thing was that, now, I didn't miss my house anymore. I didn't miss my car. I didn't miss my pretty teak outdoor furniture. I didn't miss my beautiful linens or the custom drapes or even my grandmother's china. All the stuff that surrounded me that I thought was so important in giving our children a good home had left my memory, and I didn't care. The only things I would ever miss would be the three people standing next to me. (And Zucca and Carmel Corn.)

Nights like this just added to my courage. Made me loosen my grip a little more and open my hands, palms up. Vulnerable and reaching. Though creature comforts and luxurious belongings are terrific, they don't compare to standing in the heart of Innsbruck on a star-filled, silent night … in heavenly peace. They just don't.

53 ✿ salzburg

A crowd of skaters gathered around a makeshift rink that had been hastily erected in the Old City of Salzburg to gouge money from tourists. It was the one thing that Matthew had been asking to do since we arrived here last night.

"Mom, you're the only adult putting on skates. See you over there." Katie burst out laughing as she tottered away. I looked up to see that she was right. The average age of the would-be skaters was about nine years old. This did not exactly lighten my mood.

I had pictured all of us arriving in the grand city of Salzburg, swinging by Mozart's house for a little look-see and then taking one of the famous bus tours where we all got to sing the songs from *The Sound of Music* as we drove by scenes from the movie. Okay. Maybe corny. But darn it, I knew every single word of those songs and it was to be the closest I would ever get to being Julie Andrews.

However, we awoke that morning to cold, misty, gray weather. Not very *Sound of Music*-ish. Over coffee and hot chocolate in the breakfast room, I ran my ideas past the group. Cold, blank stares told me that no one else cared about climbing every mountain or fording every stream.

We spent the day in and around the Old City. We walked around Mozartplatz and saw the famous yellow house. We toured the stately medieval castle, the Hohensalzburg Fortress, which loomed above, and walked the stone thoroughfares. Every time we would get anywhere near the rink, Matt would ask, "Can we go skating now?" and one of us would say, "Maybe later." In our adult language that meant "no." But in Matt's language that meant "maybe later."

We gave all sorts of excuses. "Not now, it's too crowded." And "Not now, it's too cold. And "Maybe later when the little kids all go home for their afternoon nap." And then, "Maybe later after *our* afternoon nap." You would think he would have gotten the message.

Matthew, not a complainer or a whiner, rarely asked for things. We had been pleasantly surprised at his ability to roll with the punches and enjoy all of this travel. I think this was the reason I didn't want to come right out and just say, "No. Of all the things to choose while visiting Salzburg for one day, we are not going to waste one minute skating on a lame twenty-five by twenty-five foot rink with plastic skates."

So after our family afternoon siesta we all got dressed for dinner and an evening on the town. We started down the stone walkways as the sun was setting in a deep golden glow and the stars were starting to dot the sky. Holiday lights were being turned on all over town, and we started to throw around ideas about where to eat.

We turned the dreaded corner and there in all its glory was the rink, now lit up by a few strings of lights. Tim, Katie and I all gave each other sideways glances and held our breath. For a few feet nothing was said. We thought that perhaps he had changed his mind. We were in the clear. But no.

"Mom?"

"Matt, we just got ready for dinner…"

"So."

Long pause. I looked to Tim and Katie for help. Nothing.

"So I don't really want …" His eyes started to glaze over. His mouth tightened. My heart caught a little. "Why don't you just go ahead and skate for a while. We'll stand here and watch."

He didn't move, and a tear dropped to his cheek. "I just wanted to skate with you," he whispered and stared at me with a naked childhood innocence that came straight from heaven. I took a deep breath and wondered when it was that I had turned into Mommie Dearest.

I looked at Tim. He looked at me. We both looked at Matthew.

"Let's go." I handed Tim my purse, and Matt and I headed toward the little shack to pick up some skates and pay the fee. At the eleventh hour Katie decided to come along.

So there I sat, lacing up my skates as I saw Matthew give up holding a place in line for us and head out onto the ice. He had played roller hockey for years and he glided effortlessly in circles. I searched the four-foot-tall crowd and easily found Katie. I hobbled toward her, knowing that we were going to be horrible at this.

"You first."

"No, you."

"Big baby," she laughed as she put one skate onto the ice and scooted down the scratched blue boards. I hobbled out and clung to the board next to her and tried to get a feel for the blades. Matt kept zooming by like he was Wayne Gretzky.

"Come on! What are you waiting for?" he called.

Katie pushed off first and immediately sprawled across the ice like a collapsed card table. It wasn't pretty. I teetered over and helped her up but we were laughing so hard that it was difficult to stay balanced. I helped her back to the boards as Matt zipped by and rolled his eyes. I heard Zucca bark from his cozy spot on the bench with Tim.

Finally, I pushed off and started to skate. Slowly at first, but then I picked up speed. I made it around a few times without falling and realized that I was starting to enjoy it. I bent my knees, leaned a little forward and tried to relax. I decided to pretend that, except for Katie, I was not two feet taller than everyone else on the ice.

Matt pulled up next to me, and we skated quietly together for a while, arm in arm.

Push. Push. Glide.

Push. Push. Glide.

"Matt, you're a great skater." He nodded his head in agreement.

Push. Push. Glide.

Push. Push. Glide.

"Aren't you going to say the same about me?"

"No." We both laughed.

"Look over here and wave!" yelled Tim from the side where he was adjusting the camera. We made funny faces and he took a few pictures as we skated past.

"Mom, look at the castle." He pointed to the Hohensalzburg Castle that sat far above us high on a hill. It was dramatically lit by hundreds of spotlights and glowed regally above the rooftops of the Old City.

"Matt, I am glad you didn't give up on this idea. This is fun."

"Told you."

We made it around the circle once more and then he was off again complaining that I was too slow, his face a study in contentment.

Katie and I stuck with it until Matt had had enough. Less than an hour all told. I was humbled once again by the realization that we could easily have robbed ourselves of this moment of deep connection with Matthew by ignoring his simple wish. The whole family loses when one member is ignored. Until I felt guilty, I didn't stop to listen to him. Those words, "I just wanted to skate with you," will haunt me forever.

We took off our skates, found our shoes, and then continued down the street to find some dinner. I have a feeling that when we think back about our short time in this spectacular city, the forty-five minutes in those skates on that tiny rink will be the ones we remember best.

54 ~ the musso treatment

Giglio parked his forest green Chevy Neon in a city lot in Recco as Pierangela pointed to the restaurant across the street, Ristorante Del Ponte, which Giglio explained meant "restaurant of the bridge." Giglio motioned for us to look way above our heads to a trestle that supported the autostrada between hills.

"The best *focaccia al formaggio* in Liguria."

We crossed the street and entered the shop to greetings that warmed us on this chilly Tuesday in January.

"*Ciao*, Giglio."

"*Ciao*, Pierangela."

"*Ciao, ciao, ciao*." A family of handsome men stood behind the counter. One of them broadly smiled and made a dramatic sweeping gesture.

"*Doviè la sua bella nipote, Carolina?*" (Where is your beautiful grand-daughter, Carolina?)

"*E`a scuola. Sei troppo vecchio!*" (She is at school. You are too old!) Giglio pretended he was disgusted. Pierangela giggled.

"*L'aspetterò!*" (I will wait for her.) The waiter put a hand over his heart and sighed. "*E poi la sposerò.*" (And then I will marry her.) Apparently they knew the Reduzzi family well.

He grabbed four menus and seated us at a center table. The place was simple, bright and cheery.

Giglio ordered for us as he sat down, "*Vino bianco e acqua naturale per tutti.*" He motioned to all of us and we nodded in agreement. "*Ricorda.*" (Remember.) Giglio held up his index finger. "Musso Treatment!"

The waiter threw his head back and laughed. Giglio explained that his daughter was married to a man named Musso, whose parents were very wealthy. Once, when Giglio and Pierangela had dinner with the Mussos at this restaurant, Giglio noticed that they were given preferential treatment. Not one to let such things pass, Giglio let the owners know that he expected to be treated as well when dining here without the Mussos. Since then, it had become a running joke, and indeed, he now also got the Musso Treatment every time he came.

Soon the table was filled with fresh seafood platters and *focaccia al formaggio*. Between bites we worked on our Italian and Pierangela worked on her English. Giglio worked on helping all of us communicate.

"Giglio, you missed your calling as a UN interpreter."

"No, this is much more challenging." He winked as he wiped his mouth on the white cloth napkin. "Who is ready for dessert?"

Giglio raised his finger in the air and caught the eye of our waiter. The waiter made a big show of coming to our table with a flourish: the Musso Treatment.

"*Sì?*"

"*Due espressi, due cappuccini, e quattro sorbetti al limone per favore,*" Giglio ordered. The waiter bowed deeply and left the table.

"I have something to ask you." Giglio was suddenly serious.

"Yes?"

"I am going to buy a new car."

"Congratulations!"

"That is not what I am trying to tell you," he scolded us like he was our dad. "Now listen to me. I have checked the trade-in value of the Neon. It is two thousand euros. If you would like to buy the car, I will keep it in my name and add you to our insurance policy. This way you won't have to wade through the miles of red tape. When you return to America, we can just junk it. What do you think?"

What did we think! Tim and I couldn't nod fast enough. Who would ever do this for someone? It was one thing to sell us his car, but to keep it in his name and put us on his insurance? I could barely think of what to say.

"I am overwhelmed by your generosity," Tim said.

"Is nothing." Giglio waved him off.

As our coffee and sorbet were set before us Tim and Giglio talked specifics. Pierangela and I kept busy with short phrases like, "*grazie mille*" and "I will drive carefully" and "I won't get any tickets."

I looked across the table at this wonderful couple. Any time we had really needed help or just a laugh or two, Giglio had ridden up like the Lone Ranger. Johnny-on-the-Spot. Asking nothing in return but friendship and a few bags of marshmallows, which he loved but could not find in Italy. Their friendship had unexpectedly become our safety net. They were fun and funny. And now I knew that they were generous beyond measure. It was no coincidence that Pierangela's name means angel.

We paid our bill and headed back to the car, which I now saw with new eyes taking in every detail. Felix Unger couldn't have taken better care of it. A '95 Neon had never looked as beautiful or luxurious. As Giglio zoomed down the autostrada toward Nervi, Tim and I looked at each other and silently high-fived behind the seat. No more walking up the hillsides with bags of groceries. No more nighttime bus rides to Matt's basketball practice. No more walking all the way to the bus stop to find that the buses were on strike. Side trips not reachable by train and bus could now be added to our list of destinations to be explored.

We pulled up to our apartment and into the driveway. The four of us sat for a moment.

"We can't thank you enough," Tim started.

"It's like you have been giving us the Musso Treatment since the day we met," I added.

"Is nothing. Now go." Giglio laughed and waved us out of the car.

"It will not be available for about another four weeks. Is that okay?"

"Yes, that is just fine."

We watched as he backed the car down the hill to his apartment and parked it with care.

"Can you imagine," I pondered out loud as we walked, "how the world would be such a different place if everyone gave each other the Musso Treatment?"

55 ✤ buses part 5

The buses were on strike again. I guess nothing had been solved during the last three strikes. I almost felt guilty in our shiny green Neon zooming by the scores of people that crowded the sidewalks and waited for the trains. But not really.

56 ⚬ trains part 2

"Amanda. It's your turn."

"I know."

"Either you have the card or you don't."

Matthew leaned back against the faded red fabric seat with a sigh and rolled his eyes. Tim and Katie leaned forward and glared into her eyes. I tapped out Beethoven's Fifth on the molded plastic armrest with my cards. Zucca barked as the train pitched and hissed to a stop. We barely noticed as passengers got on and off because we were all staring at Amanda. Waiting for her to discard.

Finally she laid down an eight. "Hearts," she announced as she swung her pin straight blonde hair over her shoulder. We each threw down a heart and then it was her turn again. And then we all waited again. We were on our way to Würzburg, where we would change trains and travel to Rothenburg, a walled medieval city on the Romantic Road in Germany.

It was Monday of *settimana bianca*, white week. The schools close for a week in February so families can go to the mountains and ski. We had decided to use this week to explore parts of Germany, Paris and Bern. Amanda, one of Katie's best friends from school, was an American from Macon, Georgia, who now lived in Genoa with her mother and Italian stepfather.

"Amanda! We're going to start giving you penalty cards if you don't hurry up."

We had always been a card playing family, but this year had brought us to a new level. We were addicted to Crazy Eights. Not your usual, run-of-the-mill Crazy Eights. This one included about fifteen homemade rules that could make your head spin. And to increase the intensity, every five-thousand point game was worth some huge wager, like who was going to have to do all of the dinner dishes for a month.

197

Even though we were annoyed by Amanda's slow pace, we understood that she was new to this and had a lot to remember. The games would often go on for days. We had started this one when we boarded the train in Genoa. We had played all the way to Munich and then throughout the following day as we toured the Marienplatz and the beer gardens. Every time we would stop for hot chocolate or a meal, we would take out the cards and the carefully folded score sheet, which we guarded like the map to the Holy Grail.

Amanda laid down a jack, a seven and then the dreaded joker. "Tim," she declared with sinister amusement. Tim's eyes narrowed as he drew four penalty cards. The train picked up speed and soon we were barreling through the German countryside once more. It was fascinating to see Europe through a train window. To study the subtle, and sometimes not so subtle, changes in architecture as we crossed borders. To notice the varying landscapes and weather differences that shaped and molded the people who lived there. To watch as the language changed on the signs and feel my brain trying to find connections in the words so that I could decipher them.

Like a voyeur, I watched the constant hellos and good-byes through the window, tearful lovers, children who searched for the face of their mother, the bored, the anxious, the well-heeled. The glamorous gal standing just far enough away from the man in the threadbare jacket. Every face told a story, if only I had the patience to sit and observe.

"Last card!" Katie triumphantly announced. This was the warning signal that she was ready to go out on her next turn. Tim laid down the ace of spades and we all breathed a sign of relief.

"Katie," he proclaimed with glee.

"No!" Katie moaned as she picked up three penalty cards. And the game continued.

Put four (or five, in this case) people together for nine hours and you can't help but interact. Cards, jokes, conversation, dialogue with other travelers, a snack from the cart. It was all entertaining and good. Like the ride to Milan when two tenors, three cabins away, practiced their opera solos, and the ride through the Alps on a stormy day that treated us to the most magnificent waterfalls I have ever seen this side of *National Geographic* magazine. Or the time that the sudden lurch of the train sent Matthew sideways into the lap of a twenty-something Swiss beauty, and the long ride to Brussels in the smoking compartment with our heads behind the curtains close to the air vents as we searched for oxygen.

Somewhere along the miles of steel rails that crisscrossed Europe, I realized that there were two ways of spending money. One was to spend it so that the world looked at us; the other was to spend it so that we could look at the world. This second approach was proving to be the better fit.

I threw down a three, which reversed the order, and said, "Last card." Because I had an eight in my hand, I felt secretly triumphant. A wild card ensured that I would win if no one else had the other joker. I smugly sat back and glanced out the window as my opponents scrambled to foil me. I caught a glimpse of a sign that raced by in a blur. I could barely make out the words *Würzburg* and *station* through the softly falling snow. Amanda laid down the other joker and slyly said, "Susan."

"No!" I screamed.

"Pick up four!" Katie and Matt laughed at me.

"No! We have to get off! Now!" I stood and slammed my hand on the bell signal to stop the train.

"What?" Everybody started to panic.

"I saw the station sign! Würzburg is next. Get your stuff!" A blur of arms and legs reached for backpacks, suitcases and puffy jackets.

The train began to slow. We were still grabbing our bags as the doors opened. Snacks scattered, cards flew, Zucca barked.

"Hurry up!"

"We'll miss our connection!"

"Grab the dog."

"Whose coat is that?"

"Our connection, our connection!"

"Alright already."

In all of our bumbling agitation, I was remotely aware that we were the only ones who seemed to be concerned about this particular train stop. No one else was getting off. But it didn't register. We scrambled to the doors with our stuff just as they started to close again. The train was moving as we jumped, one by one, onto the platform. Obviously, the conductor saw in his side view mirror that a few crazies were still disembarking because he slammed on the breaks and the train heaved unnaturally, depositing Amanda, the last of us, onto the concrete in a jumble. Phew! It wasn't graceful, but by golly—we made it.

The train closed its doors and headed on down the track. I gathered myself, caught my breath and finally stood up to look around. We were standing on a tiny platform the size of a parking space with no train station or other passengers in sight. We were in the middle of some industrial looking area, all alone as sleet began to mix with the snow. Five heads looked to the right and saw nothing. Then they looked up to the left and saw a sign that said "Würzburg Süd" (Würzburg South). We wanted plain old Würzburg.

Eight angry eyes stared at me accusingly. I shrugged.

"Sorry. I didn't see the *süd* part."

"Now what?"

"We have eleven minutes until our connection."

"I don't think we're going to make it."

57 ～ art shots and funny stories

The sun streamed through the slatted wood shades and woke me. Propping myself up by my elbows, I looked around from the canopied bed to get my bearings. The elegant room, the color of mint with dark cream moldings, was still and dust motes danced in the sun's rays. Though it was early, Tim was already up and gone. I knew exactly where he was. My feet hit the cold floor and I threw on jeans and a white turtleneck sweater. Cold water on my face and a few strokes of the hairbrush made me presentable enough to join him. I tiptoed past a cot on which Matthew was sleeping and quietly let myself out of the room. I walked down the hallway and put an ear to Katie and Amanda's door. Not a sound.

The Romantik Hotel Markusturm, in Rothenburg, was one of the nicest that we'd stayed in all year. After yesterday's Würzburg train debacle we rolled our carry-on suitcases a few hours late across a stone bridge and entered this centuries-old town filled with towers, forts, great stone archways and half-timbered Bavarian-style buildings. It sat on the Tauber River and was surrounded by a thirty-foot wall, complete with a now dry moat. It immediately cast a spell on all of us.

Heading down a flight of carpeted steps, I stopped at a window on the landing, pushed aside the white eyelet curtains and peered out. The cobblestoned street, lined with shops on both sides, was slowly coming to life. I pictured Bavarian lasses with blonde braids tucked under white caps scurrying about, holding up billowing skirts so they would not trip in their wooden clogs. Smiling from ear to ear with the memories of the day before, I took my fine mood on down the steps and followed the aroma of fresh rolls to the paneled dining room where Tim sat reading the *International Herald Tribune*. I tiptoed up behind him, put my arms around his shoulders and kissed him on the cheek.

"*Guten morgen.* I didn't even hear you get up," I said as I dropped into the chair next to him. A white china cup with gold trim was already set at my place.

"Do you ever?" His eyes twinkled as he poured me coffee from a silver pot.

"Anything newsworthy?"

"Not really."

Next to the paper lay our digital camera and a stack of brochures about the Romantic Road that Tim had grabbed from the front desk.

The first one I opened was a map of the entire road that stretched over miles of land in southern Germany, beginning in Würzburg and ending close to the Austrian border in Füssen. The colorful photos of its quaint villages and grand castles made it easy to see how the road got its nickname. It would be the perfect honeymoon.

"Someday we should travel the whole road. Start to finish," I said excitedly.

"Tim?"

"*Hmm?*"

"Don't you think that would be fun?"

"*Hmm.*"

Careful to keep my pinkie in the air, I sipped from my china cup for a few more minutes and watched as other guests filled the tables. I picked up the camera and decided to flip through yesterday's photos just for fun. I smiled at Katie, Matt and Amanda perched atop one of the old arches, Tim standing next to an ancient doorway that was chest high, the older couple who refused to wait on us last night at dinner, the bartender who took ten minutes to fill Tim's mug with beer. *Hey, what the—*

"Tim, what happened to the other pictures?"

"What?"

"I took about twenty others. The town hall, that big marketplace, the fortress and those big round pastries in that bakery window?"

"I deleted those."

"What?"

"I wanted to make room for today's and the rest of the trip."

"I loved those shots."

"They were scenery shots. We can buy postcards before we leave."

"They weren't just scenery shots, they were my art shots," I said through clenched teeth.

"Keep your voice down! Why are you getting so worked up?"

My heart pounded in my chest and I felt heat rising up my neck. "When I see things that have beauty or character I want to remember them. The moment when it captivated me, the spot where I was standing, the angle of the sun in the sky. I would never erase your photos without asking."

"Our computer is filled with your art shots from this entire year. One week without art shots isn't going to kill you."

"Look at these. Pictures of waiters? Bartenders? *Hmm.* Here's a few more: one of *you* holding a big sword, one of *you* standing next to a huge teddy bear, and here's that very interesting shot of *you* standing by the bathtub in our bathroom. Funny how most of the photos are about you. How romantic, Tim all alone on the Romantic Road."

"Those are the moments when we were laughing about something. They will remind us of our funny stories."

"Why do you think it's okay to erase other people's pictures?"

"Are you having your period?"

"Did you just say that?"

"You're acting completely irrational, and you're starting to make a scene."

"Why is it when you get angry about something, the whole world has to hold its collective breath until you are heard and get what you want, and when I get angry you tell me that I am irrational and assume that I am having my period, which I am not by the way." I put the camera on the table in front of him and stared at him, eyes narrowed.

"You have lost your mind," he said with a smirk. "Here, have some more coffee."

"I don't want more coffee," I said. "I want to know why you thought it was okay to erase my photos."

"I made an executive decision. I didn't know it would start world war three."

"Just so you know? Executive decisions usually only work for the executive. And, last time I checked, this family is not a business that you are running." I stood and turned on my heel feeling righteous and mighty, proud of myself for expressing my feelings in such a clear fashion. I strode by tables catching the eye of a few women who nodded to me with less than covert looks of triumph. I knew I was being overly dramatic but Tim had hit a hot button that we had never discussed. My period, my foot. I wasn't due to get it until tomorrow.

I headed back up the steps deciding to wake the kids and get things organized for the next leg of our trip. About an hour later Tim walked into the room, his cheeks flushed with the cold, and handed me the camera.

"I went back and took as many of them as I could remember."

art shots and funny stories

"You did?"

"You're right. I should've asked you first. When you run a company you get used to making decisions and having everyone else adjust. Doesn't work that way in a family, or at least it shouldn't. I'm sorry."

I was not expecting this reaction at all. I thought he was down there digging in his heels and ignoring me. I put down the denim shirt I was folding and put my arms around him.

"Thank you." We hugged for a moment, his jacket chilly against my skin.

"Look at some of them with me," he said like a proud father. "It was beautiful outside, the sun was just starting to rise over the rooftops and most of the streets were empty. It felt a little surreal. Very cool."

I clicked through the photos and saw the collection of moments that had captivated Tim. They were quite artistic. Matt came across the room and wiggled his head into the middle of us so he could get a look at them too.

"Oh no," whined Matt. "Not you too."

We burst out laughing and I handed the camera to Matt. "Here, take one more of Dad and me before we head out. It will remind us of this funny story."

58 ⚜ the pool

In Bern, Switzerland, on the last leg of our trip, we decided to splurge on a hotel with a pool and sauna. The kids were all very excited. The elevator jiggled its way down to the basement, where, according to the girl at the front desk, we would find the pool. Matt was dressed in his swim trunks and carried a bath towel. Tim and I, in our street clothes, just wanted to plop down on a chaise lounge with a magazine. Katie and Amanda were still up in their room and planned to join us as soon as they finished readying themselves for the *Sports Illustrated* swimsuit edition.

The elevator abruptly halted, opening into the garage. "Anyone see a sign?" Tim asked as we looked around.

"Here's a door, but there's no sign," Matt said. He pulled it open and we all stuck our heads into a nondescript hallway.

At the end, a door to a steamy locker room stood ajar.

"There's no sign anywhere."

"How do we know if it's the men's or the women's?"

"This is the only door in the entire hallway."

"Let's just go in."

We walked around a tiled partition and were immediately treated to the sight of a naked man—and not an appealing sight, at that. I gasped and zoomed back out into the hallway.

"Mom, this is the men's," said Matt.

"You think?" I teased him, and he laughed.

"I'll go in," said Tim, "and ask the guy where the women's locker room is." A moment later, Tim stuck his face out the door.

"This is it. Coed." We all looked at each other with raised eyebrows.

"Oh."

"We have to put our shoes on the rack outside. For sanitary reasons."

"Gotcha." The hairy fat man didn't look all that sanitary to me, but I'd follow the rules.

We took off our shoes and walked through the steam. Not a big deal, really, just a few middle-aged men in various stages of undress. One of them was showering with the shower curtain open and Matt looked at me askance.

I tried to act like this was normal. I didn't want to look like an uptight American. Tim found the door to the pool and we entered, the hot chlorinated air smacking us in the face. It was a small pool, but it would do. One swimmer was doing a lazy freestyle back and forth in the first lane, and another lounged at the edge near the steps. We found a few lounge chairs and made ourselves comfortable. Matt jumped in and started to swim around.

"There were no women," I said as I rolled up the legs of my jeans suddenly wishing I had put on some gym shorts.

the pool

"It's two thirty in the afternoon. Businessmen checking in. Doesn't mean anything."

"Guess you're right."

We both sat back and relaxed. I tried not to think about Katie and Amanda walking through the locker room with hairy fat man on the loose.

"Susan."

"What?"

"Those two guys in the pool. They're naked."

"No way."

I tried to act casual as I checked it out. Sure enough they were.

"Remain calm."

"I think this is all just a cultural thing. I've heard of co-ed stuff like this. It's just the way they do it here."

"Katie and Amanda are on their way down, you know."

"Maybe we should just go up and tell them not to come."

Matthew, oblivious to all but the silky feel of the water, dived for pennies. Suddenly the pool door opened and Katie and Amanda, wrapped head to toe in their towels, darted in with pinched expressions. They rushed to our sides and sat down in a fit of giggles.

"Mom."

"I know."

"But they're all—"

"Look, just grab a chair and act like this is normal for a while. Maybe these guys will leave."

As if on cue, the guy lounging by the steps got up in all of his manliness, slowly stretched and then exited.

"That was attractive."

"One down, one to go."

What exactly was that languorous stretch all about? Was that some signal or something? What exactly was going on in the locker room? I scanned the room, but there was no other exit. We were trapped in here with our innocent children.

Tim cleared his throat to get our attention. The swimmer in lane one, it seemed, had had enough of freestyle. He started the backstroke. Great. But not your typical backstroke. Sort of like a frog-style backstroke, his arms and legs spreading out wide and then pulling close at the last second.

The sight of Matthew on one side of the pool and Frogman on the other was too much. We all tried to stifle our giggles but we couldn't.

Tim called Matt out of the water. He marched over to us in a huff of irritation.

"What?"

He saw Katie and Amanda in hysterics. Katie pulled Matt down and whispered in his ear. He stared, his eyes widening like silver dollars.

"Listen, you guys," I said with authority, "in Switzerland this is normal. Let's not make anything weird out of it. Not everything has to be sexual."

Tim, amused at my weak attempt to diffuse the situation, agreed. We all took a collective deep breath and sat back in our chairs. Froggie continued his measured strokes.

"Maybe it's time to go."

Matt was clearly disappointed.

"Can I just jump in one last time?"

"Sure, go for it."

Then, in complete innocence. "Can I go in naked?"

So much for my little speech a moment ago. Now I had to act all nonchalant about it.

"I'll go ahead with the girls. Tim, you want to wait for Matt? You two can talk over the swimsuit situation."

"Yeah, this is exactly what I want to be doing right now with my son."

"Great! Then we'll see you upstairs."

59 ❦ blue funk

I scooted my black inflatable Ikea chair, Italy's answer to bean bags, over to the big glass window in the living room and put my hand on the glass knowing it would be cool to the touch. Using my index finger, I traced a raindrop on its journey down to the terrace. It had been pouring rain for four days, and I was in what my mother used to call a blue funk.

The kids were at school and Tim had gone to the New Muscle Beach. Zucca, curled in my lap, slept to the steady drum of the downpour. Loneliness crept in like a black cat and stared me down. I tried to look away, but my gaze fell upon it everywhere.

I decided to busy myself with a chore or two so I wandered down the hall and through the kids' rooms, but nothing really needed to be done. It was not hard for them to be neat and tidy when their belongings could fit into one suitcase.

I pulled up Matt's bedding and plumped up his pillow. I played with the lone decoration on his shelf, a groovy fiber optic light that changed colors. A man of action, Matt didn't seem to have the need to nest and surround himself with things. Katie was the opposite. She had decorated her room with magazine pictures of handsome models, photos of Basketball Alex and other classmates and memorabilia from home. I stood for a long time and studied each face and object. Some of them familiar, some not.

I continued on to my own room and decided to look at all of my own photos. But I had to lie on my bed and close my eyes to see them for they hung everywhere in my head. Collage upon collage of smiling faces. They all seemed to be calling to me at once, but I couldn't quite make out their words.

I was desperately homesick all of a sudden. I missed easy conversation and subtext. I missed convenience and nonverbal cues that I understood. I missed laughing and lamenting with girlfriends over coffee. I missed my parents and brothers like a ten-year-old away at camp.

Tim's key in the door pulled me from my daydream. Grabbing my book, I pretended to read as his shoes squished their way down the hall and into the room.

"I should have taken the car," he said as he peeled off a soggy black sweatshirt and grabbed a towel. "Did you see that lightning?"

"Not really. I've been totally absorbed in this book." He looked at me, then the book and then back at me. A subtle smirk.

"Must be a great story." As he turned to walk into the bathroom, I looked down at the cover, then playfully zinged it at him.

"What was that for? You're the one who was reading it upside-down."

"I wasn't even reading it," I choked out as unexpected tears sprang from my eyes.

Tim walked over and sat next to me, dripping on the bed.

"What's going on?"

"I am so homesick that I feel nauseated, and I want to buy this apartment and live here forever."

"So we're still at the same place we were a month ago."

We had been trying to decide for weeks now whether to stay another year or go home. The culture here supported the family in a way that America does not. It was this support we desperately needed when we arrived. We felt cradled in the traditions here.

"What are you feeling these days?" I asked.

"Mostly, I feel like an American on a long vacation."

At some point, the year stopped being a dream and started becoming real. I was not sure exactly when that happened, but it had a lot to do with Katie and Matthew finding happiness and deeper friendships. As they became more connected to the community, Tim and I were feeling less so. Their lives were taking root, but we still resisted.

"We could probably afford another year if we didn't travel," Tim said as he toweled off the rest of the raindrops. "Realistically, though, that would eat up our entire savings and two years out of the job market is a long time. Then there's the question of Katie's college applications."

"My biggest fear is what will happen to us."

blue funk

"Why do you have to be so pessimistic?"

"No, I'm being realistic. We're going back to the same town where the quest for power is intoxicating, the same traffic-filled highways that drove you crazy, the same population with a large number of perfect people taking antidepressants."

"Haven't we learned enough to counter all that?"

"Have we? I think it will be close to impossible not to get caught up in the materialism again."

"We'll have to deal with that whether we go back this year or next. We're different people now. We can handle it."

The drum of the rain increased. We watched with fascination through the sliding glass door as a streak of lightning splintered the iron sky. Thunder rumbled, and a second later, the storm was overhead. Bolts of lightning lacerated the sky like cuts from a whip.

"This storm is incredible. Let's get in bed and watch it," I said. We scrambled under the covers and snuggled as Mother Nature raged on. With Tim's arms around me I felt safe.

"We've been through our storm," whispered Tim. "Let's keep walking toward the rainbow. God will show us the way."

60 ~ the car accident

I loved the whole "car" thing here. For the most part, cars were not status symbols. They were modes of transportation. Sure, there were people who owned fancy vehicles, but it was not the norm.

Smart cars, the kind that were so small that they could be parked perpendicular to the curb, were the coolest. But anything tiny was perfect. It didn't matter if you could fit your entire family into the car at one time or not. The important thing seemed to be whether or not you could fit through the narrow alleyways or park on sidewalks if the spots on the streets were full. Creative parking here was impressive, but only Italians seemed to be able to get away with it. Every time Tim or I tried something creative, we got a ticket.

People here were not embarrassed about scratches and dings. Even expensive cars sported dents and rust pockets. Mishaps were commonplace.

What? You just slammed your car door into mine when you got out? Hey, no problem! Have a nice day. What? You dented my bumper because you wanted to push my car forward five inches to make the space larger so you could park? Tell your Momma I said hi. What? Your Vespa handlebar put a foot-long scratch down my door because you thought you could squeeze past us all at this red light? Hey, next time use the sidewalk, but don't worry about it.

One morning, after I had dropped the kids off at school, I was trying to get past an old woman whose car was jutting way into my lane. The space looked narrow, but after driving here for a few months I was getting pretty good at maneuvering through impossible situations. So I started to inch past her. Sure enough, my back right fender scraped against her side door. Pretty hard too.

American reaction: My heart dropped. I inhaled sharply. I thought immediately of Giglio's insurance agent and the deductible. I felt the weight of the hassle it was going to be to have to communicate with insurance companies in Italian. I panicked about having to tell Tim.

Italian reaction: The old woman looked at me. I looked at her. She did the sign of the cross and said, "*Mi dispiace*," (I'm sorry). She motioned that it was her fault for being too far over. She couldn't care less about her scratched door. She was worried about me. She smiled and waved, then moved to give me more room. I inched by and honked for good measure as we both laughed and waved good-bye.

Shifting the car into third, I zoomed along the coast road feeling reckless and free, almost giddy with the thought of showing Tim the scraped fender and feeling just fine about the whole thing. Maybe I should add a matching scrape on the other side.

61 ❧ the town that will never be named—extreme marital therapy part 3

Tim grabbed my hand and we exited the train. "This way," he said as he led me down a short flight of stairs and out onto a narrow street. "I'm so excited to show this to you."

Crossing the street, another stairwell led us down to a coast road. I caught a glimpse of the dark turquoise sea between richly painted buildings and a rocky coast that climbed high to the left with craggy trees silhouetted against an azure sky. At the bottom of the steps we turned right and followed a stream of people who seemed to know where they were going. Soon we were in an alley that was so narrow I could reach my arms out and touch each wall at the same time. All of this dark, cold stone that rarely felt the sun was eerie.

We stepped out into the open air and sunshine, and I stopped in my tracks. This little village on the sea was a life-size canvas, color-splashed by one of the grand masters and left to dry on the hillside. A wide brick thoroughfare divided a rocky beach from tall, brightly painted buildings that had been standing guard and protecting fishermen for centuries.

The architecture here was typical of Liguria. The entire façade of the beachfront, about a quarter mile long, was one smooth structure. The homes were delineated solely by paint. Like a rainbow of piano keys standing on end, each narrow section was a different color, bright and in complete contrast to its neighbor.

"Wow," I whispered. "For once, I have no words."

"Someone told me, the last time I was here, that the fishermen painted their houses those vivid colors so they could pick out their homes when they were out at sea." Trompe l'oeil cornice work and shutters added to the delight of it all. A painted cat lounging on a false windowsill looked so real I wanted to reach out and stroke its fur.

At the far end of the crescent-shaped village was a creamy yellow church of surprising grandeur poised on a throne of natural rock. We ambled slowly in that direction past restaurants and the few shops that lined the brick thoroughfare.

"Cappuccino?"

"Of course." Tim steered me in the direction of an open-air café that consisted of black iron café tables under a black-and-white striped canvas tent. Its side panels had been rolled up to maximize the view and allow the salty air to gently swirl around us. A waiter seated us and took our order.

Alone in the café, we looked into each other's eyes.

"This is when I feel the weightlessness of freedom."

"It's like a dream," Tim said.

Being relaxed and totally, emotionally present was a gift. In our harried world, it had been rare. Tim and I were now acutely aware of the power of this experience. It was something that we were learning to cherish together. Married life was rarely about being totally present with each other. In fact, I now suspected that it was a gift reserved for lovers. Once we took our vows, that intimacy had somehow slipped away in wisps so tiny that I couldn't put my finger on why our relationship didn't feel the same anymore.

Our coffees were delivered without fanfare, and we sipped them slowly. I studied the faces of the people who passed by and was not surprised that none were American. This was a town that the guidebooks had forgotten to mention. We promised each other to keep it a secret as well. Though the village had become modern in its own right, if you squinted your eyes just so, you could erase all of the restaurants and see what life had been like a hundred years ago when children played on the beach and mothers, young and old, leaned out the windows and searched the horizons for their sons and husbands. Waiting, always waiting. And praying for their safe return.

I took one last swallow of coffee. It was almost noon. "What do you say we check out the church before the pastor locks the doors for *intervallo*."

Tim threw a few euros on the table and I motioned to the waiter that we were leaving. He waved to us like we were friends and he was sad to see us go.

Holding hands, Tim and I strolled to the end of the thoroughfare and passed through an archway that led us to the harbor where the fishing vessels were docked. Over to the left the church stood near a lighthouse. The metaphor was not lost on me.

We entered the nave and my eyes adjusted to the darkness. The interior was bathed in gold with at least fifty crystal chandeliers hanging from the ceiling. The only visitors in the church, our footsteps echoed softly as we meandered, marveling at paintings and marble sculptures.

As we had done in every church we had visited so far this year we each lit a prayer candle. Although we had been to so many I had lost count, I knew we were creating a sort of "constellation in reverse." I wondered if God was watching from above and following our trek as tiny new flames appeared each week.

When we finally made our way back to the front door, I spotted a small square metal box fixed to one of the marble pillars, with instructions in Italian. We were able to make out the words "tre" and "euro."

Tim fished three euros out of his jeans and put them in. A few seconds passed, then a loud clunk, and all at once every crystal chandelier lit up. Hundreds of tiny white lights reflected off the gold and crystal. A halo of stars twinkled over the head of Mary who reigned high above the central altar. The air was thick with silence and light. If this was not a human expression of what God's love looked like, then I didn't know what was.

The experience lasted for only three minutes, but I will feel it forever. Yes, Tim, you were right. This town had stolen my heart, and I could see that it had stolen yours. But this time our hearts had been stolen together by the same thing at the same time. The way I remembered it long ago when we were just lovers.

It was almost 10:00 PM and I was sitting in bed reading *The Other Boleyn Girl*. Katie and I had been stealing the book back and forth from each other as our recent travels had made the story come alive for us. Enjoying my stint as part of the queen's court, I was in the middle of helping Anne Boleyn tighten her corset when Matthew bounded into the room and dived onto the bed.

"Hi, honey. Thought you were asleep."

"Nope. Not tired," he said as he sat up and fixed his glasses.

"How come?"

"I don't know. Just thinking about stuff."

"Hey, big fella, where do you think you're going?" Tim emerged from the bathroom and pounced on Matt putting him into a gentle head lock. Before I knew it the bedding had become a tangle of arms and legs and *The Other Boleyn Girl* went flying to the floor with a thump. We goofed around for a bit and then settled back down. Tim climbed under the covers and Matt snuggled in between us.

Matt sat up and looked at us with sudden consternation. "Easter's next week, right?"

"Next Sunday."

He looked around the room, scratched his head and took a deep breath. Tim and I looked at each other. Something was up, here.

And then he blurted it out. "There's no Easter Bunny is there?"

"No, honey, there isn't."

"I knew that."

Tim and I gave each other sideways glances. The air in the room was suddenly thick.

"There's no Santa Claus either. Right?" Hot tears sprang to my eyes, which was so stupid because Matt was eleven, and I was sure that he had

215

☜

known this in his subconscious for a few years now. Speaking it out loud just made it real. The final curtain on his childhood.

"No, honey, there isn't."

"I knew that too." With that pronouncement he quickly exited our room and entered adolescence.

"That's how it happens," said Tim, "just like that. No warning. No fanfare. One minute they're children and the next minute they aren't."

We looked at each and shrugged through our tears. Tim held out his hand and I took it, snuggling over to him at the same time.

"I was not prepared for that," Tim said as he reached over and turned off the light next to the bed. With my head on his shoulder, we lay in the dark and grieved for a few minutes.

"If we hadn't come to Italy, that would have happened at either your house or my house. One of us would have missed it," I said.

"That would have broken my heart even more."

"Me too," I said as I pulled the covers up around us. "Will you hold me tonight while I fall asleep?"

"I wasn't about to let you go."

63 ✻ under the tuscan sun

"April showers bring May flowers!" My mother, Lois, stood by the glass paned window and adjusted its worn gingham curtains, which were the same moss green color as her sweater. Harry, my dad, was busy stoking an early morning fire in an old stone fireplace that took up an entire wall of the small living room. The smoky scent coupled with the rustic décor was reminiscent of our summer vacations years ago on Crescent Lake in Maine.

My parents were on one of the "Dream Trips" that my mother could now cross off her "All the Things Left to Do Before I Leave the Earth" list.

Our sudden departure last July pushed this one to top priority. Our family was thrilled when my parents rented this farmhouse villa, Le Chiuse, nestled in the middle of a Brunello vineyard near Montalcino. Katie and I had arrived the day before to spend a few days before Tim, Matt and Zucca arrived. They would join us after their trip to the island of Elba to search for the ghost of Napoleon.

"Here, Mom." I handed her a mug of freshly brewed coffee and we both snuggled in around the hearth. My dad settled into a sturdy wooden rocker that had probably sat in the same spot for a hundred years. The stories it could tell. The warm golden light of the fire took years off our faces and I felt about fourteen again.

"So what should we do today?"

"Here," my mother pulled a white piece of paper from her pocket. "These are the names of the towns that I heard were cute." On it, in her precise handwriting, was a short list of names: Murlo, Pienza, Buonconvento, Cortona.

"Let's take a look at the map."

"It's such a crummy day, let's go to the farthest one."

"I guess that would be Cortona."

I had seen Frances Mayes' book, *Under the Tuscan Sun*, sitting on my mother's bedside table for years, literally. I suspected that she wished she was Frances. So though we both acted like our decision to drive to Cortona for the day was random, we both knew that it was not. It was something that had to be done. Paying tribute to the Goddess of "You Did What I Want to Do and Never Will."

Before we left for Italy, I had gotten three copies of *Under the Tuscan Sun* as going-away presents. I threw one in the suitcase, but upon our arrival decided to just leave it there. I wanted to experience Italy without prejudice or expectation.

Then as March, my least favorite month, dragged on cold and dismal, I got itchy for something to read in English. Suddenly, I remembered my suitcase, pulled it out of the closet and opened it. There sat the book, with its binding smooth and creaseless.

So I started to read all about how Frances and Ed found a perfect farmhouse in Cortona, which they refurbished and transformed into a paradise by anyone's standards. How they flew back and forth all the time from San Francisco taking breaks from their teaching positions. How they cleaned up the property and planted roses and lavender and got all of those olive trees back up to snuff. And had a huge yellow picnic table built and put it under a stand of trees so they and their friends could while away the hours drinking wine from their own wine cellar and nibbling on all sorts of fine meals prepared by Frances in the kitchen, without, it seemed, any effort at all.

It appeared to me that Frances and Ed were having a much more poetic experience than old Sue and Tim. All of this "you cook and take naps, darling, while I clean and renovate stuff," I mean, what was that? Frances and Ed never had so much as a tiff through all of these goings on? Please, you're spending your life savings on an old abandoned building half a world away and working with people you've never met and with whom you can barely communicate. There's going to be a little stress. Of course a book was going to sound romantic when you left out all of the little irritations that make us real, make us human.

You can't tell me that Frances never looked out the window and said to herself, "He's at it again. Hauling those rocks. What is up with all of the rocks, Ed? It's not like the Great Wall of China we're building here. *Humph.* Guess I'll pour myself a glass of wine." Or that Ed didn't look down the road, checking his watch and muttering, "She's been to that stupid market seven times in the past three days. I could use some help around here. I thought we'd agreed to a budget! *Humph.* Maybe I'll pour myself a glass of wine."

Let's see you throw a teen into the mix, Ed, and let's hear you whistle above the whines and moans about how you are ruining her very existence on the planet. Let's see how you pleasantly ignore her eye rolling as you lecture her on the science of pressing olives and extracting water from ancient wells.

Or how about an eleven-year-old, Frances, who fights back tears as he asks why we can't just have chicken strips and meatloaf?

"You know," my mother said knowingly, pulling me out of my resentful daydream, "Frances Mayes is from Cortona."

"Oh yeah?" I played along, "Now that I think about it."

"So did you ever read it?"

"Just last month," I said, deciding not to share any of my immature thoughts on the subject.

Katie poked her sleepy head around the corner. "Can't a girl get some sleep around here? Geez, it's the crack of dawn."

"It's seven forty-five," I said. "We're leaving in a half hour for Cortona so go jump in the shower."

"We don't want to keep Frances and Ed waiting," my dad joked.

We threw together a simple picnic basket and soon we were driving down a pitted and bumpy dirt road toward a local highway in a tiny white rental car with our tiny map.

We didn't drive through Tuscany so much as we zigzagged through it. The rolling green hills fanned out in every direction as far as the eye could see. This time of year, many of them wore mohair sweaters of teeny yellow flowers. Needle straight cypress stood here and there, like soldiers guarding against the modern world. The steel gray sky and angry clouds provided a dramatic and ever-changing backdrop. It was "stop your heart" magnificent.

To the rhythm of the windshield wipers, we oohed and aahed over this villa and that. I wondered (besides Frances) who could be wealthy enough and lucky enough to own these. Katie numbered countless flocks of sheep grazing lazily and wondered why there were no signs of any horses in this seemingly perfect horse country.

But we spent most of the ride discussing Frances. I, of course, weakened and revealed my feelings about the book. That gave everyone else permission to throw in a few zingers of their own.

"Exactly how did she and Ed afford this adventure on two teachers' salaries?" asked my mother.

"How did they find the villa they eventually refurbished? Did they work with a Realtor?" my dad wanted to know.

"Did you notice how much wine they drank?" asked Katie.

219

"Did we put a bottle in the picnic basket?" I asked.

"No."

"Bummer."

And the general chorus was "Who really cooks like that every day?"

As we neared Cortona, I noticed my mother examining every villa on the hilltops looking for "the one" that resembled the villa on the cover of the paperback, which we just happened to have. There was an intensity about her manner, an emotion below the surface that I could not put my finger on.

"Look at that one up the hill to the left."

"Too many cypresses. But the one up on the right …"

"The color doesn't match. And I don't see any olive trees."

"I wonder if that villa on the cover is a picture of just any old place, to thwart people like us. I am sure the last thing they want at this point are more looky-loos," said my dad, ever the voice of reason.

"Look." Katie pointed ahead to Cortona in the distance. A respectful hush fell over the car. I was surprised to see that the town sat high atop a mountain. Up we drove through winding streets lined with tents and mobbed with shoppers out for market day. Scores of older men stood on corners gabbing away while the women folk clogged the markets behind them doing all of the work.

Up and up we climbed until we arrived at the top and parked the car. Founded by the Etruscans, Cortona was one of the oldest hill towns in Tuscany. It had stopped raining, so we ditched our umbrellas and made our way through the medieval streets.

"Keep your eyes peeled." I said.

"For what?" Katie asked.

"For Frances!" my mother and I said in unison.

"She could be here right now!"

"Do we even know what she looks like?" Katie exhaled a sigh of disgust. I pulled the paperback from my bag and showed her the tiny photo on the back, and we all laughed.

"All of these shop owners probably know her."

"Whatever. I'm going to go look for a leather bound journal."

"And I am just going to walk around and take in the architecture, maybe stop into a bookstore," my dad added. We all made plans to meet back at the car in an hour.

My mother and I sauntered along looking in store windows and at the passersby. The sky was starting to clear and the air felt clean and cool around us. We halfheartedly searched for a gift for one of her neighbors who was watering her flowers while she was gone.

"So how are things going with you and Tim?"

"We've grown in ways that neither of us could have imagined. I am at peace with the ups and downs of who we are together. Once we forgave each other for not being perfect, it got easier."

"Any regrets?"

"Honestly, no. But it's not like we have a fancy villa to show off to the world now."

"Enough," my mother said, a sudden edge to her voice. "It's not like you're suffering in that apartment on the Italian Riviera."

Shaken by her tone, I stopped and looked squarely at her. "I thought we were having fun. All of that stuff about Frances and Ed. I was trying to be funny." She took a deep breath and exhaled loudly avoiding my eyes.

"Is something wrong?" I asked. An awkward stillness hung between us.

"Nothing is wrong. I'm proud of you. What you both did took extraordinary courage."

"Thank you."

"A person can take real chances," she stopped for a moment and fished around in her oversized brown leather purse. "Or," she stated as she held up *Under the Tuscan Sun*, "she can just read about it, like me, in somebody's book and wonder why it is that only other people do things like this." A crack in her voice surprised both of us. She looked away and we stood in silence.

"You could still do something like this, Mom," I said as I took the book from her. "If you really want to."

"Maybe I just will." The set to her jaw told me that the conversation was finished.

After an hour of window shopping, our moods back on an even keel, we ended up back at the car and decided to find a place for a picnic. From our high vantage point we spotted a big lake in the distance.

"Here it is." Katie pointed to it on the map. "It's called Castiglione del Lago."

"A lovely picnic on the shores of a lake in Tuscany. Who could ask for more?"

We slowly drove back down the mountain and followed various road signs according to the map. We drove and drove and drove some more.

"Where the heck is it?" my dad grumbled. "I'm hungry."

"It didn't look this far."

"Why don't we just open the chips?"

"The food's in the trunk."

After another silent twenty minutes we saw the exit. Hallelujah. Soon enough we arrived and found a castle in the center of town overlooking the lake. But we wanted to sit at the water's edge, so we wound around in the maze of streets in search of the shore. Suddenly, and without notice, the road became a one-way street and dumped us squarely in front of an unkempt patch of grass next to a dumpy trailer park.

"I thought trailer parks were an American thing."

"There's no outlet. Just the same street we came from."

"Well, I can kind of see some water beyond those tall reeds over there."

"This place looked a lot prettier from far away."

"Should we just keep driving?"

"Let's just park and get the sandwiches out of the trunk. Just get this over with."

"Nice mood."

I pulled the picnic bag from the trunk and distributed the food. Sitting in the car to stay warm, we peeled open our Saran wrap in silence. As I chewed my sandwich, I glanced out the window to my right and began to giggle. In the center of the patch of unkempt grass was a lone, squashed, white molded plastic chair. Punchy with hunger, we guffawed over who could have last sat in it. We agreed that it must have been another wayward American because all of the Italians were skinny. We could not have been in a more unpicturesque place. Of all the choices in Tuscany to have lunch, here we sat.

"I know one thing for sure." My mother giggled as she chewed. "Frances has never been here."

The laughter filled me more than the lunch. It didn't matter if we were sitting in Newark, New Jersey, or Tuscany, Italy. Whether we were sitting with Frances and Ed at their big yellow table or in a cramped rental car parked by rusty trailers. Our hearts knew no view nor sense of place but merely that we were together, laughing at nothing, looking for a person we would never know and searching for a villa we would never set foot in.

We wrapped up our little pit stop and headed back. We made a pact to tell anyone who asked that we had picnicked on the shores of a sapphire blue lake under the guard of a famous castle. A thoroughly Tuscan experience.

It would be our little secret to enjoy. Another thread added to the already thick bundle of heartstrings that connected us over the miles. We drove home in quiet contentment. As my parents and I watched each other age, we both knew, though it was unspoken, that our times of connection like this were numbered. The thought of that was excruciating because once one of those hearts was gone, the others would be left with all of those strings waving in the lonely wind.

But there was no time for melancholy now. For we were Montalcino bound and a bottle of Le Chiuse Brunello and a welcoming fire awaited us.

6 4 ❦ the abbey

It was almost 6:00 PM when my father parked the white rental car just outside the massive, wrought iron gate. My parents had been here a week before for Easter services and were captivated by the beauty of the place and the singing of the monks during the Mass. We started down the cypress-lined lane that led to the stunning Monte Oliveto Maggiore Abbey, high on a crest in the Tuscan hills. A soft rain fell, but the mist was fine, a gray gossamer.

The grounds were woodsy and our walk down the path was quiet and respectful. My parents shared a red umbrella, but Tim, Matt and I let the budding leaves of the trees overhead shield us as best they could. The scent of pine and wet leaves clung to us like smoke. The days were getting longer and the sky still held a grayish light.

"I wish Katie were here," I whispered. She was back at the farmhouse with a stomachache.

"Why are you whispering?" Matt whispered back.

"I'm not sure."

At the end of the path, the fifteenth-century church, stately and austere, came into view. We entered through the side door into a dimly lit, gothic masterpiece. Only a few candles lit the way, revealing artwork and sumptuous carvings. We had come to Vespers. Even the word was mysterious.

A monk in a white robe nodded and directed us to some traditional, plain wooden pews close to the altar. Against the walls were ornately carved wooden seats with high backs and hard benches, the kind you see lining the walls of Westminster Abbey, where the church elders sit and watch the royal family pass before them.

"Let's sit in those," I said.

The five of us moved to a row of the carved chairs. Matthew, thrilled with their thronelike appearance, put on the airs of a young prince. I responded by acting like the queen.

Others filtered in and sat directly across from us in the other set of thrones. The only problem with this seating arrangement was that we squarely faced each other. Eye contact was inevitable and uncomfortable. I didn't mind a good hearty staring contest once in a while, but I could tell that these were not the sort of folks who would appreciate the sport. I wondered if this was what led to the more modern pew arrangement of theater seating.

A few monks appeared, floating down the aisle like angels in their white robes. Many held books as they glided in alone or in groups of two or three. All of them looked serious and focused as they took their places in the wooden thrones on either side of the aisle in the rear half of the church. The lights were turned on, and the room had a golden glow.

The monks were of all ages, with as many youthful faces as those lined with wisdom and depth. I wondered what drew these young men to such a life. I wondered if it was an escape from a tumultuous world or a calling to a life more noble than most.

More monks drifted in and found their places. At the top of the hour, the last two monks appeared and took their spots in the center of the aisle at podiums set up just for them. I assumed they were the cantors, the leaders of the choir. I studied each and every monk. I wanted to know who they were: their quirks and secret fears, who was the funny one, the quiet one, the one who was not sure if he should be here or not. I wondered who the leader was, and who wanted to be. Who the others secretly envied as the one most holy in his ways.

Then, a deep and resonant voice filled the church with Latin phrases. The rest of the men joined in. Melodious prayer. The Latin made me close my eyes, a language so ancient that only my soul knew the words, or cared because the sound was so seductive that it was enough. I sat back and relaxed into the hymns. One cantor sang and then the other. Then a chorus of deep voices followed: calm, harmonious and seemingly effortless. It went on and on until I was mesmerized with the ritual. I felt tranquil and the thought of ending each day this way was suddenly very appealing.

I opened my eyes and took in the scene once again, but this time I was aware of something more. The high ceilings seemed to be filled with the spirits of six hundred years of monks elbowing their way in to join the others in a chorus so sweet. A communion of saints who found such peace here that they stayed forever. I felt them, their voices captured by these walls that had listened to their every joy and pain. The monks here followed St. Benedict's rule, *ora et labora*. Pray and Work. Their version of the road to peaceful living. Perhaps we could walk that path in our own lives a little more. Tim and I exchanged glances. For some reason, the spell was broken. The monks were not yet finished, but we were ready to go.

The five of us filed out the door in a silence that we felt compelled to preserve all the way up the wooded path. We piled into the car and headed home. I snuggled close to Tim and held his hand. Sometimes there were no words. Sometimes it was enough to be together without them.

65 poppies in tuscany

I had been waiting all year to see them so it was no surprise when I felt an overwhelming compulsion to pull my car off the wandering Tuscan road and park near an ancient cypress. I got out and walked to the edge of a field of poppies and stood, the sun warm upon my face. They bloomed on the hillsides, these blood red wildflowers, like thousands of cherry life-savers thrown upon a lush emerald carpet. The essence of red, upon the essence of green. It was, somehow, better than Christmas.

The rolling hills spread out in all directions making me feel that I could run as fast as I could all day just for the sake of it. But running was not an option in my skimpy sandals so I made my way carefully through the flowers like a botanist on her first field trip. The poppies had a tangled nature and didn't part with precision. It was a challenge not to crush any of the papery blooms, and I worked hard at it as they were perfect in their simplicity.

Soon I was in the middle of the field. I fought the immediate pull to run back to the car. I knew I looked foolish, a lost soul. But I stood fast and took a deep breath. It was bright and deathly quiet, a luminous moment untouched by any other human being. And it was all mine.

Something caught my eye. Off to the side. A stirring. At first I saw nothing. And then it moved again. A rebel bouquet breaking free and rising above its peers. And up she stood in her midnight blue coat with that black and white brooch that she always wore. Firmly set upon her silver waves was a hat made of oversized red silk poppies. The one my mother and I convinced her to buy one Easter when I was twelve. The one she tried on at the hat shop on a whim, but which transformed her into a fashion statement with an exclamation point. The one she wore for years even after hats went out of style.

We stood eye to eye. She smiled, her head tilted a bit to the side like it always did. Her sweet blue eyes magnified through those corrective cataract glasses that she hated so much. I waved my hand to show her that I still wore her gold signet ring on my right hand as I had since she gave it to me when I was sixteen. I told her that I had named my firstborn after her, but she already knew that.

I knew my grandmother in the latter part of her fifty-four-year marriage to my grandfather. The part beyond the struggle when couples settle into acceptance and simple pleasures. They were a courageous twosome, choosing each other despite religious differences in an era when that was not readily accepted; she a devout Catholic and he a Protestant.

My recollection of their relationship was clear. Even into his eighties, he drove her to weekday Mass every morning and waited in the car until she was through. And she cooked him grand meals and ironed his clothes as he sat smoking his pipe in a big cocoa colored easy chair with doilies on the arms. They took care of each other. A humble life of surrender, a belief that family matters.

My grandmother exemplified the transformative power of simplicity and service. White sheets on a clothesline, a broom whisking away the dirt from the front stoop, veal and peppers bubbling on the stove, a

227

thimbled finger mending an embroidered pillowcase. Her sacred sanctuary was her home and she showed me that there was pleasure and healing in daily routine, shuffling between rooms, between grandchildren, between laughs. She reigned queen in a world of constancy, the rest of us growing secure, strong and courageous because of it.

"Good Night, Dolly," she would say to me after prayers, in the dusky light of the bedroom off the kitchen where she would put my cot. A cool hand across my forehead, a caress of my cheek and she would be gone, leaving the door cracked in case I called out in the night.

I would strain to listen to the hushed conversation between my mother and her as they sat in the kitchen, happy to be reunited for a weekend. My mother sharing her joys as well as her disillusionments about married life. Sometimes I would dare to peek out and see them, heads together, giggling.

I had a thousand questions I wanted to ask my grandmother about who she was when she was my age. I wanted to ask her how to be a better mother, a better wife and a finer friend. How to weather storms in life with class and courage. How to put one foot in front of the other when sometimes I felt so tired that I just wanted to sit right down in a field like this and sleep forever like Dorothy and her friends in the *Wizard of Oz*.

But before I could utter a sound, she turned and walked, fading gently until I had to shake my head to return to my senses. Without a sound I walked back to the car aware that I really wasn't alone out there. It felt good. I felt stronger.

So much of how we relate to a partner is dependent upon the generations that lived and loved before us. The hows and whys of couplehood passed down like fine china wrapped in muslin. How we treat each other, how we resolve our conflicts and handle life's challenges are deeply ingrained, the result of witnessing a million interactions between parents and grandparents. Somehow, Tim's and my ability to find renewed happiness together would affect children who were yet to be born.

I didn't come here today in search of my grandmother. I hadn't thought about that Easter hat in twenty-five years. But there she was. It's funny how memories found me. How they'd look for a quiet moment to steal my breath away when I was perfectly happy doing something else. How they'd leave me changed for the better, handing me bits of wisdom and food for thought. My grandmother must have been the reason I felt compelled to see the poppies. I think she had waited a long time to come and remind me of the power of simple deeds when done for each other with great love. Or maybe she had stood waving frantically in front of my eyes a thousand times over the years, and I had just been too busy to notice.

66 ✤ buses part 6

The last few days the buses *and* the trains have been on strike. Nothing had been solved in the last four strikes. No one seemed to care. I am starting to wonder why these strikes didn't take up a whole chapter in Giglio's book, *The Unsolved Problems of Italy*.

67 ✤ two women, one house

It was pitch black and I waited for my eyes to adjust. I was not sure what had awakened me. I got up and tiptoed down the hall, checked on Matthew and found him sound asleep. I snuggled the covers around him, kissed his sleepy face and then stood for a moment just to watch him. A parent's privilege.

I left his room and continued down the hall and around the corner. That's when I heard it. The soft murmurings. A giggle. Katie was on the phone. At two in the morning. That could only mean one thing.

I stood outside her door for a moment and listened, but I couldn't distinguish the words. Not that I needed to. The tone of her voice told the story. I decided not to disturb her. Not to remind her that it was the middle of the night and she should hang up.

I leaned for a moment against the smooth white wall and smiled to myself, remembering the days, long ago, when love was the only sleep I needed. When tired mornings were worth every silly word that had passed between me and Tim. I was happy for Katie, and I wondered who he was.

Now wide-awake, I tiptoed into the kitchen and poured myself a glass of water. I wasn't really thirsty, I just needed something to do. I took my glass into the living room and sat on the couch. Suddenly I felt all of my forty-four years at once. It wasn't a bad feeling, it just took up a lot of space.

Knowing that my daughter was now old enough to be in love pushed me further into middle age. Something I had yet to come to terms with. Does anyone ever come to terms with that?

I gazed out the sliding glass door at the moon hanging high above the sea and the water below that danced with its light. Young love was like that, making all things within its reach glow and shimmer. Mature love— not so shimmery. More like gravity. Invisible, but the force that holds it all together.

Though I missed the glow and shimmer, I understood that they were like the moon, alluring but powerless on their own. Until now, I had had it backward. Mature love is the greater prize because when you have that you become the source of the light and others glimmer and glow because of you.

I drank up my water, set the glass on the table and headed back to bed. Passing Katie's door one last time, I heard her singing a stanza from one of her current favorite songs. Then there was silence. I imagined that he was singing the next stanza back to her. Another giggle confirmed it. I love you because it is romantic when you sing back to me on the phone in the middle of the night.

I promised myself that, in the morning, I would not ask her why she looked tired. I would not intrude. I would let her bask in these moments all by herself. Maybe she would confide in me, but I wouldn't be hurt if she didn't. A female heart was a complicated place.

And our home would now bear a new weight. One that I knew would be difficult to juggle for a while until we all could adjust. There were two women now in the house, and Katie had a right to her own life. How would I move over without stepping down?

68 pisa

The three of us looked everywhere but at each other. Tim handed Katie an extra napkin to catch the tear that was slipping down her cheek. I was suddenly very attentive to the fine weave of the white linen tablecloth and the pattern on the silver in this tiny restaurant in Pisa. I fortified myself with a deep breath and a gulp of *acqua frizzante*. Matthew was back in a hotel room with Tim's parents who had come for a two-week visit. We wanted to tell Katie first that we had decided to move back to America. We knew it would be more difficult for her.

"But *this* is our home now."

"Katie."

"You don't understand. I have *never* been happy like this. I don't want to go back."

"We know."

"No, you don't. You don't know. Everything is real here. The kids, my friends...they don't care about material stuff. It's so much easier."

"We're running out of money. We thought we could stretch it two years, but we just can't."

"I have a life here. I don't have to wait around for you to drive me places. I earn my own money babysitting, and I love teaching English to those kids."

Tim and I were now passing the napkin back and forth so we could all mop up our tears. It was true. We had never seen her so happy. Teen life here was pretty idyllic, as it did not revolve largely around famous brand clothing and binge drinking.

"It's not fair. You make me come here and fall in love with this place, and then you make me leave."

There wasn't much more to say so we all just sat with heavy hearts and waited to pay our bill. I searched Katie's wet eyes, but she looked away.

"Katie, if nothing else, this experience has opened up your world." Katie looked back at me suddenly with a new fierceness that I had never seen in her.

"No. You've got it all wrong, Mom. It gave me a world."

69 ～ the leaning tower

"Okay, everybody, lean to your left to the same degree as the tower and I'll just tilt the camera." The five of us, Tim's parents, Katie, Tim and I all leaned in unison to the left until Matt motioned for us to stop.

Tim and I were humoring Matt's every whim. We wanted him to be in the best mood possible when we dropped the bomb about going back to Los Angeles. Katie was still mute and uncommunicative after last night's episode so Tim and I were hoping not to repeat it.

We walked past the scores of white vendors' tents that lined the street. Picking through the cheesy souvenirs, Tim, Matt and I enjoyed a few moments of family camaraderie, poking fun at as many things as possible.

Matt wandered over to check out some soccer jerseys. Tim and I gave each other the secret nod. As we pretended to look at prices and colors Tim casually said, "Hey, Matt. How would you feel about moving back to Los Angeles when the school year is over?"

"Really?"

"Yes. You know, our money is not—"

"Okay. Can I get this blue jersey here? The one from Milano?"

10 ✦ globalization

Ring. Ring.

I could hear my cell phone but I couldn't find it. I ran into the kitchen and searched the counters and windowsill over the sink. Nope.

Ring. Ring.

"Would you answer your phone?" Tim called from the couch.

"I'm trying." I shouted as I ran past him down the hall toward our room.

Ring. Ring.

"Why can't you ever find your phone?" he called as I rounded the bend and spied the little silver devil lying on my bedside table.

"Hello?"

"Mom, finally." There was an unfamiliar urgency in Katie's voice.

"What's wrong?"

"I'm a little scared. Can you come down and get me? There is an enormous crowd at the bus stop and the police won't let me through."

"A crowd?"

"It's like a demonstration or something."

"I'll be right there."

I grabbed my jean jacket, raced out the door and jogged down to the bottom of our hill in record time. As I stepped out of the stone stairwell onto the main road, I encountered a sight that I could only remember seeing in the pages of *Time* magazine.

There were at least a thousand people. The crowd had been split into two groups with a wide swath of empty street between them like a huge game of Red Rover. Overhead was the train trestle which provided a natural midline. Each group was being held in place by carabinieri in full riot gear equipped with shields and batons.

Red Rover, Red Rover, please let Katie come over.

233

ॐ

The crowds were calm and restrained, certainly not Rodney King's version of a riot. I walked to the outskirts of group number one while keeping my eye on Katie whose blonde hair I spotted on the outer reaches of group number two. I dialed my cell phone and saw her answer as her eyes swept the crowd for me.

"Katie, just relax and stand away from the crowd if you can. I'll try to get some help from this side." I looked around. People were quietly whispering to each other or just staring across the way. "Does anyone speak English?" I said rather loudly. I got a few hostile stares. I pushed my way toward a friendly looking policeman who didn't seem the least bit bothered by all of this.

"*Si parle inglese?*"

"*Un poco.*" (A little.)

"What is this?"

"A demonstration." With that a beer bottle came flying down from the trestle above our heads and splintered on the street below close to where we were standing.

"For what?"

"Globalization."

"Globalization?" That's what this is all about? "See that tall girl with the blonde hair and pink scarf over there? That's my daughter. She just got off the bus. Can I just go get her? We live up that hill." I pointed high up the mountainside to our apartment. He just shrugged.

"There are angry people up there." He pointed to the overpass.

"Apparently."

I called Katie again and told her that I would be there in a few minutes after I found a safe way to cross. This was not our fight and we could figure out a way to safely sidestep it.

I observed the crowd for about ten more minutes. The more I watched, the more nothing happened. It appeared that the throngs of people were just onlookers. The demonstrators were up hiding along the railroad tracks.

Breaking free from the throng I marched purposefully across the empty swath of pavement. A zillion eyes were on me at once. Whispering. Pointing. Halfway across, my feet stopped, fear turning the pavement to quicksand. I turned in a slow circle, faces blurring around me. I was suddenly and keenly aware that I was in the middle of something profound. I was the perfect example of what this demonstration was all about. The arrogance of the West. Here I was, the lone American, worried only about my own agenda disregarding a national debate that was threatening the very fiber of Italian society.

I kept an eye on the overpass so as not to be hit with another errant missile. I flushed, feeling the heat rise up the back of my neck to my face. Quickening my pace I said loudly, "I am just going to get my daughter!" After what seemed like an eternity, I made it to the opposite side. The crowd parted a bit to let me through, and I kept my eyes straight ahead until I reached Katie.

"Thanks for coming," she sighed.

"Let's go find someone who really speaks English." We searched the crowd and Katie spotted a tall redhead with her arm linked through the arm of her blond boyfriend.

We wiggled our way over to them and I tapped her on the shoulder. "Excuse me, do you speak English?"

"Why, yes, we are from England."

"Can you tell us what is happening here?"

"The westernization of Italy is bringing all sorts of badly needed conveniences and advancements," said the blond boyfriend.

"However, those in opposition, like us," said the redhead, her voice impassioned, "feel that the international free market benefits multinational corporations in the Western world at the expense of local enterprise and culture."

"Down girl," the boyfriend started to laugh. "You're scaring the poor people."

"Quite sorry," she put her hand on my arm. "It's just that I feel for them. What they are losing."

I chewed this over as I watched the carabinieri march back and forth and confer with each other. I wondered if they were starting to feel foolish holding up their big shields.

Katie leaned over and whispered into my ear, "What did she mean?"

How would I put into words what I felt as I looked up the road at the string of tiny shops and restaurants I had come to love, each with its proud owner standing at the front door looking on in concern wringing his or her hands under an aged sign that had boasted the family name for generations.

"She means progress is something to watch out for. It can ruin the very life we think we are improving."

"Oh."

I felt deep sadness as Katie and I stood together in silence and waited until the demonstration ended. We walked back through the crowd and up the ancient steps toward home.

"Maybe the side against globalization will win," said Katie.

"Let's hope so."

236

71 ⁓ zucca

Our family was in crisis mode. We had just found out that, due to airline regulations concerning the transatlantic transport of animals, Zucca had to leave us two months before our scheduled return to the United States in July. Tim paced the living room floor, the phone pressed to his ear. Katie and Matt sat rigidly on either side of Zucca like bookends. Four hands holding on to him for dear life.

"What are our options?" Tim asked. He listened intently, eyes widening and head nodding.

He hung up the phone and stood squarely before us. "Something to do with regulating temperature in the cargo area. May is the cutoff."

"Can't he ride in the main cabin with us?" asked Katie.

"Too big to fit under the seat."

Matt pulled Zucca tightly to his side and buried his face in his black curls. Katie swung her blonde hair as she readjusted her position on the couch folding her long legs beneath her. Matt looked up at us, his eyes filled with tears. "Does this mean we have to give him away?"

"No," cried Katie as she pried Matt's fingers from Zucca's body.

"We're not giving him away," I said. "Let's just figure it out."

We discussed various scenarios and options and finally called Tim's sister, Mary, and asked her if she would dog sit for two months. Tim could fly with Zucca to Ohio in May and deliver him. She graciously said yes, Zucca could keep her two dogs company. I could imagine her husband, Don, cringing in the background.

We breathed a collective sigh of relief though this unexpected development would throw the balance of our carefully itemized budget severely off kilter. We sat on our L-shaped couch and passed Zucca back and forth as we settled into this new reality.

"What will he do without us?" Katie's eyes also filling with tears. "He's going to think we deserted him."

"Let's not forget that he's a dog," Tim said.

But Zucca had become more than a dog. He had literally been by our side every step of every day. When we would journey together, he would walk before us stopping at times to check that we were all together before proceeding. As if he were a new baby, we had recorded every inch of his growth and examined every nuance of his emerging personality. How he always needed to rest his chin on something elevated, slept nestled against our legs and loved to chew rawhide bones that he held upright between two deft paws.

We lapsed into a "remember when" episode recounting every cute thing we could think of: his scary haircut that was so short we could sense his own embarrassment, the day he needed to be rescued when he wiggled through the wrought iron bars on the balcony and slid backward down Annalisa's roof six stories above the ground. The time he broke loose from the leash at St. Mark's Square in Venice and raced in huge circles delighting scores of amateur photographers as he sent thousands of pigeons into swirling flight.

"What if he forgets us?" said Matt.

"What if he likes living in the country with Aunt Mary?"

"How are we going to get him back to California?"

"Well," Tim said as he thought this through out loud, "I guess I'll fly back to Ohio once we're settled and drive him back." More money.

"That'll give us a little time to spend with Carmel before he arrives," I said.

"What if Carmel Corn doesn't like him?"

"That's enough," Tim said as he looked up the number to the airline. "It'll all work out."

Katie stood and started back to her room. "I call he sleeps with me tonight."

"No," said Matt. "I already called it."

"Why don't one of you treat him with a nice long walk and the other sleep with him?" I offered. Katie and Matt both looked at each other for a long moment. Then they looked at the leash hanging by the door.

"I call he sleeps with me tonight."

"No, I already called it."

72 ✽ basket part 3

Matt's team played the longest basketball season on the planet. It began in September and ended in May. I think their record was something like 1-267. The kids played with heart and ran their legs to a nub, but darned if that basketball ever went into the net. Errant passes went long, exuberant dribbling left the ball wide open for steals, and shots went up without ever being aimed.

It was demoralizing at first, but then Tim and I started appreciating the good points. We learned to navigate through the many back roads and alleys of the neighboring towns. Looking for the gyms for away games was like looking for a hidden basement speakeasy in the back alleys of some barrio in New York. I knew it was back there somewhere but I felt nervous and edgy as I peered though doors and listened through open windows for the sounds of sneakers squeaking on a gym floor. And finally finding it was always accompanied with the sentence, "How would you even know that there was a gym back here?"

I think we went through three coaches. The last of whom was an elderly man who worked at the sports center at the park where the team was based. I loved to just sit in the stands and watch his body language and facial expressions as he yelled at and to the boys. I would silently review the steps for CPR knowing, by the looks of the veins that popped out of his neck, I could be called upon at any moment.

But the best part of the whole experience was sitting with the other parents in the stands. We all showed up to cheer every week. Everyone was polite. No one berated his or her child. And not one person ever spoke poorly of the coaches. There were no tirades, no blaming and no disrespect toward the other teams.

These parents wanted their children to win. But they kept it in perspective, and their attitudes were reflected in the behavior of the players. Throughout the entire year, Matt was never once bullied. No one made fun of him for being different. No one taunted him for not knowing the language. These parents made us feel welcome. And their sons, in turn, did the same for Matt. Funny how it works that way.

As Matt and I drove home from his very last practice, we talked about the season. I asked him to tell me what he had learned from this experience. He sat for a while and thought about it. "Winning does matter," he said, "It's not fun to lose all of the time."

I agreed with him and then asked if there was anything else. Maybe something he had learned about Italian boys his age and how they might be different from American boys.

Again he thought long and hard and then turned to me with a serious face. "Everyone on the team except for me wears tighty whiteys," Matt said. "I'm the only boxer guy in the crowd." Who would have known?

239

73 ✢ buses part 7

The buses and trains were on strike again. Nobody cared again. Nothing was solved. Again. On my way to the grocery store I bent down and kissed the steering wheel of the Neon.

74 ✢ boob rock

June arrived and so did Dick and Sandy, friends from LA we had met through the radio business. Dick was turning sixty, and they were renting a villa above Lucca for a month to celebrate. They were the two people I would choose to be with if Tim and I were stranded on a deserted island because at least we would be laughing together while we were dying.

The four of us stood on our rooftop enjoying the view that would be ours for only another two months.

"How can you leave this?" asked Dick as he spread his arms out wide parallel to the horizon.

"It's a sore subject," laughed Tim.

Matthew bounded up the steps with a handful of cookies and heard us discussing what to do on such a beautiful afternoon.

"Let's go swimming," said Matthew with a spray of crumbs.

We threw on our suits and headed down to the car. Matt led the way with an air of confidence that had blossomed recently. Something about him was changing. Tim and I exchanged smiles as we watched Matt converse effortlessly with Dick and Sandy.

We squeezed into our little green Chevy Neon and snaked down the winding roads.

"We always go to 'The Rock' to swim," Matt explained. "It's big and flat and you can jump off of it. And right above it there is a place to get ice cream."

"That's the crucial ingredient," laughed Sandy as she checked her camera to make sure it was working. Matt had assured her that the scenery was to die for.

We parked in an alley near the old port and walked down to the red brick passageway that ran alongside the sea. The sun was fierce and the salty air was sticky on our skin so we walked purposefully toward the Rock, stopping only for a few photos along the way.

"There it is." Matt pointed to the jagged boulder far below.

Sandy looked at me behind Matt's back and mouthed, "How do we get down there?" I pointed to a lone rusted wire gate about two hundred feet ahead of us that led to a crumbling stone stairway that descended haphazardly. Soon enough we were standing before it. The only down side to the Rock was that you had to scale this locked gate and land safely on the other side without barreling to your demise.

Matt climbed over, explaining confidently that we could all ignore the big rusty padlock.

"Come on," Tim threw his long leg over the top, "You can do it. I'll help you." A few contortions later, we began our descent in single file.

Unfortunately, a few other people had discovered our favorite spot and were lying on towels and puffing away on cigarettes. I nudged Sandy and cocked my head in the direction of a portly fellow lying, with his eyes closed, at the base of the Rock. Half of his body was slowly sliding on the dark green moss into the water. We all set up our towels on the opposite side of the boulder and relaxed. The water was too rough to swim in, but the random sea spray that ricocheted off the beached man felt refreshing.

We all lay side by side and pointed out boats and gnarled rock formations and ancient villas that were being restored. Soon, more people arrived, and it started to get a little crowded. A teenaged girl and her boyfriend climbed down and squeezed their way in right beside us.

"Can they *not* see that there is not much room here?" Sandy whispered through her teeth. "It's never this crowded." I whispered back.

boob rock

Oblivious, the couple spread out their towels and lay down. After a bit I noticed Matthew's eyes erratically moving. His face was forward, but his eyes were glued to the side. I elbowed Sandy, and we watched for a second following his stare. Matt caught us and started into a fit of giggles.

"Sandy. Tell me this is not happening."

"Oh, it's already happened."

The girl next to us had taken off her top. And the fact that she wore only a thong just added to the illusion of total nakedness. No one else on the Rock gave it any notice. But this was not just your average topless Italian woman who was usually well over fifty—someone you wouldn't necessarily want to see topless. This young girl had the largest natural breasts this side of Mount Vesuvius.

Breasts are everywhere in Europe. They are on billboards, magazine covers, TV shows and beaches. Europeans are fine with that. No big deal. It's handled much more naturally than in the States. It's only during times like this that I am reminded of how deeply our Puritan roots are embedded.

We four adults could handle this situation no better than a preteenage boy. None of us could concentrate or think of any thing of consequence to say other than, "Oh my goodness," and "Would you stop looking over there?" "You are being so obvious," and "Grow up already."

Matt buried his head in the towel, trying to contain the giggles that shook his body like he was in the grips of a seizure. Sandy and I dissolved into silent, suppressed laughter. To make matters worse, the boyfriend decided that he needed to put suntan lotion on his girlfriend's back.

After about fifteen minutes of this nonsense, Sandy and I decided to take our immaturity elsewhere before Matthew burst a blood vessel and Tim or Dick had a heart attack.

"Come on you guys. Show's over."

"Let's go get some ice cream." We threw our shorts and shirts back on over our suits and headed back up the stone steps.

"Matt," I scolded as I walked behind him, "if you turn around and look back there one more time you will turn into a pillar of salt."

We made it to the top and back over the high fence with even less grace than before. We stood, our backs to the Rock gasping for breath between laughs and wiping tears from our eyes.

"So that was the Rock?" asked Dick.

"No," said Tim. "That was Boob Rock."

75 · lourdes—extreme marital therapy part 4

"How much longer?" moaned Matthew as he laid his head against the car window.

"Just a little bit."

I shook out the map and held it up for all to see. "We passed this town, here, five minutes ago," I pointed to a town I could not pronounce just over the Spanish border into France.

"It has to be right up ahead," Tim added.

"You always say the same thing no matter how far away we are," Matthew grumbled.

"Then stop asking."

I refolded the map and took a swig of bottled water. I wanted to empty the bottle so we could fill it with holy water at the natural spring. It was late in the afternoon and we were tired after driving all day through the Pyrenees. As we rounded a bend in the verdant French countryside, a large sign said Lourdes.

"Thank God."

"No. Thank Mary."

After a few blocks we saw the large expanse of a field surrounded by a hedged fence. In the distance, above the hedge, was a church steeple.

Tim pulled over and parked. We got out, smoothed the wrinkles from our shorts and shirts and headed toward an opening. We walked across a grassy meadow about the size of a football field. On the far side of the meadow was a stone bridge that stretched over the Gave River, which separated the meadow from the grotto and the imposing Basilica of the Immaculate Conception that had been built above it.

We passed over the river in silence though I was not sure why. There was something in the air that drew me inward. The bridge was wide and throngs of people crossed with us, but it was unnaturally quiet. The grotto stood up ahead. It was smaller than I expected, a rocky alcove on the side of a hill. Hundreds of people waited in line to walk close to its walls and rub their hands on the dark rough surface.

We looked around to get our bearings. Katie pointed to a long tan colored structure that housed the baths, but they were closed for the day.

We lined up behind the rest of the pilgrims. People carried candles of all sizes, so Katie and I went to buy a few while Tim and Matt held our place. We returned minutes later with a twenty-four inch taper, which had been one of the smaller ones for sale.

"Can I hold it?" Matthew asked.

"I'm holding it," said Katie. "I bought it."

"Mom paid for it so that doesn't count."

"*Sh*," whispered Tim.

Katie and Matthew looked at each other with narrowed eyes.

"Okay," said Katie as she handed the candle to Matthew. "But this is holy. You have to be very careful not to break it. And don't poke anyone."

We inched our way forward. As we stood in silence, I heard snippets of hushed conversations in many languages. Up high, in an inconspicuous hollow like a cupped hand, in the exact spot of the vision, stood a statue of Mary. I imagined being Bernadette for a moment, looking up and seeing the Blessed Virgin and wondering why she had been chosen. How she came back to this spot eighteen times to see Mary and listen to her words and wishes. Off to the side I saw the spring, now connected to an elaborate system of pipes and spigots that pumped out countless gallons of water every week.

I thought of the day when Mary instructed Bernadette to dig at a dry spot in the dirt and bathe in the healing water. How Bernadette must have thought it strange to be digging where it was dry as a bone but had the faith to go on though she probably felt foolish before the crowd of jeering onlookers. Then the moment that she felt the cool water and knew that she had been right to heed Mary's instructions. And it dawned on me how this was a perfect metaphor for my own spiritual journey this past year. How I had felt like I had been digging in the driest of deserts and wondering when the pay off would occur.

Matt kept close to me. I put my arm around him as I watched him take it all in. The wheelchairs, the visible disabilities, the pilgrims who sat or knelt in fervent prayer. I wondered what he was thinking.

The closer we got, the quieter the crowd became. The air was thick with pain and introspection. For some reason, just being here made me aware of hurts hidden deep inside of me as well as of how I had hurt others. Pain and remorse surfaced like bubbles in a pond, no matter how I wanted to suppress them. Just as if I were sitting in a room with my own mother, I could not hide from Mary, the one who had known me most intimately from the moment of my first breath.

I could read distress in people's eyes. I winced at the sound of heavy sighs and sobs that escaped without warning. Pain was an equalizer. And everyone here was concentrating on his or her own for a moment. Here you were allowed to be selfish, to hope and pray for healing and grace without holding back. It was a relief to lay it all out for the world to see. And to see that everyone suffers from something.

I finally reached the wall, but I was not sure where to touch it. Which crevice or hollowed area was best for divine intervention? I ran my hand along the entire length of the grotto. The black rock was rough and cold and I was aware of every bump that passed under my palm. When I came to the spot nearest Mary I reached as high as I could but of course it was not high enough to be anywhere near the tiny niche where she stood.

The flow of the crowd pushed us silently and respectfully through the grotto and then down a long corridor of hutlike structures filled with lit candles of all sizes. Some of them were as tall as I was.

"I guess this is where we light our candle."

"I don't even see an open spot."

"Here's one down here." Tim waved us over to a place where a candle had burned itself out. Tim scraped away the old wax and positioned our family candle upright in a tiny metal clasp.

"Why don't we say a prayer."

"Let's join hands in a circle," I said as I looked at Katie and Matt. No one was making fun of this and that made me start to cry.

"Mom, we didn't even say anything yet." Matt shook his head. Looking straight into my eyes as he spoke, Tim said a beautiful and heartfelt prayer about the sanctity of our family and asked for Mary's intervention in our journey and, finally, God's blessings. I felt a greater power at work.

Extreme Marital Therapy Part 4 was all about accepting that we can't always do it alone. That if God was not a part of the union, it would lack strength. That there would most certainly be pain or emptiness or disillusionment at times, but our faith would give us a place to rest when it all became too heavy.

A family, in a circle unbroken, that stands together in prayer. That was how we could handle the tough times that each of us would invariably encounter along the way. That was Mary's message today. It was not about each of us reaching, separately, as high as we could to touch her, it was about all of us standing below, together, in her care.

As we walked the rest of the way down the path, I took in the sight of the hundreds, perhaps even thousands of candles that were burning brightly around me. The heat they generated was astounding. Each of these candles stood for a situation that needed guidance, that needed God. The heat of pain, but the light of hope.

From the looks of it around here, no one had it easy. And, maybe, no one was supposed to.

76 american barbecue

"Katie, hand me those kidney beans over there. Then the pinto and lima beans."

I was making the best baked bean recipe on the planet called Delicious Beans. Not the most creative title, but certainly the most accurate. They were a sure hit at every barbecue I had ever brought them to. Tim was outside cooking on our tiny charcoal grill. He had been out there for about two hours now as he could only do about four chicken thighs at a time and there was a lot of chicken to cook before the party started.

After a year of being fed gourmet dishes by Annalisa we were finally reciprocating. We had been dragging our feet about cooking for their family for a few reasons ... all of them lame by anyone's standards. We were not great cooks. Nothing short of Julia Child could compare to her feasts, so it was a little intimidating. We had only six place settings of cheesy white Ikea dishes. We didn't even have enough chairs for everyone to sit on. And it was still difficult to communicate. An entire evening was a long time to rely on facial expressions and sign language. By this point it was a disgrace that we didn't know more Italian than we did.

Tim and I had tossed around a few ideas and came up with this one. We would wait until it was warm so we could all eat outside on the *terrazza*. And we would have a traditional American barbecue. Barbecue we could handle, and it let us off the hook about anything fancy.

Our menu included barbecued chicken, baked beans, corn on the cob and a fancy salad that included pine nuts, blue cheese and apples. For dessert we would offer watermelon and brownies topped with vanilla ice cream. Did it get any more American than this?

I had found barbecue sauce, brownie mix and brown sugar during our recent trip to Spain, items that were relatively unknown in Nervi. I was excited to find them because I wouldn't have to cook anything from scratch.

247

american barbecue

Tim entered the kitchen with another tray of cooked chicken. He began adding it to the pan in the oven that was keeping it warm.

"So how are we going to figure out his name?" he asked. "They're going to be here in ten minutes."

"Maybe Katie can do it."

"Do what?" Katie said as she walked into the kitchen with Windex and paper towels.

"Figure out what the father's name is."

"No way," says Katie.

"Come on," I pleaded, "You're the only one who can do it without looking conspicuous." We were dying because we had been here eleven months and still couldn't figure out what Annalisa's husband's name was. We had been to this wonderful man's home many times when he had served us delicious meals and had graced us with much generosity of spirit. But he mumbled. And he mumbled only in Italian. How were we going to greet him at the door?

"Just ask Elisabetta some time during the evening, Katie. She won't care. She won't think a thing about it."

"No."

Tim and I exchanged shrugs. The doorbell rang. Tim gave me a quick kiss and then went to answer it.

"*Permesso?*"

"*Sì, sì. Buona sera*, Annalisa."

"*Buona sera*, Tim."

I walked to the front hall to greet everyone and saw that it was only part of the family. Annalisa, the two boys and Ester stood with big smiles.

"Elisabetta. She will be here in a few minutes. She needs, *uh* ... some time. *Sorelle!*" (Sisters!) Annalisa said as she threw up her hands. "A very big fight." We had gotten used to hearing Ester's and Elisabetta's screaming and door slamming below so we all took it in stride. Annalisa didn't offer an explanation as to where her husband was. He had been late to every dinner we had shared thus far, so his absence didn't really surprise me.

"Please come in and make yourselves comfortable," I said as I showed them the dining room table filled with snacks.

"You can eat them anytime you want." Matt threw this in for good measure. "You don't have to wait for everyone to be here and then eat them all together."

They timidly reached for chips and salsa, but I could tell that eating this way made them nervous.

Elisabetta arrived, her eyes puffy from crying, and sheepishly joined Annalisa and the kids outside on the *terrazza*. They gathered around Tim and watched as he flipped the chicken and brushed on barbecue sauce explaining every step like he was the star of a cooking show.

I heard another knock at the door and opened it. There stood Mr. Annalisa in his usual dark slacks and pressed white shirt.

"Hey, you! How's it going?"

"*Buona sera.*"

"*Buona sera.* Come in, come in. Everyone is out on the *terrazza.*" He followed me through the apartment. "So how was your day?"

Mumble, mumble.

"We're so happy to be able to cook for you tonight for a change!"

Big smile. Head nodding. More mumbling.

"Tim," I said as we stepped out onto the *terrazza*, "look who's here."

"Hey … big guy. Great to see you!"

Tim poured him a glass of wine and ushered him over to Annalisa where they stood to relax and take in the view of the late afternoon sun over the water. Matt took the boys up to the rooftop to play ball.

Soon, with dinner ready, I called everyone to the table outside. Tim proudly stood with the loaded tray of barbecued chicken. He made a big deal out of explaining that we were having an American barbecue and that all of the dishes were very traditional. Then he put the tray down in the center of the table and motioned for everyone to take a seat.

"In America we put all of the food on the table at once, wait for everyone to be seated, say grace, put all of the food on our plate at one time and then eat." This was a completely foreign concept to Italians who ate one course at a time. Everyone nodded like they understood me.

"Now, I'm going to go get the last item out of the oven and then we can start." More nodding.

american barbecue

I ran into the kitchen and opened the oven door. I put on my heavy Ikea oven mitts and took out the bubbling casserole dish filled with Delicious Beans suddenly thinking about the first time I had tried them at Lauren Schuermann's house in Columbus, Ohio, twenty years earlier. I smiled to myself about the power of a recipe to connect friends for life.

As I carried the casserole through the house toward the terrazza it dawned on me that this was our first farewell dinner. That this recipe might be the only thing that reminded Annalisa of me twenty years from now. I stopped for a moment to swallow the lump that was rising in my throat. The bacon scented steam that rose from the dish filled my nose and calmed me.

By the time I had made it back out to the patio, everyone had already taken a lone chicken leg from the platter, put it on their plates and had begun to eat. I shot Tim a look, and we both just shrugged and laughed. I took a seat and guessed that we would do this barbecue the Italian way. We all ate our chicken leg. When that was gone we passed the beans around. After those were finished, we passed the corn on the cob around and gnawed on those for a while. Then, though it was now way past the collapsed state, we passed the salad. Tim handed it first to the dad who looked at it with disgust. Annalisa blurted out, "Adriano!" Tim, Katie and I looked at each other with relief. Adriano!

"Here, Adriano, let me help you." His name sprang off my tongue as I jumped to my feet to toss the leaves and try to revive the wilted greens. Salads here were different beasts entirely, usually just comprised of lettuce and a little oil and vinegar. It was served at the end of a meal as a digestive. That for some reason a handful of field greens would help the entire glutinous episode zoom more easily through the intestinal tract was, in my opinion, wishful thinking.

I walked around and put some salad on everyone's empty plate. Annalisa shot Adriano a look of shock and I remembered that this was supposed to be the husband's role. I was pretty sure that the sight of a digestive mixed with other food items was throwing them for a loop. But they all ate it nonetheless, swallowing slowly, as if it were poison.

"So, Adriano," Tim said, "what do you think of American food?" Adriano stared back blankly until Annalisa translated for him. He continued to chew thoughtfully for a moment and said, "Good."

As the sun dipped below the horizon, the last of the tea lights that Matt had lit and placed artfully down the center of the table cast a golden light on our faces. Laughter and effortless conversation filled the air. Instinctively, I pushed my chair back to get up to start clearing the table, but then caught myself. Why rush from this moment? The lump was starting to creep back up my throat.

"I know," said Tim. "How about a few songs from Carlo before dessert?" Carlo looked up and smiled.

"*Sì sì sì sì,*" Annalisa cried. "Go! Go!" Carlo went downstairs to retrieve his guitar.

At age twelve, Carlo played like a grand master. He traveled all over Europe and competed with other advanced musicians. Within moments he returned with his prized guitar and a few American songbooks as well.

We all sat around the living room and listened to his concert fare and then took turns choosing Beatles tunes. At one point we were all belting out "Yellow Submarine," and I caught Annalisa's eye. Both of us smiled. Then our eyes teared up, and we started to laugh as we reached for our Kleenex.

"It is hard to say good-bye."

"Yes, it is." I said as I dabbed at my tears.

"Then we must have one more dinner for you! Wednesday night! A farewell party."

"You are too good to us."

"When we come to America, you will do the same for us." We both continued to cry silently as the rest of the crowd started into "Hey Jude."

We finished up the night with brownies, gelato and some limoncello, another digestive. Tim and I made it a point to say Adriano's name with every comment we steered his way to make up for every vague "what's up?" and "how are you?" that we had handed him over and over these past eleven months. By this point in the night he had been Adriano'd to death and announced that it was time for his family to leave.

Soon enough they were gone and the four of us were left staring at the countless dishes and glasses strewn throughout the apartment.

"That was fun," Katie said out loud what we all were thinking. "We're going to miss them." We all nodded in agreement avoiding each other's eyes. More words were just not necessary so we all got up and started to clean in a silence that lasted until bedtime.

77 &c. the kiss from robert frost

Searing sunshine. Turquoise pool. Vineyards marching down the hillside. Butterflies. Hedges of lavender. Orange lilies and honeysuckle vines in bloom along an ancient wall. The smell of jasmine and peace. Wind through the leaves. Birds making lazy circles in the dry air. A stillness that cities had long forgotten.

I was sitting on the terrace of a five-bedroom villa high on a mountaintop that overlooked a Tuscan countryside. The valley spread out below and rushed to the horizon in shades of green and brown. And I was all alone. For the moment at least.

Tim and the kids were inside the villa having a late breakfast. We were here as guests of Dick and Sandy. Sandy's family from Minnesota, to whom we were so eloquently introduced as "the ones from Boob Rock," filled the other bedrooms.

I was thankful to have a few minutes to myself to just sit and soak in the beauty. I was acutely aware that we would be back in Los Angeles just four weeks from now. I felt a panic rise in my chest because a part of me didn't ever want to leave this country, this year, this newfound sense of wholeness. Ever.

A few stray piano chords floated on the wind. Then a sonata coaxed from the keys by skilled hands. Someone was playing the piano in a villa far up the hillside. Oh, of course there needed to be piano music. As if this moment wasn't perfect already.

I spied a pair of fluorescent green goggles forgotten at the edge of the pool and wondered when I had last swum laps. I remembered swimming when I was eight months pregnant with Katie when we lived in Atlanta. But that was not about the joy of swimming, that was about exercise and the fear of cellulite growing in places I couldn't see anymore due to my swollen belly. That was sixteen years ago.

I reached for the goggles and adjusted them to fit. I eased myself into the cool water and fanned away a few bugs that were swimming frantically for their lives. I positioned myself dead center on the back wall of the rectangular pool and tried to think of the old movie actress who was so good at swimming. What was her name? Esther Williams, that's it. I decided that if it weren't for the green plastic goggles, I would look just like her. I struck a pose in case anyone was looking.

I pushed off and started a slow crawl feeling sluggish and clumsy. I tried to recall how to breathe properly so that I could relax. I got about three fourths of the way to the other side and felt completely exhausted. I reached out and floated until I could grab onto the other wall, then stopped and gasped for a few minutes. This was not what I had been picturing in my mind's eye a few moments ago.

Turning over on my back, I started a slow backstroke. With my ears in the water, I was suddenly deaf. All I could hear was the swishing of my strokes. That muted underwater sound that for some reason reminded me of childhood summers. Of an infant safe within its mother's womb.

This year had been like that. Safe, nourishing, life giving. Though we had toured Europe extensively, our personal world had grown very small. We had few friends, few social engagements and a glaring lack of pressure to do anything or be anywhere. And, surprisingly, we had paid very little attention to the media, the palliative effect of which was unexpected. For years my decisions had been molded by what I had read on the printed page or heard on the news. To suddenly be free of shoulds and coulds

253

for these last few months had been liberating in a way I never knew possible.

With each leisurely lap of the pool I reminded myself of all the things I didn't know. I did not know the crime rate. I didn't know who had been kidnapped or molested nearby. I didn't know who had been caught stealing or what part of town was considered taboo. I didn't know which politician was having an affair or which Hollywood star had anorexia and/or had entered rehab, again. I was unaware of traffic or weather problems until I happened upon them.

I was not up-to-date on how unhip and old I was becoming or which of my clothes were "out." I was starting to forget about how many wrinkles I had and the fact that those age spots appearing on my hands were an absolute giveaway to my decade in life.

I had become a happily uninformed citizen. I was trusting my own instincts and doing just fine. For the first time in my life I was not riddled with doubts or in a state of constant consternation. There was more room in my brain now for matters close at hand and close to the heart. I felt God's constant presence and the deep peace that such awareness brings.

With my face to the sun I continued, feeling the heat on my nose and cheeks though the water kept the rest of my body cool. It was mesmerizing. I loved this feeling. I loved the solitude and the slippery feel of my skin through the water. The buoyancy that I couldn't take for granted.

I felt like Sleeping Beauty finally awakened after all of those years. But it was not the kiss of a prince that broke the spell. Rather, it was more like the kiss of the poet in me. The kiss from, *uhm*, maybe Robert Frost. That crazy moment last May when I took the road less traveled.

I made it to the shallow end and stood with my back to the wall one final time. In my Ester persona once again, I struck a swimmer's pose. I bid a tearful adieu to the searing sunshine and the turquoise pool. To the vineyards marching down the hillside. To the butterflies balancing on the hedges of lavender. To the honeysuckle vines in bloom along the ancient wall. To the smell of jasmine and peace. To the dry wind through the leaves. And to the stillness that cities and lost human hearts had long forgotten. But I did not say good-bye to the orange lilies in the field nor the birds in the air as I knew that I would see them again.

I climbed out of the pool, swallowed the lump in my throat and looked down one last time upon the valley that rushed to the horizon in shades of brown and green and the great walled city of Lucca. For "knowing how way leads on to way, I doubted if I should ever come back."

78 ⸙ egizio's II

Tim loved to visit Egizio at his restaurant early in the mornings from time to time when Egizio came to prepare the mountain of dough for the night ahead. They had forged a deep friendship over the year helping each other learn words in their respective languages and sharing their separate experiences of life. They had brought light to each other's days. When Tim invited me to come this morning, I was honored, as I knew that these visits were like gold to him, and as yet he had not shared them.

Egizio, relaxed and smiling, crossed the floor of the restaurant with a round silver tray on which he balanced three cups of cappuccino. Tim and I sat facing each other at a table by a window covered with freshly pressed white cotton curtains. I could picture Christina, hot iron in hand, searching diligently for every wrinkle. Egizio placed the cups before us with flour dusted hands.

"Not many days more?" Egizio asked referring to our impending departure. The words were like a punch in the stomach.

"Don't remind us!" Tim and I said at once as Egizio's dark eyes turned sad.

"We come to Malibu!" He laughed and the topic of the dream of bringing Egizio's to California was on the table once again.

Tim, ever the list-maker, turned over a place mat and took out his pen.

255

"The Ralph's shopping center by the Malibu Colony would be ideal." He scribbled it down as he spoke.

"All the movie stars would come because the crust is not fattening," I said as he jotted it down as point number two. Egizio's black eyebrows were knitted together in thought.

"The money is too much," he said.

"You don't use your own money," Tim explained. "Here are the names of some venture capital companies." Tim carefully added the names to his list in precise handwriting. "All they would need to do is try one piece of your pizza. They would fight over you."

"But my back, it bothers me many days." Egizio put his hands on the small of his back. "Maybe I am too old."

"You stay here, in Italy," I said. "Send Simone. It will be Egizio's II."

"He no like planes," said Egizio.

"We'll give him a sleeping pill." Tim laughed.

We continued the elaborate list of plans with enthusiasm until the place mat was full. By the time we had finished a second cup of cappuccino, I could fully visualize Egizio's II tucked in next to Dietrich's Coffee Shop giving Wolfgang Puck a run for his money.

"I check on dough. One minute." Egizio held up his finger and disappeared down the steps.

"You know this will never happen," I said to Tim as he carefully folded the place mat.

"I know." He laughed as he put the list in his shirt pocket. "Sometimes the dream itself is enough. They don't all have to come true."

We held hands across the table and quietly looked around the room. I pointed to a forgotten shelf far up the wall near the ceiling. That would be the spot, we agreed, where we would secretly leave the list propped up by tiny pieces of our hearts before we left to go back home.

79 ❧ serendipity

Tim was typing up a list of items for sale so he could post it at the American School for anyone who might be relocating. I was wandering around the apartment bumping into blank walls and empty shelves.

We were starting to get rid of our things. We had shipped off most of our belongings the week before. An unmarked vehicle showed up with an unmarked male who said he was there to pick up the shipment. So we gave him everything we owned, and he gave us an old piece of paper torn in half with his name on it.

We were not bringing home the TV, an iron, a DVD player, our huge air conditioner—anything Euro that did not match American electric currents or American tastes was being left behind. We asked Giglio if he thought a garage sale was a good idea. He had looked at us in horror.

"No one will buy anything. It is considered distasteful."

"Oh. Well, do you want any of this stuff?"

"*Hmm*, maybe the iron."

"Great, and we are going to give you all of our spices and any food that hasn't been opened. We don't want to just throw it out."

"Fine."

Tim and I, in our newfound ability to partner in all things, decided on prices and proofread the list together. I hoped it would all sell. I was counting every penny these days as reality was looming like Goliath running toward us from a not so distant horizon. I kept searching for my slingshot, but I couldn't find it.

This last month had been extremely emotional. Matthew was blossoming at an unexpected rate and enjoying his newfound independence and the affections of Sonia. Katie was unsure of how to say good-bye to her first love—who turned out to be Basketball Alex—as well as the quality of life she had found here. Tim and I just alternated between tears and wistful sighing.

257

❧

"Have you heard from Mike?" Tim had been interviewing with an old college friend in San Francisco.

"Not for two days."

"Oh."

"I'm not worried, though. If it's meant to be and all that."

"Right."

"Have you heard from Ron?"

"Yes, the house will be ready when we arrive." A friend of ours had e-mailed us out of the blue and asked if we needed a place to stay upon our return. Talk about serendipity.

"At least we know where we'll be living."

"Yeah, at least that." And only that. It was all we knew about our return. We were plunging back into LA with only a roof over our heads, enough money for a few months of unemployment and some recently purchased short-term health insurance. A few years ago such a plan would have been cause for suicide. But we were surprisingly fine with it.

We had learned to recognize serendipity as God's grace in our lives. I couldn't begin to say how much stress that relieved. We would move into this rental and see what doors he opened next for us to peek into. I was not fooling myself that it would be easy. It wouldn't. But it would evolve, and it would be okay. Our marriage was back on track, and our family ties had never been stronger. We were all enjoying each other, and that was all we really cared about.

"Veronica called. She and Thomas are moving back to Sweden."

"I'm not surprised."

"She can't take this place anymore. It's too disorganized for her."

"Did they get their furniture back yet?"

The saga of Veronica and Thomas was woven tightly into the fabric of our year. We had followed them through every move and every emotional up and down. When they finally got their loan to go through while they were living in Recco, they moved all of their worldly belongings from Sweden to Busalla where the owner of the villa let them store it all until the documents were finalized. The documents never finalized. Now they had to move all of their worldly belongings back to Sweden.

So we were both leaving Italy and each other. It was a friendship I would sorely miss. I couldn't even think of the moment when I would have to say good-bye to Veronica. My new soul sister. That was the nature of life as an expatriate. It was part of the territory. Part of why every day had to count. Every laugh had to be from the pit of your stomach. Every friendship opened deep and real right off the bat. You just didn't know when someone would have to move on. Or for what reason.

Tim finished the list and printed it up as the sun was starting to dip low in the sky. It was one more sunset on the Riviera that we had the opportunity to enjoy together.

"That's enough of that for one afternoon."

"You get the wine and I'll wipe down the chairs."

"Meet you on the roof in five minutes."

I went to the kitchen and poured two glasses of local wine. I picked up one in each hand and started to cross the wood floor toward the open door. I paused for a moment in the stillness and scanned the room and the view of the coastline from each window treasuring every inch. I watched the sun for a moment by myself as it slid from bright yellow to a fiery orange. It took some fancy maneuvering to wipe my tears with my shirt sleeve without spilling.

But somehow I managed.

80 ❧ the dawn of a new era

I opened my eyes to the gray light of predawn. Achy with fatigue, I snuggled close to Tim though I knew I was finished sleeping.

"I'm awake too," he said as he pulled me close.

"What time did Katie get home?"

"About two hours ago."

"Well, I guess we can all sleep on the train later."

"Coffee?"

My bare feet padded across the cool wood floor to the kitchen. The empty apartment echoed and its blank white walls were now screens on which played the many farewell scenes we had endured these past two weeks. They kept playing over and over. And morbidly, we kept watching.

I busied myself measuring coffee grinds and lighting the gas stove with our last book of matches all the time wondering how Katie's final date with Alex went. Last night, a full moon had descended upon our little village and bathed the coast in its milky light. Tim, Matt and I had spent our final midnight with Alex's parents, Tony and Marissa, on their rooftop terrace watching fireworks from a nearby town that was celebrating its feast day. A reluctant farewell to one's first love in such a romantic setting would be hard to get over.

I poured the steaming coffee into two mugs and carried them carefully back to bed. I handed one to Tim and crawled in next to him. We sat with our backs to the headboard and knees drawn up to our chins. Tim had opened up the sliding glass door so we could breathe in the cool sea air.

We reminisced about the year—what had happened and what hadn't.

"Well, we never saw a Gypsy."

"And the high school was voted back for another year."

"Not one person ever asked for our documents to see if we were legal."

I took a long sip and felt the heat of the coffee slide down my throat. The sky was turning pink and a bird began to sing nearby.

"Do you think we're doing the right thing?" I asked.

"Yes."

"I'm more nervous about going home than I was coming here."

"I love you. And I love our children. Whatever home we make in Los Angeles can only be about that."

Tim's eyes were suddenly moist with tears.

"We hung in there together, didn't we?"

We sat in comfortable silence for a while and watched a fishing boat head out to sea. The sounds of traffic began to find their way up the hillside and a dog began to bark for its breakfast. I watched as a few neighbors threw back their shutters and opened their windows.

The muted whistle of the morning's first train still down the coast a way cut through the quiet. We looked at each other knowingly and Tim began to sing, "Everybody loves the sound of a train in the distance."

We clinked our mugs in a toast to our future as I finished the verse, knowing full well what the song was about but, once again, only caring that we both knew enough words to sing it together with abandon on a lovely Italian morning.

"Everybody thinks it's true."

81   all roads lead to home

In silence we left the apartment for the last time. All morning long Matt had felt the need to announce every "last" as it occurred.

"This is the last time I will brush my teeth at this sink. This is the last bowl of cereal I will eat at this table. This is the last time we will stand on this balcony. This is the last time I will push this button."

"This is the last time I am going to tell you to be quiet," Katie hissed through clenched teeth as we began our final descent in the elevator. It jiggled its way downward and as I had hoped, God was there with us.

"We're a little nervous about going home."

"Not worried though?"

"No, here let me show you this." I fished around in my back pocket and pulled out a new card, fresh and crisp, on which I had typed Matthew 6:25–34 in a lovely Lucida Calligraphy font.

"Very nice. Modern."

"Check this out." I turned the card over and pointed to a new verse printed on the back: Matthew 7:7–8. "'Ask and it will be given to you; seek and you will find, knock and the door will be opened to you.' Winning combination, don't You think?"

"Perceptive."

"We could use a little help on the job front in LA."

"I will guide you. Just listen."

"I trust you."

We exited the elevator and walked, slump shouldered, down to our last Mass at the tiny chapel in the neighborhood. As luck would have it, all of the regulars were there. Giglio and Pierangela told the priest that we were on our way home that very day, so he, in turn, announced it to the tiny congregation before Mass started. As every eye turned toward us, he added that he would offer up that Mass for our safe return.

Throughout the ceremony, Carmelina threw us happy sighs, and other neighbors gave us sideways glances and wistful smiles. Tim, Katie and I kept blinking back our tears and then had to give up and just let them flow down our cheeks and onto the pages of our trusty St. Joseph missals. Matthew stood as the altar server one last time, and Pierangela put her bashfulness aside and proudly did the readings.

Then, at the end, Giglio orchestrated a group photo before the altar table. And the neighborhood stood as one in the tiny courtyard and wished us Godspeed. Afterward as we all walked back up to the apartment with Giglio and Pierangela, we tried to keep the conversation light.

"What was all of that stuff in the bag you left on our doorstep last night?" Giglio asked with a twinkle in his eye.

"I told you we would give you our left-over groceries," I said.

"We only recognized a few things. What is that ... that Crisco stuff?"

"Giglio, stop it," laughed Pierangela.

"We sat on either side of that big blue can at the kitchen table for two hours trying to figure out what it was. Pierangela wanted to keep it, but I was afraid it would take an entire shelf in our refrigerator forever. What do you do with it?"

"It's like ... lard, I guess," I said. "You can use it to fry things in, or make pie crust."

"It is paste."

"Just throw it out," said Tim.

"I already did." Giglio laughed as we came to a halt in front of their apartment building where both Giglio's new car and our Chevy Neon were packed with half of our luggage. It would take two trips to the train station to get it all there. I would have to go on the first trip to watch the bags.

I scanned the neighborhood one last time. I looked up at our now lifeless terrace, the rooftop clothesline and the empty Adirondack chairs. I caught a glimpse of the orange trumpet flowers cascading around the entrance to the ancient steps, and I looked through the trees, with Katie, at the blue horizon speckled with sailboats.

Hot tears leaked through my already soaked lashes, and I walked over to Pierangela with a heavy heart. The air was suddenly thick, dreamlike.

"I guess this is good-bye," I started.

"I have a gift." Pierangela pulled a small wrapped box from her purse. "A birthday present for you."

"How did you know?"

"Tim."

I unwrapped the box and took out a small cloisonné turtle. "I will put this on my dresser as a reminder to take life more slowly. Thank you."

"You are welcome, my American friend." Her soft brown eyes brimmed with tears. "Be well." I hugged her tight, her perfume a comfort. Then she walked to Katie who collapsed in exhausted sobs against her shoulder. "Bella, Katerina."

Then she put her two hands on each of Matt's cheeks and said, "You take care of your sister, Matteo. You have become a man."

Bravely, he nodded. "Sì, sì. I will."

"The train will not wait for you," Giglio gently called from his car where he sat patiently behind the wheel.

"You will come to Nova Scotia next summer to see us at our cottage, no?"

"Dad, can we?"

"We'll try," said Tim as he climbed into the Neon. Matt hugged Pierangela quickly and we squeezed into the cars contorting our bodies to fit around the luggage.

Pierangela stood in her crisp white blouse with her elegant paisley scarf

tucked in around the collar and waved as we pulled away. I put my fingertips to my lips and threw her a final kiss as we rounded the first bend.

Minutes later, Tim and Giglio dropped us off with the first load of
suitcases. Katie, Matt and I stood outside the Nervi train station and
waited. If melancholy looked like dust, we would all be Pigpen.

I sat on one of the red bags and stared up the street admiring the
tall palms that marched up either side. I memorized the blue sky, the
gelato stand off to the left, the Hotel Astor, where we had begun our year,
and the people milling about as if this were an ordinary Sunday. How
could they be so nonchalant? Did they not know that we were broken-
hearted to leave them? Could they not read our pathetic postures? Our
oversized Linus heads hanging in despair?

Before long I saw Giglio's car headed back toward us. The Neon had
been left back at the apartment. My heart dropped because I knew that
this was finally it. No more stalling. No more reasons to stay. Tim and
Giglio unloaded the trunk and then the five of us just stood, looking
everywhere but at each other.

"We'll miss you," I said to Giglio. But the words felt too light in my
mouth. Like they were not enough to carry the load of what I was feeling.

"Go on now. No talking." Giglio said. He was not going to be one for
showy emotion. He gave everyone a bearhug and a handshake, jumped in
his car and drove away with his hand in the air out of the side window, a
final wave all the way up the street. Just like that it was over. Just the four
of us. All alone in the world. Again.

The bell started to ring on the platform. We had two minutes to move
a half ton of luggage to *binario* two. Like Pavlov's dogs, we moved into
action. By now, we were a well-oiled travel machine. Four people who
knew that in order to get the job done, you had to work together.

We were headed to an unknown future. New house, new schools, no
jobs. But we held no fear. We were together. And we were a family. And
nothing else really mattered.

afterword

The Pohlman family returned home to Los Angeles and slowly rebuilt their lives. Tim fulfilled a dream of starting his own company, Katie and Matthew enrolled in new schools, Susan became an assistant principal at a nearby elementary school, and Zucca was introduced to an incensed Carmel Corn, who to this day remains annoyed at his presence.

In June 2007, they relocated to Scottsdale, Arizona, for business and family reasons. Tim and Susan remain happily married and continue to recognize God's grace at work in their lives and in those of their children. And though the pace of American culture has seeped back into their daily routine, their hearts remain peaceful and focused on the truths revealed to them through their magical time in Liguria.

265

four years later:
a life of being led

I rested my head against the airplane window to watch the sun set over the desert. Fiery rays of light streaming from behind jagged mountains washed the desolate terrain in ginger, a momentary glow. I felt numb. Other than missing Katie and Matt, I was not glad to be coming home to the scorching heat of Arizona in July. Tim and I were returning from Italy where we had celebrated his fiftieth birthday at Egizio's Pizzeria with all of the cherished friends we had met during our time abroad.

Two weeks in Nervi was enough to convince us that nothing had changed. The sun still shone bright upon the cerulean sea, the cappuccinos were still thick and rich, and the language was still filled with vowels and music. Egizio continued to pull perfect pizzas from the wood-burning oven, and Giglio and Pierangela were busy with their grandchildren, though two more had been born since we saw them.

Just last night Annalisa, Adriano and the kids had fixed another multicourse feast for us, for old time's sake. We had sat, once again, at the long, candlelit table on their terrace under the twinkling stars and laughed until the wee hours of the morning as the moon rose over Genoa and slid across the sky.

It was painful to look up at our old apartment and know that we could not climb the cool marble steps as we had on so many other evenings and drift off to sleep with visions of gypsies scaling the building, armed with their secret spray. Someone else was living there now: a businessman from London who flew home every weekend. From the looks of the dark windows and empty flower boxes, I had a feeling that the apartment missed us too.

A few weeks in Nervi was enough to reduce us to the blathering fools we had been just four years ago. I ached once again to own nothing, but possess everything. To hang laundry in the hot sun and wander through time like it was all I had to do. I ached for simplicity and our life as a family before Katie left for college and Matthew grew twelve inches and learned how to grunt. I was officially homesick for our home away from home. Again. It was my second time back to Genoa in four years, so I knew I was in for it. The intensity of that experience had changed me. Like the emancipated slave who had finally tasted freedom, there was no going back to the woman I had been before.

When people ask me how our time abroad changed our lives—if we were able to retain the joy of that year—I smile inside. I want to take them by the arm, sit them down on the nearest bench and share my new inner beauty secret: the marvelous lift of a deeply peaceful life.

This trip has reaffirmed that I am to continue down the life path I have been awkwardly navigating, the one still so new that the blades of grass are softly bent and the pebbles barely disturbed by my tip toes. I have begun to lead a life of being led. The person I am now knows what peace feels like. Rich, penetrating serenity. The kind of peace that allows me to sleep through the night regardless of life's complexities. The kind of equanimity that helps me accept that it is okay to be lost in life and not understand why things happen the way they do. To accept that times of instability are necessary and filled with opportunity to lift us toward heaven if we so wish. To realize that life is about becoming, and relationships are about transforming.

Such peace lies in surrender. Plain and simple. I changed my approach to living upon our return to America. I climbed out from behind the wheel and buckled myself into the backseat. I used to maneuver with fingers clenched tightly around the steering wheel, shouting directions and weaving through traffic to get ahead. Now, after following God's lead through that magnificent year of wonder and healing, I have realized that my old perspective was off, like a camera lens one turn short of focus. I now understand that there is vast, transformative power in being led.

Giving up control and truly putting my destiny in God's hands was the singular most terrifying event of my life, but the lesson learned was stunning in its simplicity. I did not belong up front behind the wheel. Who did I think I was, leading the way in my little world? How could I possibly know the intricacies of God's plans? Instead of helping, I had been getting in the way with my good intentions, like a young child on moving day who runs amuck between the packing boxes, pulling out her belongings and insisting they be packed another way.

"Excuse me," chirped the flight attendant. "Please put your seat back up and tray table back."

I gave her my best annoyed look. Did she not notice my wistful expression and my head against the window? Surely we had at least twenty minutes before landing. And everybody knows you can't properly conduct a self-pity party in an upright and locked position.

"Fine," I said. It was time to steel myself for reentry into our life in Phoenix. After we returned from Italy, we lived in Los Angeles for three years until life moved us to Arizona. We had been there exactly a year, and I was barely feeling settled and had yet to find a job. I had been on several interviews, but schools were laying off teachers these days, not hiring them. But I was totally relaxed about it, knowing that God was in control. Too relaxed, if you were to ask Tim.

Surrender is a process. I must remind myself every morning when I awake that the day will unfold as it is supposed to. That it is my job to use my talents where I can. It doesn't mean I jump for joy as I juggle the often unpleasant intricacies of life. It means that I have complete confidence that God is taking care of business so that I do not have to. I have reinstituted my faith in Matthew 6:25–34 and once again look to the birds of the air and lilies of the field.

"Almost there," Tim said as he pointed out the small oval window. He grabbed my hand, and we sat in peaceful silence, watching the valley below slowly embrace nightfall. As the afterglow faded from orange to rust, twinkling lights appeared, outlining neighborhoods and highways. I loved the perspective from this height. How insignificant those tiny lights looked, though each illuminated personal worlds of great depth and yearning. One porch light waiting for a son to return from Iraq, one kitchen light shining upon a young family gathered for the evening meal, one bedroom light haunting a husband as he worried about the whereabouts of his wife, one closet light scaring away monsters, one dark home where someone sits alone. On impulse I said a quick prayer for all of the people below. People who had no idea that someone was praying for them.

I tightened my seat belt and tucked the airline magazine into the seat pocket next to the well-worn *Sky Mall* magazine that now bore circles around certain items of interest that only seem relevant to my life while at thirty-five thousand feet.

"Tim."

"*Hmm?*"

"Thanks for a great trip." We looked at each other and smiled. "Sorry you're fifty."

"Yeah, I hate that," he said. "Do I look fifty?"

"No." He kind of does.

"Next year's your turn."

"*Ugh*. Do I look forty-nine?"

"No." I kind of do.

"Can't wait to see the kids."

"Me too."

"Matt's basketball camp starts tomorrow."

Matt's reentry into American life was seamless. Ever the good natured and flexible guy, he fell into step without skipping a beat. We enrolled him in a lovely Catholic school in the San Fernando Valley that welcomed him and our family into their community with smiles and open hearts. It's not easy being the new kid in the sixth grade when all of the others had known each other since kindergarten. But he blended right in, like they had been waiting for him all of those years.

"Matt," I would ask every day when I picked him up at three o'clock, "how was school today?"

"Good," he'd say as he tossed his backpack in the car.

"Anything new happen?"

"Nope."

269

☙☙

"Are the kids still being nice to you?"

"Yup."

"I put my name on the substitute list. You okay with that?"

"Long as you don't substitute in the sixth grade."

Katie's reentry did not go as smoothly. Her heart and soul did not travel with us back to the states that summer. Try as she might, she was unable to connect with the girls in her classes on a level that was meaningful for her. After living a year free from the pressures of materialism and experiencing the inherent joys of global diversity, she had trouble relating to the culture of her new LA high school. By the end of the first semester, we could see that her struggles were getting the best of her.

"Katie," I had said to her late one Friday night as she sat alone and stared at the TV, "have you made any plans to see any of the girls over Christmas break?"

"Funny." She would not meet my gaze.

"I'm serious. How's it going?" I knew the answer before I asked the question because Katie's smile had disappeared weeks earlier. "What about April? You said she was really nice."

"She is. She goes out of her way to include me, but she has her own credit card, Mom. She drives a Lexus."

"People have money, Katie. There's nothing wrong with that. She's a wonderful girl."

"I know. It's not her, really. I'm just different. I don't fit in." Tears pooled in Katie's eyes. "All of the 'who hates who' drama feels empty. I want to care about it, but I don't."

I cozied up next to her on the couch and handed her a tissue. "Maybe this school isn't for you. Maybe we should look at some of the other schools in town over Christmas vacation," I said gently, knowing I was treading on fragile territory.

"What? And start over again? It would kill me."

"*This* is killing you. You aren't eating well. You're having trouble sleeping—"

"Think about my transcript! Four schools in four years? No college will look at me."

"Dad and I don't care about your transcript. It's a piece of paper. Your health and happiness are more important. Let's not waste the whole year." Her tears were flowing freely now, and mine were not far behind. We sat awhile in silence, petting Zucca and pretending to care about David Letterman.

"My friend Donna's daughter goes to the school just up the road. We could meet them for lunch one day and you can ask her about it. Donna says Kaley loves it there," I said.

"I guess that wouldn't hurt," Katie said, a hint of relief creeping around the edge of her voice.

"I'll call her tomorrow," I said, blowing my nose.

"You really think it wouldn't be terrible for my transcripts?"

"Colleges will fight over you. Schools love problem solvers."

A life of being led is about understanding the potency of adventure. Not the swashbuckling, travel the world sort of adventure, rather, a hushed more daring sort: a sincere openness to change. An embracing of the possibility that our long sought-after dreams may not be the right ones after all. I have loosened my grip on goal-setting and thrown away words like *should* and *must*. I have begun seeing myself as one of God's divine chess pieces moved from place to place when He sees fit. I may love life in my little square on the chessboard, but perhaps I can do more good in the square of His choosing.

This whole surrender business has been confusing. Because this philosophy runs contrary to social norm, it has not been easy. We are taught from an early age that surrender is a sign of weakness. But now I see that belief as misguided. I am not used to moving forward without the end in sight, but I am learning to live in shades of gray while knowing that I am somehow contributing to the rainbow down the road.

God continues to lead me down unexpected paths where I am blessed with grace-filled moments that teach and inspire me. I am learning that the key to this way of life is to become adept at listening. This has also been difficult. How do I know when God is calling me? How do I tell the difference between the whisperings of the Holy Spirit and my own random thoughts? How do I not take advantage of this way of thinking by claiming that it was God Who insisted that I buy those amazing black leather boots?

Thus far it is something I sense deeply. A knowing. A push. All of which used to be easily ignored in my busy life. He lays His requests on my heart with a touch so tender that often I barely feel it. When weeks go by with the same persistent nudge, I awaken to it and follow even if it doesn't make complete sense. The reasons often become clear as I travel along, and I am reminded of our days of wandering through the Italian countryside. Every road held a treasure that waited for us to discover. Living life this way—accepting that I don't need to know why I am being asked to travel a certain path—gives my days and my decisions an element of excitement.

Tim put down his *Time* magazine, let out a deep sigh and closed his eyes. The flight attendant grabbed one end of the magazine as she walked by with her garbage bag.

"I'm not finished with it yet," said Tim, engaging in a little tug-of-war as the attendant raised a penciled auburn eyebrow. He made a face behind her back as she bustled on up the aisle. "What's her deal?"

"Overachiever."

"You've got to read this," he said, pointing to a headline that spelled disaster for our economy in the upcoming year.

"Please. Let's change the subject. I don't want to know. Not right now."

"There's a chance the stations won't make it."

"Do we have to have this conversation here?"

"Can't put your head in the sand."

"Whatever happens, we'll deal with it."

It was this sense of adventure that led us to Arizona and gave us the opportunity to live near my parents, something I had not been able to do since I graduated college. The year we spent plunging back into American culture in Los Angeles and trying to rebuild our lives was especially complicated. When Tim came to me after months of job- and soul-searching and told me that he wanted to invest the last of our savings in a start-up broadcasting company, I looked to the sky and thought, *You've got to be kidding.*

"You want to do what?" I asked as we stood face-to-face in the morning sunshine that poured through the kitchen window.

"I had a long talk with Bill yesterday and he convinced me that I should go out on my own. Start my own company just like he did," Tim said, his eyes glittering with excitement. I could not wait to get my hands on Bill!

"Tim. If this doesn't work, we'll be homeless."

"I know I can do it. I feel it in my bones."

"You'd be competing against huge companies like CBS and Clear Channel."

"I'll look for small stations in small markets."

"Are you envisioning us moving to one of these small markets? Because that will never happen. I don't have another move in me."

"Bill didn't move. He runs the company from home."

"Bill's been building his business for years. His girls are already out of college. It's a different situation."

"Once you get a teaching job, we'll be fine."

"First of all, I haven't been in the classroom since Matt was born. So I don't anticipate school districts fighting over me. Secondly, do you recall what my salary was?"

"You have no faith in me."

"I do too! You are one of the most talented people I know. I'm trying to be responsible."

Tim opened one of the kitchen cabinets and grabbed a glass. He filled it with water and leaned against the sink. Zucca and Carmel Corn scampered into the room to see what the ruckus was about.

"Give me six months to find investors and a station to buy," he said. "If it doesn't take off, I'll look for an industry position with another company."

We stared at each other for the longest time. I looked past him, out the window and noticed that the huge oak tree that anchored the back deck of our new rented home had tiny green buds sticking out from beneath last season's withered leaves yet holding on. The seasons were so mild in the West that trees often did not shed their leaves entirely before spring sneaked in. It was as if they were more comfortable with the old rather than the pain and energy it would take to nourish the new. Suddenly I had that deep sense that God was somehow involved in this as it went against all I knew to be safe and logical. This was one of those paths He wanted us to wander. Somewhere up ahead we would happen upon the treasure He was waiting for us to discover. I had lived long enough to know that the "treasure" often comes in packages one isn't expecting, and that treasure isn't necessarily monetary. Sometimes it is a person to be met or a tough life lesson to be learned.

Then, for the second time in my life I heard myself saying words that I could not believe were coming from my lips. I said, "Well, if you absolutely have to try this, try it now because neither of us knows what we're doing."

He smiled from ear to ear, grabbed his Day-Timer off the counter, unplugged an old phone from the wall and walked down the hallway.

"Where are you going?" I asked.

"Into my office," he said as I followed him into an unfurnished room. He bent down, plugged the phone into the wall and sat cross-legged on the tan shag carpet. He thumbed through his address book and dialed the phone.

"Wish me luck," he said.

"Break a leg," I answered as I pushed back the aging white vertical blinds to let some light into the room. I marveled at his courage as he began calling contact after contact. That was the day Riviera Broadcast Group was born. And Tim proved to be right is all areas. He found a partner and a venture capitalist company to back them, and before we knew it, they had four stations to run.

As Tim was launching his new company, I blew the dust off of my teaching credentials and began to fill out applications. It didn't bother me when I bombed an interview because I knew that I would be led to the right place. It was just a matter of time.

One day, after my third interview for a Language Arts position at another highly regarded Catholic school in the Valley, the principal offered me a job. The shock of it was that it was not the job for which I had interviewed.

"I would like to offer you the assistant principal position," the principal said as my mouth fell open.

"Excuse me?"

"The position has come open unexpectedly and I think you would be a perfect fit."

"I haven't been in the classroom for thirteen years. I'm a little rusty."

"You have a degree in administration."

"But I've never had a chance to put it to use."

"Well this is your chance. I have an overwhelming feeling that you are the one." Ah yes, the old "overwhelming feeling" again. I looked deep into her eyes and liked the way they held a smile. I could tell that we were going to get along just fine.

I wiped the fear from my brow and said, "Well, you're the boss. I'm telling you right up front that I have no idea what I'm doing, but I promise that I'll do the best I can. If, after the year is up, I'm a dismal failure, you can fire me."

"Deal."

The job was a good fit. I loved it. I loved working with the students, supporting the teachers and gently redirecting parents when their good intentions clouded good judgement. It was familiar terrain.

Sometimes, this new guide to life is about good old-fashioned faith. When an unexpected opportunity or challenge lands in my lap, I now do my best to look at it with new eyes. Eyes that see possibility rather than the ones that used to see roadblocks and hazard warnings.

I was enjoying our newly reconstructed life in Los Angeles when we both realized that we were slowly sinking back into our old ways. Tim was traveling between radio markets during the week to nurture this new baby of a company, and I was busy establishing a rhythm to balance my job and a happy home life for all of us. Though we were a team on all levels, we knew the dangers of such a lifestyle and were not eager to repeat our mistakes.

"Maybe we should move to one of the radio markets," Tim said gently one evening as we sat on our patio and shared a glass of wine.

"M-move?" I stuttered. Oh no. Not that word again.

"We promised to put family first, right?"

"We have been."

"All of this traveling is wearing me out. Katie's at college, but I feel like I'm missing out on the little things with Matt. I barely see him until the weekend and then he has ball games. I miss all of our family time. If we moved to one of the radio markets, I could be home almost every night."

"So that means Vegas or Phoenix. Vegas is out of the question."

"Your parents live in Phoenix now." Ultimately this was the only thing that would drive my decision in that direction. Though we had been there to visit countless times, at that moment I couldn't visualize life among enormous cacti and homes with parched pebbles for lawns.

"The company's too young to wrap a move around it. Don't you think?" Yes, Miss Cautionary Tale, keep talking. "I don't want to leave my job. I feel like I'm just getting started. We're going to ask Matt to relocate again?"

"Matt starts high school next year. He would change schools anyway."

"But this is his home. This is our home."

"It's not the right home if we aren't all together." His words settled in the stillness of the September evening. I sensed he was right, but the thought of it made my head hurt.

"I'm going to have to pray on this one," I said as dusk fell and a lone coyote yelped in the distance. "I told you before, I don't know if I have another move in me."

We allowed the idea into our home where it promptly claimed a bedroom and wandered through the house at inopportune times. It shook its head knowingly if we had a silly argument borne of travel fatigue. When Matt and I would eat dinner together at the kitchen table, it would perch on Tim's empty chair. And sometimes late on a sleepless night, it would lure me to the patio to gaze at the heavens and tearfully consider that our time in Los Angeles was coming to a close.

"Excuse me, sir." The flight attendant glared at Tim. "Your seat back."

"My seat back is broken."

"No, it's not."

"Actually, it is." Tim stared her down. I briefly considered telling her to relax, that all of her hard work had little or no effect on the pilot's ability to land the plane.

"I checked them myself before the flight. Put it up." Her tone was what one might call condescending. Tim unbuckled his seat belt and stood in the aisle, all six foot eight of him towering over her.

"I'll let you do it," he replied with a politeness that would have frightened Hannibal Lector.

She pushed and pulled and slammed the seat back with enough force to dislodge a wiry swath of red hair from her Wilma Flintstone bun.

"*Hrumpf*," she huffed, "I guess it is." She turned on her shiny black pump and strode up the aisle.

"Apology accepted," Tim called after her as he plopped back down into the seat. "Speaking of seats . . . ," he murmured as he fastened the seat belt. "That reminds me of furniture." He gave me one of those raised-eyebrow-sideways-smirk sort of looks.

"This week. I promise I'll start looking," I said.

"We've been in the house a year."

"I know."

"You've had plenty of time."

"Sorry."

"It would be nice to open the front door and see furniture in the living room. If you don't handle this, I *will* pick out the furniture myself in about ten minutes at the nearest furniture store, regardless of style or quality."

"Consider it done."

This was my final hurdle. I continued to wrestle with the concept of ownership. Renting an apartment and living with limited possessions had been intoxicating for me. The freedom it had allowed was liberating beyond words. Overseas I had stopped spending time taking care of things and instead spent time taking care of people. On weekends we were free to read, walk along the sea, explore a nearby town or while away the minutes eating gelato in the park. I had begun to view many "things" as unnecessary and was having trouble finding meaning in housework.

Renting, when we returned to California, had been blissful. The fact that we were "not allowed" to paint or put holes in the wall to hang pictures was music to my ears. I loved decorating with plants and flowers rather than exotic knick-knacks and perfect end tables that took me weeks to hunt down. We enjoyed calling someone else when the plumbing backed up, and saying things like, "We have no idea how long we'll rent here, so why put the money into new drapes?" The order and peace that simple living brought to our lives was hard to beat. I was painfully aware of every "thing" we "had" to purchase as we fell back into step with American life. I watched the silent accumulation of items that drifted into our corners. They reminded me of beautiful snowflakes that were perfect alone but deadly enough to smother if you fell into a drift.

The night before we signed the contract to buy our house in Phoenix, I quietly excused myself from the table and went into the bathroom for a good cry. *Here we go again*, I thought. So all of this foot-dragging had nothing to do with the fact that I was unable to pick out furniture. It was symbolic. Tim said I was being ridiculous. I guess I was.

I squeezed Tim's hand as the plane began to descend. Glancing outside, we contemplated the full moon, bold and luminous.

"Hard to believe that the last time we saw the moon, it was on the other side of the world shining above the Mediterranean," Tim said. "Now, here it is, hovering above cactus and rocky soil."

"Somehow it's just as pretty."

"We can be happy both places."

"I think we could be happy anywhere," I said as I laid my head against his shoulder.

"Yeah, I think we could."

Through all the ups and downs of starting over, our marriage did not skip a beat. It was not easy to rebuild our life, but we did not see each other as the root of any of the difficulties. We stayed on the same side of the fence and continued to work together while maintaining a sense of humor through triumphs and disaster. We were, we decided, stronger together than apart.

Whatever we gave up in terms of accumulated wealth and social standing to live in Liguria was a small price to pay for the family richness we now enjoy. Not a day goes by that I do not travel to Genoa in my heart and bless the moment we raised our pathetic white flags together and gave up. Surrendered. Found peace.

279

acknowledgments

When something extraordinary happens, when something real and profound finds its way into your life, there is an insatiable need to proclaim it to everyone kind enough to act interested. Upon moving to Italy, I had no idea that the experience would end up on the pages of a book, but I could not keep myself from putting it all down on paper. It simply poured out of me. My journey in writing and publishing was as unexpected as the move itself.

It would take another chapter to thank all of the people involved in the evolution of this book. Many of them you have already met on the preceding pages, but the ones who worked behind the scenes are the individuals I would like to introduce to you now.

I will be forever grateful to my agent and friend, Judith Riven, who has guided me through this often-arduous process and championed our story from the beginning. To Anita Bartholomew, who took my manuscript, helped me polish it, and taught me more about the craft of writing than I ever thought I'd need to know.

I want to thank Guideposts for publishing the first two editions of this book. The organization was supportive in every way. I am fortunate to have worked with them and am grateful to Linda Cunningham for taking a chance on a new author.

An overdue thank you to my parents, Harry and Lois Hall. You raised six children to love and cherish their families. Your example is and always has been the compass by which I direct my life. To all of my extended family and to Tim's for your constant love and support. I cherish all of you.

Heartfelt thanks to Carol Firenze, The Bunko Girls, Kim, Beth, Debbie, Karen, Sharon, Mary Lou, Mary Kay, my amazing writing group, and all of the women who have marked my life's journey. You are too numerous to name but I treasure each and every one of you.

Last and most important, I offer my deep and loving gratitude to my husband, Tim, and my beautiful children, Katie and Matthew. Life only makes sense when we stand as one.

Made in the USA
Coppell, TX
10 March 2022